Walking with Stones:

A SPIRITUAL ODYSSEY ON THE PILGRIMAGE TO SANTIAGO

WILLIAM S. SCHMIDT

 www.trafford.com

North America & international
toll-free: 1 888 232 4444 (USA & Canada)
phone: 250 383 6864 ♦ fax: 812 355 4082

For

Michael

Thomas

Matthew

TABLE OF CONTENTS

In Blackwater Woods (An excerpt)
Every year
Everything
I have ever learned
In my lifetime
Leads back to this: the fires
And the black river of loss
Whose other side
is salvation,
whose meaning
none of us will ever know.
To live in this world
you must be able
to do three things:
to love what is mortal;
to hold it
against your bones knowing
your own life depends on it;
and, when the time comes to let it go,
to let it go.
Mary Oliver

INTRODUCTION

*S*ometimes in life we do things we never in our wildest dreams imagined we would ever do. Walking 500 miles/800 kilometers from southern France, across all of northern Spain, to the ancient Pilgrim city of Santiago is one such "never even imagined" event that I did in fact accomplish. For five weeks in July-August, 2009, I traversed those rigorous, challenging, up and down mountains, plains, and cities, all on 59 year old legs.

Sometimes things happen to us in life that are beyond anything we ever expected would happen to us. Divorce, for me, was such an event. Of course, no one gets married believing that divorce is likely, so I share that illusion with everyone. But after 35 years of marriage there is a quality of permanence that enters the picture in that your identity is wrapped around the person with whom you have shaped your life. Besides, I also made my marital vows to God, and those promises one does not easily break, and if they are broken, they tend to shatter something very deep inside of us. They shatter our fundamental sense of how the universe operates and how we are connected to its truth.

This story is a story of how these two formally unimagined possibilities intersected for me. The summer of 2009 found me nearing the end of an almost 2 year separation from my life partner, Margita, with hopes for renewal fading, and divorce looming. My life was in great turmoil and my pain burden intense. One would think that my professional roles in ministry, paralleling all my years of marriage, would help me avoid such a fate, or if not, at least get me through reasonably unscathed. Yes, being a former chaplain and ordained minister, functioning for 35 years as a counselor, and serving as a Professor of Counseling, did give me some tools and perhaps equipped me better than others who must navigate these waters of loss and collapse of family structure. But in other ways these roles made my burdens worse.

The classic line thrown at Jesus sums it up well: "Others he can help, himself he cannot?" Having so-called skills or know-how is no protection from human frailty or vulnerability and it certainly did not inoculate me. Furthermore, maintaining a sense of personal integrity and authenticity in all of one's relationships, including family, friends, counselees, and students, when your own life is falling apart, is not easy. Everything about a person is up for grabs, one's sense of identity, one's sense of worth, and one's deepest values. I even began to wonder if I retained any basis for doing the work I do, and furthermore, I was concerned that my spiritual center would give way. In short, I was thrown into the middle of the greatest crisis of my life.

In this state of confusion and turmoil a desire for a healing journey of some sort first stirred within me. Spiritual traditions have long known and utilized such an undertaking for healing and renewal under the label of "Pilgrimage," and now this prospect was calling out to me. But this is not how the seed for pilgrimage was first planted.

In early 1993, shortly after arriving in Chicago the previous summer in order to begin teaching at Loyola University Chicago, I began to set up my counseling practice. One of my first clients was a Christian minister in midlife undergoing a painful divorce. We worked together for well over half a year when toward the end of his therapy he announced a rather odd intention. He spontaneously decided to buy a used VW Jetta and drive from Chicago through Western Canada to the Alaska Highway and on to the Arctic Ocean and return. This he did in only three weeks, staying at the Arctic Ocean only long enough to jump in, undergoing a kind of baptism in its icy waters, and immediately turning around to return to Chicago and his unknown, yet open future. He returned feeling surprisingly cleansed and free of many of the emotional burdens he had been carrying. Something profound had happened to him on this unofficial pilgrimage which seemed to accelerate and bring to greater closure what he could not accomplish in his everyday world.

Beyond noticing with some surprise how profoundly this man was helped by his dramatic act, I never thought much about how the intentional journey itself was part of his healing. Over the years other such situations presented themselves to me, in which persons undergoing often massive and traumatic loss, would find profound comfort and renewal in what in retrospect clearly were pilgrimage events, and over time I was more explicitly recognizing them as such, and sometimes even intentionally helping persons structure them as potentially healing events. And now, unexpectedly, it became my turn to take this medicine.

When I first began to observe the profound renewal that these healing journeys facilitated, I initially studied the history of pilgrimage itself, and discovered that it has been a consistently utilized spiritual resource which has been present for millennia across all possible religious and spiritual traditions. What I discovered is that there are various types of pilgrimage such as healing (Lourdes), devotional (Fatima), obligatory (Hajj), wandering (Way of the Pilgrim), and ritual cycle traditions (esp. Buddhist and Hindu traditions).[1] But one element that seems present in all types of pilgrimages centers around the personal changes it evokes in the participants. For this reason, I have found that the term "transformational," is a useful overarching category to cover most all pilgrimage commitments. Transformation is ultimately what all these types seem to have in common and this is the commitment I was now prepared to make on this 500 mile/800 kilometer trek called the pilgrimage to Santiago de Compostela (The Camino).[2]

---

[1] Morinis, Alan, Ed. (1992). **Sacred Journeys: The Anthropology of Pilgrimage**. Connecticut: Greenwood Press.

[2] Schmidt, William S. "Transformative Pilgrimage," **The Spiritual Horizon of Psychotherapy**, William S. Schmidt and Merle Jordan, Eds., (2010), London: Taylor and Frances.

A BRIEF HISTORY OF THE PILGRIMAGE TO SANTIAGO

This ancient pilgrimage to Santiago actually has pre-Christian origins and had as its initial destination a spot on the northwest coast of Spain called Finisterre, the so-called "end of the Earth." This spot marks the furthest point of land known by the Western world until around 1400, when it was "discovered" that our earth is round. For as long as the earth was held to be flat, Finisterre was the dropping-off point, the place where the earthly transitioned to the heavenly. It was the spot where eternity began. This "boundary" zone quality of the temporal and eternal, of time and space, permeates the air in that region of Spain, and I believe is one of the reasons for its abiding attraction as a pilgrimage site across time and traditions.

With the arrival of the Christian era and the diaspora of the Christian community after the death of Jesus, his disciples undertook missionary journeys throughout the ancient world. While the travels of Paul and Peter are well known and documented, the travels of the disciple James to Spain to minister to the local pagan population are less well known, and have faded into the mists of legend. What is known is that James returned to Jerusalem from his Spanish sojourn, and was promptly beheaded by Herod in 42 A.D. (Acts 12:1-2), as the first of Jesus twelve disciples to be executed. Following his martyrdom, legend suggests that James' followers brought his body back to Spain to be buried near the modern city of Santiago.

It took until the year 813 A.D., however, for the story of Saint James to reappear in the form of a shepherd named Pelayo, who one night is drawn to a field by a "bright light" of stars there to miraculously find the grave of the Saint. It is from this "field of stars" description that we get the combined name of the Saint, his city, and his pilgrimage: "Saint Iago de Compostela." This "discovery" of the

Saints' bones was "confirmed" by the local Bishop at the time, and the powerful presence of the bones of a Jesus' disciple was conscripted in the service of liberating Spain from the Moors, a process that took all of 400 years to complete.

This legend, then, of a missionary Saint James eventually morphed into a warrior "Moor-slayer" Saint James, a transformation he himself would surely find hard to believe. But so works of the projective power of our needs. We get the saints we want, and Spain appropriated his relics in the service of war and liberation, and so James became the patron saint of Spain. By the 14th century, as Christian armies themselves were driven out of Palestine, Jerusalem could no longer serve as a prime Christian pilgrimage destination, and Santiago emerged as a vital replacement, perhaps even eclipsing Rome. Thus by the Middle Ages the focus of the pilgrimage had shifted away from Jerusalem and liberating conquest, toward more devotional and healing pilgrimages, and with the accessibility of Santiago for persons from all over Europe, it became a destination for tens of thousands of pilgrims annually for literally centuries, and hence a profound cultural and spiritual unifier for all of Europe.

Protestant resistance to pilgrimage emerged due to the corruption that crept into pilgrim practices, which included the purchase of indulgences for those unwilling or unable to walk for themselves. While this did cut into its popularity somewhat, it did not truly fade as a spiritual and cultural practice until after the Napoleonic era and the Enlightenment. By the middle of the twentieth century, however, the devastation and division wrought by two World Wars, had given way to a new desire to find new bonds of connection in the modern era, at least as far as Europe was concerned. Miraculously, one could say, the patron saint of Spain, Saint James, provided the seed in the form of his trail that spreads like a web throughout Europe. Given the many ancient Camino pilgrim narratives, the many still-standing churches, shrines, monasteries and hostels, whose actual locations are still visible, even if only in ruin form, it became possible to re-create the entire network.

By the 1950's a small number of persons had rediscovered this ancient pathway and slowly growing numbers were walking it on annual basis. The numbers grew consistently in the latter years of the twentieth century and by the 1990's, tens of thousands were walking this route

William S. Schmidt

for at least the last 100 kilometers/60 miles which qualifies pilgrims to receive the coveted "Compostela," the certificate of completion. This dramatic increase in pilgrim traffic can be seen from official statistics.

Official Compostela Recipients

YEAR	PILGRIMS	YEAR	PILGRIMS
1986	2491	2000	55004
1989	5760	2002	68952
1992	9764	2004	179944*
1993	99439*	2006	100377
1996	23218	2008	125141
1999	154613*	2009	145877

* Holy Year

There are over a dozen Camino routes, all of which are used to varying degrees, but by far the most popular is the Via Frances, essentially because it offers the "easiest" route over the Pyrenees, the mountains that mark the border between France and Spain. But essentially any path will do. You simply have to step out of your front door and keep walking as increasing numbers of pilgrims are choosing to do.

HOW TO BE A PILGRIM

*B*ecause pilgrimage is at its heart a spiritual commitment, it is strengthened by following a simple ritual structure which involves (1) taking along something from home which one leaves behind; (2) utilizing symbolic/ritual acts both along the way and at one's destination such as hugging the statue of the saint at the Cathedral; burning of one's clothes at the beach in Finisterre; offering up prayers etc. at sacred sites along the way; (3) taking something home, which for most pilgrims is a scallop shell, the abiding symbol of the Camino.

My pilgrimage to Santiago follows this simple script by taking along a ritual object to be left at the high point of the pilgrimage, the Cruz de Ferro. For me this object is a heart-shaped stone given to me as a gift by Margita many years ago. Another key practice I intend to use along the way is to find prayer stones on a daily basis, small pebbles of rock, presumably lying on the ground, which will represent the joy and sorrow themes of my life, and serve as daily reminders to prayer and inviting God's sacred presence into my feelings of joy and sorrow on each day. I intend to leave these stones on "cairns," those piles of rock that guide any wanderer who follows on the path. I also intend to utilize the singing of songs and favorite hymns as I walk, as well as rely on the practice known as "walking meditation." And finally, I am committed to the discipline of keeping a journal to track my daily experiences. I also know I will need to create rituals of closure and completion, but do not have any initial ideas as to what they will be.

My deep hope and desire for the entire journey is to do the work of the heart. The work of the heart has many elements to it but it includes the work of honest naming of our reality, claiming it as our own, and releasing any false or illusory attachments to our life. It is the dual work of ownership and release which is asked of all of us. I know I need to embark on a journey of embracing my life and my history of loving for better or for worse. My story of loving is intimately interwoven with my spiritual story, and thus my journey with God.

Even though my marital pain is one prompter for this pilgrimage, I am not going on this pilgrimage to be healed, nor to have my pain necessarily "fixed." I do not believe that we can command our own inner processes, nor the timelines and pathways of our inner life, and we certainly do not have the power to command God. Making a commitment for renewal is also not about feeling better or worse, happier or more focused, or any other grand self-improvement agenda. It is really about being able to "own" oneself more fully, to be able to say, "yes, this is my life, this is my story, this is who I am."

This is also not a book about my marriage, but rather about how God and all that is sacred meets us in our pain. God does so through sacred texts, traditions, practices, as well as through nature, through other people, and in all the stirrings of our own hearts. But we must show up. We must bear the burdens of our lives as we currently live them. When we offer our burdens to God we must be willing to feel the burdens, to actually carry them and be willing to do so consciously. When we consciously carry our burdens in the presence of the sacred, they become amazingly lighter. The burdens are not lifted necessarily, but they miraculously do become lighter. This book is my testimony to that lightening.

When Jesus carried his cross on the way to Golgotha, he had others carry it for him for a while. But it was still his cross and ultimately it remained fully his. And so too are our crosses. They can and must be shared, but they remain our own.

This book could not have been written without the loving support of family, friends, and colleagues at Loyola University Chicago, and elsewhere. Special mention needs to be given to those who read drafts, offered support, and in ways large and small brought encouragement, inspiration, and grounding. I especially wish to mention the helpful support and critique of Priscilla Boyd, Bill Epperly, Peter Gilmour, Elizabeth Landers, and Connie Vitale. Martha Bartholomew's spiritual wisdom and guidance has been a further source of strengthening and grounding. Special mention needs to go to my clients who have graced me with their pilgrimage stories and arduous healing journeys, whether we ever called them that or not. My students also deserve my gratitude as they are also champions of the commitment to honest ownership of our lived experience. Finally, my deep and profound thanks goes to all my Camino Pilgrims, those trail "soul friends" who helped make the journey what it was. You, the reader, are about to meet some amazing people.[3]

---

[3]   Names and all identifying information have been changed in all cases where it was requested.

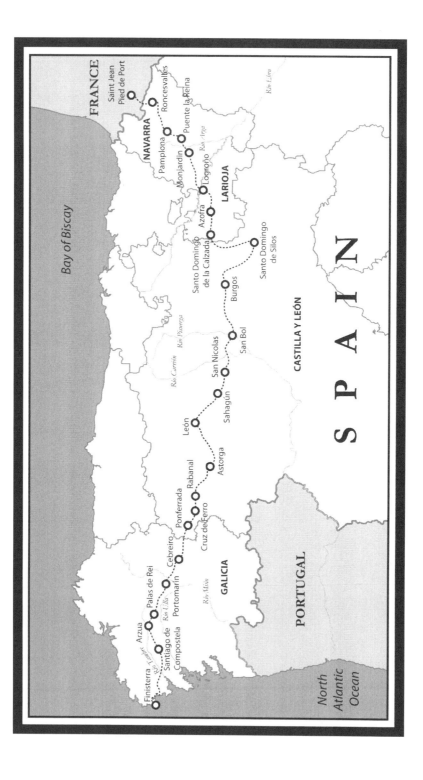

CHAPTER 1

The Way of the Scallop Shell

"Pilgrims are poets who create by taking journeys."
Traveling With Pomegranates, Sue Monk Kidd, 2010, p. 143

"So, why are you walking the Camino?" Such is the question that enters most any pilgrim conversation. Why, in our modern era, do well over one hundred thousand of us on an annual basis walk hundreds of miles/kilometers, in all seasons, under all possible conditions, with all manner of challenges: physical, emotional, or spiritual, to reach this relatively obscure northern Spanish city of Santiago, there to hug the statue of this saint called James? Why do we cry the tears and laugh the gut-splitting laughter the path seems to squeeze out of us? Why did I walk over 500 miles/800 kilometers (mostly) from St. Jean Pied de Port in southern France, through all of northern Spain, across three mountain ranges, to reach Santiago, finishing in Finisterre, the so-called "end of the earth," all in thirty five days?

I believe I share with most pilgrims a combination of pain and hope that leaves us with an inner yearning. For what? Perhaps some healing, a resolution of some dilemma, possibly renewal of some sort, or perhaps finding our way again in the midst of the storms and confusion that life churns up for us. For me, there were very specific burdens I was carrying on my pilgrimage, the most intense of which was the collapse of my 35 year marriage, and my yearning to find healing and perhaps some closure of the wound that this loss generated. But an even deeper struggle I was less aware of, even as it touched more of me, was a disconnect from my own true center, and with that a disconnect from God.

These revelations come with some embarrassment because I of all people should not be in such a predicament. After all, I have been a counselor and psychotherapist for the same number of years as my marriage. I have worked with well over 100 couples in that time span, and supposedly helped a good number of them. So what gives? Others he can help, himself he cannot? It feels even worse when it comes to the God question. I was an ordained minister for a quarter of a century. I teach counseling and spirituality at a Jesuit University, and directed two Master's degree programs in Counseling and Spirituality for over a decade. I should know how to find my way to God and be able to stay there. How can my head and heart be so disconnected?

A glimmer of why the Camino might be a partial remedy for my problems is seen in its supreme symbol, the scallop shell. The scallop has represented a deep truth about the Camino going back even into pre-Christian eras when the town of Finisterre on the Atlantic shore was the final goal, the furthest point of land known to persons in the Western Hemisphere. There, at this final shore, the scallop shells on the beach were used by pilgrims as a ritual object to symbolize the completion of their journey. But perhaps the shell also reveals something about the path itself. A close look at a scallop shell reveals its truth. Its many grooves all point to the center and every groove reaches the center, but the spiritual mystery of the scallop is that the grooves at the center of the shell are longer and thus further from its end, therefore covering more distance than those grooves at the perimeter. But how does this relate to the Camino or any spiritual truths?

The Scallop: Symbol of the Camino

Just because I think I am living close to my spiritual center does not mean I will get to my destination faster. If anything, it may take longer because I might actually be further away. According to the symbolism of the scallop, the one who seeks the center from the outside, from the hard margins of one's life, has a shorter distance to travel. Maybe that is why I need all of 500 mi/800 km to work on myself. When we begin the search for God from the perimeter, from a more painful place of searching, we may have less ground to cover because we are then perhaps hungrier for the Sacred, and may have less accumulated spiritual clutter to cut through. I, who am a spiritual fat cat, will have further to travel because I have to lose some spiritual weight first to get any real momentum. After all, Jesus noted how the first often arrive last, while the last seem to arrive first. For me, this may mean getting out of my head, out of my knowledge, out of my scripts, out of my habits, and into my need for God, into my need for healing.

Saturday, July 11, 2009 begins for me well before dawn when I awake at 5:30 a.m., nervous and excited, a combination of eagerness and trepidation. I have been preparing for almost a year, have read over two dozen Camino memoirs, walked for months in my neighborhood with my poles and backpack, surely a strange sight in suburban Morton Grove, Illinois. I have purchased a state-of-the-art backpack, high-end boots, kept the weight of my pack under 10% of my body weight (185 pounds), packed with precision, and have decided on several spiritual practices and disciplines I will use on the Camino to whip myself into spiritual shape (prayer, walking meditation, journaling, singing, use of prayer stones, Scripture, etc.). In short, I am ready.

I am so ready, that I see no problem with having still scheduled four counseling sessions in the morning, beginning at 8 AM. For someone like myself who constantly flirts with overextension, I don't question my packed schedule or the price I might be paying for my hyper-responsibility. My flight does not leave until 5 PM, and I have time to call and say goodbye to my oldest son Michael in Western Canada, my middle son Thomas in upstate New York, and to my youngest son Matthew, who lives with me at home.

My first pangs of sharp pain are felt as I sit down to write my thirty fifth and final anniversary card to Margita. The anniversary is in nine days, and while she is currently in Europe, the card will be waiting for her when she returns. I am given the grace to write from a place of gratitude, even as I am full of grief and longing for another outcome. Because my journey covers 35 travel days, one day for each year of my marriage, I contemplate doing a cathartic tour of my 35 years of marriage, one Camino day per year of marriage. But if the waves of sadness I am feeling at this moment are any indicator of what is to come, I don't think I can do this for 34 more days. I ask God to guide me onto a healthy path of ownership and release, and not one of fixation or morbid attachment. In that spirit I climb into my taxi, and say goodbye to a home and a life that will not return. The journey into a great unknown has begun.

I pride myself on being well organized and an excellent packer. My backpack is a model of compactness, efficiency, and thorough German standards of organization. As I pass through the airport security checkpoint my bag is pulled out and the attendant says everything must be removed. I stand by helplessly as she takes each item out and examines it in full public view. Out come my toiletries, two pairs of underwear, two T-shirts, sandals, one long and one short pants, a book of poetry, a second book, a journal, special hiking towels, three pairs of socks, trail-mix nuts, sunscreen, a large stone (to be used later for a sacred Camino ritual), and finally, at the very bottom of the pack, a wine bottle opener which I had thrown into the pack and forgotten about. That was the culprit. "Do you want to mail it somewhere?" the security officer asks, "or have us confiscate it?" Since mailing will cost $14.95, and the opener only costs $2.95, I do not spend a long time thinking about it, and point to the garbage can.

At this point the line behind me has grown long and impatient, and she summarily dumps my whole jumbled pile onto a nearby table for my repacking job. I now get to show my skill before a hostile audience, and I start to sweat. "Oh hell", I think, and throw everything in as fast as I can so I can escape the gazes. Of course not everything fits, so my sandals will have to be attached on the outside where they will remain until they encounter a new adventure in approximately three weeks.

After the security screening scene I hurry to my gate, picking up a Starbucks coffee on my way to soothe my frayed spirit, and look forward to relaxing there before departure. What do I discover when I arrive? This is the very gate where Margita and I departed for our last trip together only four months ago, to Glastonbury and Oxford,

England, where she declared her final intention to leave the marriage. Not only is it the same gate, but all seats seem taken except the two that we sat in before our departure. What kind of divine conspiracy is this? I feel her absence and my loss so deeply. All I know is, I am being driven deep down into myself toward my pain, my deepest truth, my personal path. I say a quiet prayer: "Be my strength and my guide, O God," as I board the plane. As my plane picks up speed and lifts its wheels, I see Chicago recede behind me. I know I am heading into the sacred fire of God's purifying furnace. I don't know how this will occur, but I harbor no doubt that occur it will. I am apprehensive, yet strangely at peace.

As one who loves books, I cherish times when uninterrupted reading is possible. Flying lends itself to this pastime beautifully, and within the hour I have plunged into "Physics of the Impossible," by Michio Kaku, a cofounder of String Theory. After an hour or so of reading I become restless and disturbed, even though I am enjoying the book. I come to realize that my reading is a distraction from the deeper invitation to go inward on this journey. I need to disengage from my head if I am to make headway on the spiritual path. Realizing this, it becomes an easy decision to set the book aside, and leave it on the plane, perhaps for someone else to enjoy. I am left with only one small book in addition to my Camino guidebook, a book of poems by Robert Hass.

Why a book of poetry? Poetry is a language of the soul and because it is not linear, it takes us into realms of knowing and of truth that can only be accessed indirectly. I feel myself breathing more deeply as I open this little volume and read a few lines from a poem called:

Poet's Work

If there is a way in, it may be
Through the corolla of the cinquefoil
With its pale yellow petals,
In the next smell of dust and water

> At trailside in the middle reaches of July.
> Soft: an almost phosphor gleam in twilight.[4]

The poem calms and centers me; it tells me there is a way in through the combination of dust and water and the faded blossom that is my life. This dust and water will be the physical and existential context of my life for these next five weeks.

I doze off and on but am brought into full alertness by mild chest pain which I have been experiencing for several days now. A few weeks before departure I underwent a physical examination which determined I have high blood pressure and some mild heart irregularity. I conclude that this is the physical manifestation of emotional pain, and am actually reassured by this thought. My being is an integrated whole after all, and my body is just speaking in the language it knows.

As I try to listen to myself more deeply, I feel the full force of my aloneness and the pain that seems to accompany it. I am experiencing both a sense of existential aloneness in the universe, but I am also struggling with the isolation and abandonment that loss brings with it. Perhaps these have become tangled up for me. I am of course always alone in the universe in the sense that no one can live my life for me, and I must face life as myself. On the other hand, this relationship rupture has thrown me into a solitude that overrides everything else. Perhaps I have been given this solitude as a vessel, as God's cauldron, to burn off what is impure and untrue in my life. In that sense it might be a gift, but I am far from ready to call it that.

The sounds of people rustling paper and plastic and shifting in their seats awakens me, and we are told that we are beginning our descent into Paris. Within the hour we have landed, on a gray and cloudy Sunday morning. I disembark, eager for my bonus ten hours to explore Paris before my evening flight to Biarritz in southern France. Yet at the same time I am feeling nervous and apprehensive without really knowing why.

Then it hits me. It is virtually ten years to the day since my only other trip to Paris, this time with Margita, in what was one of the happiest days of our life together. The summer of 1999 had me teaching at the Katholique Universiteit in Leuven, Belgium, with my

---

4   Robert Hass. <u>Time and Materials</u>, New York, Harper and Collins, p. 77.

responsibilities ending soon before our anniversary on July 20. Margita had been traveling in Europe on her own, and we had prearranged to rendezvous in Leuven around the 11th. This we did on the train platform with flowers, hugs and kisses, all in grand romantic fashion. At dinner that evening a surprise was waiting under Margita's dinner plate: tickets for two on the bullet train to Paris the next morning.

Romance filled the air, and Paris did not disappoint. No one can walk down the Seine and not be swept up by the combination of soft light, music, gentle breezes, architecture, the sexiest bridges around, and overall atmosphere. There are probably more kissing couples per square foot along the Seine than in any other comparable piece of real estate on Earth. It was a day of wonder and joy. And now I am back, only this time alone. No wonder I am anxious, and soon start berating myself. Why did I fly into Paris? I could have just as easily flown into Madrid to make my Camino connections. Was my unconscious working overtime again, conspiring with some scheming deity to push me ever deeper into sadness?

My fractured emotional state must have short-circuited my brain because I spend well over an hour wandering around Charles de Gaulle airport looking for a locker to store my backpack. I walk round and round in circles and eventually find the lockers virtually steps from where I first started. This does not bode well for the long trek which begins the next morning. Nonetheless, I resolutely stride off into the Paris subway system aiming for no particular central location. Surely I can find central Paris?

Find it I do in glorious fashion, coming up from the tunnels at Notre Dame station. Next to the Eiffel Tower, Notre Dame in its grace and grandeur, represents the best of Paris. And here it is immediately in front of me with long lines snaking around the plaza in front of the church. Since it is Sunday morning in time for Mass, I join the line entering the "International Mass," which is about to begin.

The scene which awaits me is surreal. Those of us entering to "worship," are directed to the center of the cathedral where there are seats for well over 2000 worshipers, where I take my place. This area is surrounded by a waist high picket fence. On the other side of this fence marches an army of tourists, at least six to eight people across, a constantly flowing river of humanity, circling around us as Mass proceeds. The flow never stops, with talking, pointing, looking, picture taking, and general commotion. I have landed in a religious zoo or theme park, and I am one of the exhibits. We on the inside, are as distracted by those on the outside, as they are intrigued and puzzled by us. This detached and passive mutual curiosity matches our engagement with the Liturgy. Few worshipers seem to be paying much attention, and do not seem moved by it. We are distant observers of a ritual that seems to carry little if any relevance or emotional connection for us.

I become very sad in the middle of this spectacle. Have we as Christians succeeded in taking the drama of salvation, of God becoming flesh and dwelling among us, and have turned it into a dusty, ancient, and remote fable, and trapped it in an other-worldly realm of non-relevance? I stumble out of Mass in a spiritual fog. Has the personal encounter with God become lost even in its sacramental moments? I am yearning for spiritual food, but wonder where I will find it in any formal or communal way on the Camino? Will I be left only with my private musings? Will I find the necessary spiritual guidance for what awaits me?

A shift in focus is needed, and so I decide to walk along the Seine toward the Museum D' Orsey where my son Thomas, a sculptor, has recommended I spend some time. I unfurl my large and detailed map of Paris to get my bearings. With confidence I march off down the Seine only to be stopped by a young Chinese tourist asking directions to a particular landmark. I didn't realize I look so Parisian, but nevertheless, I confidently open my map and proceed to tell her in what direction to walk from where we stand. We say goodbye and I march on, and twenty minutes later realize I am walking in the totally wrong direction. I need to go in the opposite direction along the Seine, which by now amounts to a forty minute detour. Worse yet, I have led this poor Chinese woman astray who was probably wandering for hours because of my assumptions. I really should know where I am before I presume to tell others where they are. That is a rather basic life principle which I have just violated, and I have a strange feeling that I may have to pay a karmic price for this subtle arrogance.

I realize that I am also experiencing jet-lag, am tired and hungry, and conclude I need to treat myself to a special French meal. A restaurant next to the Seine looks appealing and I settle in and order, only to discover that I have inadvertently ordered two specialty salads in addition to my main course. It turns out my French is rustier than I thought. The waiter will not hear of returning one salad because they are specially made. The salads come to €25, with a total bill of over €50, including my wine of course. I have just blown a week's worth of Pilgrim meals in one French meal. This is not a good start but I will not let it deter me from a spirit of goodwill.

I see that while my table has a nice bouquet of fresh flowers, the two elderly ladies sitting next to me have none. I get up and offer them my flowers and they give me puzzled, if not dirty, looks. Maybe it was something I said. I don't understand their reply, but all the French customers in the establishment certainly do because they start to snicker and look my way. I now get to sit there and feel embarrassed while my waiter takes his sweet time taking my money. Random acts of kindness seem to seldom go unpunished.

A one hour walk to the D' Orsay lifts my spirits a bit, although I miss Margita and feel the sadness gnawing at the edges of my awareness. I arrive at the Museum only to find amazing long lines. It will take a few hours to get in I am told, and with only about three hours left before I must return to the airport I realize my day in Paris will not include the Museum. A great fatigue overtakes me, all out of proportion to the walking I have done today. I sit down on a bench overlooking the river and come to an insight that I come to realize is my first real "pilgrim" awareness.

I have been treating this day as a "tourist," thinking my real pilgrimage will start tomorrow. A tourist sight sees, and looks outside of himself for stimulation, interests, and all the satisfactions that sightseeing can provide. A pilgrim does not sight see in that sense, but goes inside first and foremost. A pilgrim may well look outward, but more as a stimulus or mirror for one's inner world. Today, I have been trying to be both tourist and pilgrim simultaneously, and have not been doing either one particularly well. I have been challenged in so many ways today, and my expectations for a happy little excursion in Paris have not been realized.

As I slowly wind my way back along the Seine toward Notre Dame and my subway stop, intense feelings of loss and aloneness overtake me. My day in Paris is ending, and as I walk alone along the very paths I have walked with Margita ten years earlier, my memory of her presence with me becomes overwhelming. The ache of aloneness is so strong it feels like an actual weight on my body. In this state I stumble into the underworld of the subway system and wind my way back to the airport and the final phase of my arrival on the Camino.

Fortunately, I find my locker with backpack with relative ease, and shortly thereafter board my plane for Bayonne in southern France at the foot of the Pyrenees. As we lift off from Paris I receive an answer to my "Why Paris?" question. Perhaps I needed to travel through Paris to begin my Camino. Perhaps I needed my distinct memory of Margita in this place to take me more directly into my pain. Perhaps the path of pain in all its forms is how the work of letting go will be accomplished.

Arrival in Bayonne near sundown brings a glorious view of mountains in the distance, bathed in the setting sun. The air feels fresh, warm, and salty, not surprising since I am only a short distance from the ocean. A brief taxi ride later, and I arrive at the non-descript hotel next to the train station. Because I arrive later than expected, the proprietor is about to give my room away to a young couple who have arrived just before me. It is the last open room in the hotel and I feel badly that they must continue their room quest. But by now I have been awake for over twenty hours, and am extremely tired and therefore very relieved not to have to begin a new room hunt myself. It turns out my room is on the top floor, and with no elevators it means I must grunt up four flights of stairs and I quickly come to wonder how my backpack became so heavy? My room is very spartan, old and scruffy, with poor ventilation and a very soft mattress, but I don't care! A bed is a bed and I suspect I will be seeing a lot worse soon enough. Surely I will sleep like a log tonight.

At 2 AM I suddenly awake, perhaps from noise coming from the street below, and immediately I feel the intense pain of aloneness. The Paris feelings have come right along in my inner baggage compartment, and they are stronger than ever. I can't believe it. I have not even slept four hours and here I am wide awake. Rather than fighting with myself and becoming frustrated and upset about my sleep agenda going up in smoke, I get up, turn on the light, and begin to journal. A thread of clarity emerges which is a continuation of hints already sensed in recent days. The conclusion dawns on me with a force and a certainty so strong that it feels conversion-like.

The insight that my middle of the night journaling reveals to me is that this pilgrimage is supposed to be about coming home to God, not just about coming to terms with my marriage. It cannot just be about grieving the loss of Margita and our life together. It must also concern itself with my distance from God if not also from myself. All my pain experiences, whatever their source, are my inner Camino. They are my pointer, my inner scallop shell, and they will guide me to where I need healing and renewal, but I cannot become exclusively fixated only on loss as the sources of my pain. Yes, I will grieve on the Camino, but that cannot be the sole purpose for being on this journey. I am also being called onto a more conscious path toward God and toward myself.

It occurs to me that perhaps I have made my marriage into a fixation, whether in pain or joy. Maybe I need to see it more as a doorway, an important path, or even an icon perhaps, whose ultimate purpose is to take me closer to God's heart, but it should not be held onto as an end unto itself. By 4 AM I have finally fallen asleep again with the Hymn "He Hides My Soul In The Cleft Of The Rock," echoing in my head. I feel a gentle calmness around me even as a nervous anticipation rumbles in my stomach. Two short hours later I awake at dawn and begin my final packing task, making sure this time that my pack is properly balanced, and everything secured. One last look around the room, and before leaving I offer a prayer of gratitude to the Spirit that has brought me to this threshold. I step out of my room into the Spirit adventure that awaits me.

CHAPTER 2

Prayer Stones

Cairns

Eternal pilgrims we,
on the sometimes broken
sometimes silken
path
we call our lives.
Longing pilgrims we,
hungrily seeking
stones and rocks
all shapes and sizes
to point the way.
Blessed pilgrims we,
when the stories of our lives
sometimes broken
sometimes silken
are deemed cairns
by the one who truly listens.
Grateful pilgrims we,
Gathering stones and rocks,

And with the one who truly listens

patiently creating

a cairn of balance

that reaches toward

heaven.

Wise pilgrims we,

as we bless the cairn

bless the sometimes broken

sometimes silken

path

we call our lives,

and know that

heaven is the gift

of welcoming

the broken and the silken

with equal measure.

Jennifer (Jinks) Hoffmann

A lack of clear signage at the train station in Bayonne leaves me fretting that I might miss my train. Noticing there are only four tracks calms me. Surely I can find the right train with so few possibilities. A small two-car train with St Jean Pied du Port signage sits right in front of me. Lo and behold I have found the correct train, or, better said, it has found me.

I am flooded with excitement and anticipation as I board my train. It feels as if I have prepared a whole lifetime for this moment and in a sense I have. I am bringing everything I am to this journey and no doubt I will meet all parts of myself, including the lost and the hurting me, as well as the confident and courageous me. After all, I am both sinner and saint, and they belong together, and are both on a journey home.

Only one other passenger is in the car with me, obviously a pilgrim with his backpack and walking stick. We nod to acknowledge one another, but no words are exchanged. I suspect we are both somewhat numb and are trying to keep hold of ourselves in this final hour. The scenery is spectacular as we climb higher and higher with deep forests cut through by sharp ravines. Some distant mountains are bare and treeless and I know that is where I am headed. I give thanks that I don't have to climb this particular grueling stretch which my train is traversing right now, as most pilgrims in ages past have had to do.

One hour later a plateau is reached and we pull into the train station at St. Jean. Crisp mountain air awaits me in bright morning sunshine. My first act after leaving the station is to find the two small stones I will use as my prayer talismans. I will carry these "joy" and "sorrow" stones in my pockets and from time to time during my day will touch or hold them in my hands as I encounter either joy or sorrow in my daily Camino experiences. These "touchstones" are going to serve as my prayer stones, and will be daily tangible reminders and invitations to focus on my emotional states of desolation and consolation. This spiritual practice is an application of the Ignatian spiritual practice called the "Examen of Awareness" or "Examen of Consciousness". This daily examen is a central tool developed by Ignatius of Loyola to gain awareness of one's self-states. A practitioner of this discipline focuses daily on one's deeper feelings, both positive and negative, with the cumulative effect of this work to hopefully grow in trust of self, other, and God, and most importantly, in a loving response toward self, other, and God. Discernment of spirits is the gift that such a discipline can bring and I am greatly desiring such discernment.[5]

My plan is to use these stones as a daily reminder for prayer, and then on a regular basis place them in cairns, those wonderful piles of rocks that countless pilgrims have left as markers for those who follow. For ages, travelers, pilgrims, walkers of every description, have used these stone mounds to guide fellow travelers. I want my story, my pain and my joy to become a marker for those who follow me, and these small stones are a symbolic reminder for me of that hope. For every stone I leave behind, I intend to find new ones to replace those that will serve to guide others.

---

[5]   More information on the spiritual practice called "The Examen" can be found at http://ignatianspirituality.com

Stone Cairns Guide the Way

I smile internally as I remember the hymn that I was singing in my sleep last night in my turmoil: "He Hides My Soul In The Cleft Of The Rock," and feel the surge of warmth that comes with the recognition that God is the protector of my soul, my center. Within a few steps of the station I spot my first stone on the roadway. It is in the middle of the road and has jagged edges, and given where it is lying, has obviously been run over a few times. Perfect! I have found my sorrow stone. I pick it up, kiss it, and give thanks that it will walk with me for a while, as I enter the medieval town.

My first stop is the Pilgrim Center where I must get my pilgrim passport stamped and authorized. My pilgrim passport will give me admission to the pilgrim hostels (albergues in Spanish), which are sprinkled along the route to Santiago. About eight volunteers are checking pilgrims in, and all spots are taken so I await my turn. A few minutes later, I am at a station, and am asked a few basic questions: name, citizenship, address, reason for walking the Camino (religious/ devotional/spiritual/or cultural)? I choose spiritual, but I'm not paying attention all that closely. I am too nervous and excited. In a few minutes I will be climbing and can't believe the moment has arrived.

After a handshake and best wishes from my volunteer, I step into the street only to turn around and go right back inside to find a bathroom. Who knows when the next facilities might be available, and little do I know how hard finding a bathroom will be. One final backpack adjustment, and I take my first steps. I feel stiff and a bit shaky. They say it takes about 1 million steps to walk from St. Jean to Santiago. I think, "one down, 999,999 to go." After only a few steps I am already at the medieval city gate, next to which is an old church. I feel compelled to go in, and have a strong inclination to stop, linger, and pray. I take off my backpack, light a large prayer candle, and begin to pray for all those I love. This includes first and foremost my broken family and beyond. An unexpected peace washes over me. My heart becomes quiet and I lose any sense of how long I have been sitting. In time I depart the church, undergo the necessary rituals of stretching my legs once again, filling my water bottles at the fountain in front of the church, and I am off! Just as I pass through the town medieval wall, my second stone appears, lying at its base. It is very rough on one side, but very smooth on the other. I have my joy stone. It too has suffered, but has been made soft along the way. I place it in my pocket wondering how that process of softening will unfold in my life in the weeks ahead.

You would think that simply crossing the street at the city gate would be too early to be confused about the direction, but confused I am. Two scallop shells are visible on two separate posts, each next to a road going in opposite directions. After months of reading guidebooks, how can I be stumped after only twenty steps? Then it hits me. Of course, there is one route which parallels the main highway, and another route which I am looking for, which climbs over the Pyrenees, the so-called route Napoleon. Bright boy that I am, I pick the path that climbs sharply upward, concluding that climbing over a mountain range probably means going steeply up. I grimly smirk at my powers of deduction and begin my assent.

Barely twenty minutes into my climb I hear my first "Buen Camino" sent my way. This is the greeting and encouraging wish that pilgrims consistently direct to one another, in this instance given by one of a group of approximately twenty cyclists who pass me going up the hill.

They speak English and I discover they are a group of young men from a school in Wales. One of them is struggling to make it up the hill, and the leader hangs back to keep an eye on him, and so he bikes slowly next to me while I walk. In the middle of this my first pilgrim conversation, he blurts out in full earshot of his young underling, "this kid is unbelievably clumsy." The young man turns beet red with embarrassment and tries to defend himself. I immediately feel the ego blow he has just taken and offer a prayer of support for him as the leader speeds off after the others. As the young man strains to catch up, I find memories welling up of similar messages I received as a boy and adolescent. Could it be, I wonder, that I may still be compensating for my version of those messages? As I plod on the thought occurs to me: "If these first thirty minutes of the Camino can dredge up those buried memories so quickly, this is going to be one hell of a trip."

Speaking of clumsy, barely one hour after this exchange I stumble on a large rock and mildly twist my left (strong) ankle. I have broken my right ankle twice while in my twenties through sports injuries, and have always been weaker on that side. Now, for some reason, my left side has given out, but since the pain is only modest I walk it off. I become instantly grateful that I purchased high-top hiking boots rather than low-cut trail shoes. I take this opportunity to claim my first fifteen minute rest which many guidebooks recommend one does every two hours or so. This includes taking one's boots and socks off to let one's feet and footwear dry which is supposed to help with blister prevention. I hope they are right, but even as I sit and stretch my legs and feet, I sense some ligament pain in my now slightly swollen left foot. So-called "heel spurs" have sometimes been a problem for me during the many years I was an active runner and I know how painful and persistent they can be. I swallow hard, because any ligament issues such as that can become totally disabling often requiring complete rest. This is an unexpected source of anxiety that finds its way into the pit of my stomach.

But, I soon forget my foot worries since the sky is gloriously blue and cloudless, the vistas breathtaking, and my stamina holding up as I lean into the steep country lane that unfolds in front of me. I encounter few pilgrims since most probably left St. Jean long before I did, likely aiming for Roncesvalles, the first village one encounters when entering Spain. It is famous for an ancient monastery which contains a large pilgrim hostel of over two hundred beds. It has been a familiar pilgrim stop since well before the Middle Ages, and I hope to stay there tomorrow.

My destination for today, however, is Orisson on the French side of the Pyrenees, still a good 12 mi/18 km from Roncesvalles. As steep as the trail is, and as much as I am huffing, puffing, and perspiring, I congratulate myself to have been so wise to have picked a closer destination for my first day. This will be the last time I so praise myself for many a week. A few hours later as afternoon shadows lengthen, a beautiful stone building appears, with a stunning panoramic patio with tables, overlooking mountains and valleys as far as the eye can see.

My first act is to register, claim one of the eighteen beds in the hostel, and have my pilgrim passport stamped. My second act is to purchase the largest glass of beer they have and head for the patio teetering on the crest of the hill. I find a table and chair right at the edge, and feel as if I am sitting on the rim of a cloud peering into the world below. Perhaps I have died and gone to heaven? If so, I am delighted to know they serve such good beer. I think to myself, this pilgrim business is all right! What on earth could I have been so anxious about?

The dinner hour brings with it my first extended contact with fellow pilgrims. What an experience of sociability and human connection across cultures, languages, traditions, and ages. We include four Canadians, six Irish, two Poles, three Germans, two French, and myself, a hybrid, a German-born Canadian, residing in the USA for eighteen years. The conversations during the pilgrim meal are rich and deep. I immediately realize one reason why people may walk the Camino more than once. It is the perfect counterpoint to our insular and isolated modern world.

Sheila, one of the Irish six, sits across from me and in the process of telling her what I hope to gain from my Camino journey, I show her my prayer stones and explain their purpose. She immediately tells me the story of the dying journey of her best friend. This friend invited all of her family and friends to bring a stone to her bedside. She instructed them to each rub their stone, and as they held it in their hands, they were asked to put all of their thoughts, feelings, love, and pain into that stone. The dying friend also rubbed and held each stone in the same manner and returned each stone to its giver. When she said her final goodbye to them before she died, she gave them a final instruction to put the stone in a special sacred place of their choosing, but only when they were ready to let her go after her death. They could take as much or as little time with this step as each person needed. What a powerful ritual of blessing and release, I think to myself, and here I am, now a beneficiary of this wonderful narrative on my first day on the Camino.

Noteworthy characters abound. Gregor, an approximately thirty five year old Polish professor of German at Warsaw University, and his Polish friend, Bogdan, who is soon to leave for China to teach German; Hanna, a wild and lively Berliner whose wit flows like the long sleeves of her medieval style red robe in which she walks; Sean, a sweet easy-going Irishman, husband of the aforementioned Sheila, and four other animated Irish women who are all walking as a group. I call them Sean and his harem. Our pilgrim company also includes Barbara and Michelle from Toronto, with whom I can satisfy my Canadian nostalgia. Finally, there is Claude, a Frenchman with whom I exchange robust laughter even though neither of us knows what the other is saying. Chaucer's Canterbury pilgrims are no weirder than this bunch.

Perhaps at youth camp in my teens was the last time I shared a tight room with five other people in bunk beds such as I now do on my first night. Since I am the oldest, with an old man's bladder, I grab a bottom bunk. Claude, the Frenchman, is above me, with the two Canadian women in bunks on one side of me, and the two German men on the other. "Reach out and touch," is the motto in most Camino hostels' bed arrangements and Orisson is no exception. Why I hardly sleep this night has many possible explanations. Is it jet lag? Claude and a German snoring incessantly? The heat in the room? Too much excitement? Too much wine? People getting up all night to go to the bathroom? Whatever the reason, I can hardly find sleep, and by six AM the rustling and packing begins with headlamps slicing through the dark. By seven AM we have all stumbled down to breakfast, which in my case involves going outside first to retrieve my washed clothes which are hanging outside to dry, but which are now drenched because of an all-night drizzle. Survival lessons come quickly on the Camino.

A simple breakfast of bread and fruit preserves is all I can manage given my nervous stomach, and out into the fog I step. Most of my fellow pilgrims have already left and I expect to see them out ahead of me. To no avail. A dense fog envelops me and I see no one, barely even the trail at my feet. The steep climb is constant and physically taxing. I remember from my guidebook that the trail does branch off in two or three places so I remain on the lookout for Camino markers which will be hard to see in this soup of a fog. At one such junction I linger because the painted arrows on the ground are ambiguous. Do I go straight or veer off?

Suddenly, out of the fog steps Claude, my French bunk mate from last night. We don't understand each other any better this morning than last night, but he seems confident enough, so I trudge after him which is not easy because he walks faster than I, and is soon out of sight. Now the trail is fading and has become a treeless meadow. In this heavy fog I run the risk of losing all bearings and either going in circles, or walking off a cliff. I come to realize I have been led astray by my French friend. I let out a grim chuckle. It has taken the Camino less than twenty four hours to give me pay back for leading the Chinese woman astray. At least when the Camino punishes, it does so quickly.

I retrace my steps by following my footprints in the wet grass. To my great relief the earlier path appears and at least I am not lost. Who then shows up? My French friend bursts out of the fog from the other direction. He has also realized his error and looped back around finding his own way back to our point of departure. This time I take the lead, and pick up the pace. He can do what he likes, but I am going to trust my instincts, rather than riding on the coattails of someone else's confidence or enthusiasm.

After another two hours of heavy uphill slogging, I feel growing exhaustion, but also the first pangs of doubt that I can really do this Camino thing. My left foot ligament problem is acting up and becoming very painful. I should rest, but with the fog and drizzle, with everything wet and muddy, with no place to properly rest, I march on. An hour later I am still grinding it out, although I do resort to some singing to lift my spirits, but have to stop because I am breathing too hard. I force myself to stop and rest, even without sitting, and lean on my poles and nibble a few nuts for energy. I wonder aloud: "how am I going to keep this up for thirty three more days?"

Within minutes the trail levels and I realize I have passed the crest of the Pyrenees. A surge of joy and satisfaction passes through me as I realize that my first serious climb is over and I will be passing into

Spain shortly. Sure enough, there is the opening in the fence, with the stone marker indicating I have entered the province of Navarre. As if on cue the fog lifts, and I see a thick forest of birch trees emerging on my right, and a short hour later the sun breaks through as I approach a fork in the path with several pilgrims congregating and resting ahead of me. Surprisingly, I see none of my mates from last night, but decide this is a perfect lunch stop and dig into my small supply of wonderful French salami and bread rolls, all purchased in St. Jean yesterday. It all gets washed down with yesterday's fountain water and I feel as if I have feasted. The sun is burning off more and more of the fog, and I see deep valleys emerging ahead of me. Somewhere down there is the monastery at Roncesvalles, my first destination in Spain.

In the midst of my blissful interlude, a large group of about thirty young people with some adult chaperones appears. They seem to be Italian day hikers since none of them have backpacks, and they have likely sent them on ahead by bus or taxi. They too decide this is a good lunch spot, and soon they settle in all around me. They are in party mode, and I feel totally overwhelmed by the commotion around me. I am losing my just-achieved emotional equilibrium and I am losing it fast. I make an immediate decision to cut short my break, and get on the trail before this noisy group does.

At this spot the trail begins its descent into Roncesvalles and in places quite steeply. I look back up the hill and see the Italian group beginning to gather for their descent, so I decide to pick up the pace in order to retain my peace and quiet. All of a sudden the ankle weakened yesterday buckles, and this time, perhaps because of my momentum or the weight of my backpack, the ankle gives way as I am thrown into the ditch next to the path, directly on top of a thorny bush. I have sharp pain in my ankle, and can barely move because every move pushes thorns deeper into my skin. A vision of the Camino being over for me on only day two, flashes through my mind and my heart sinks. I slowly attempt to wiggle my ankle, and although there is strong pain, it does not feel broken.

With careful maneuvering and occasional swearing as another thorn punctures my clothes, I slowly roll over onto the trail and lie there with simultaneous shock, shame, and relief to at least be on my back. A grim joke forms in my head. Jesus received his crown of thorns at the end of his journey; I get mine at the beginning. If Jesus' script is the model, however, then I know things can only get worse. As I slowly sit up and try to move my foot, I feel the anger at myself welling up. Yes, the trail was very uneven; yes, I have had two nights of little sleep, never mind jet lag; yes, I am physically fatigued, but this was brought on primarily by my haste. In trying to outrun the Italians, I set my own trap and now the damage is done.

I slowly maneuver myself up and am surprised I can weight bear. It hurts like hell to move, but if I hobble gently on my bad leg, and use my poles to redistribute my weight, I find I can hobble on. Slowly I limp downhill, awkward looking I'm sure, but at least I am mobile. Within an hour the pain has lessened a bit and a first hint of optimism appears. Maybe I can survive this and not have to stop or curtail my Camino. The realization dawns on me that my excessive need to shape the Camino into **my** vision of what I needed contributed to this. My demand for peace and quiet, for solitude, for contemplation even, prompted me to want to push beyond what my body or the trail could bear, and here is the result.

Perhaps it was becoming stuck in this self-analysis, or my pain preoccupation, or both, but whatever the reason, I now miss the fork in the trail which would have taken me more directly through a soft forest path into Roncesvalles. It turns out I have now inadvertently ended up on the main highway (N165) leading into Roncesvalles. So while I am not lost, I am now having to walk the final twenty minutes on a winding highway with trucks and cars zooming by, and me hobbling gingerly to stay out of their way. I feel foolish and very vulnerable in mind, body, and spirit. My Camino lesson in all of this: don't let even worthwhile needs override other considerations, in this case, the caution I should have exercised for my already compromised ankle. Now I have really put myself in a very tough spot.

Suddenly, out of the last lingering fog of the valley floor, a great stone edifice appears. Could this be the famous monastery of Roncesvalles? I can scarcely believe my eyes as the entire array of buildings appears. As I approach the complex, I see a cairn where I deposit my joy and sorrow stones. It seems odd to have a cairn where the destination is so obvious, but maybe some pilgrims like me need extra reinforcement lest we get lost, just steps before our goal. Maybe the point is to offer gratitude, which I do as I linger over the stones. I sense the gift of this moment even in my pain and exhaustion. Here I am, almost fifty nine years of age, aching in body and soul, yet I sense myself to be in communion with the Sacred Spirit which has guided me to this path and is keeping my soul supple even if I seem to have become too hasty in this quest.

I hobble a bit further toward the maze of buildings and find the sign pointing to the registration office. The place is bustling. I feel as if I have entered a pilgrim village and soon discover that to be literally true. This is the starting point for many other pilgrims, especially those from Spain, with several hundred pilgrims passing through here every day. I leave my backpack and poles at the office and hobble to the adjacent restaurant and spot on the terrace enjoying the late afternoon sun, eight of my companions from last night. At the one table sit the Irish six, and at the other the Polish two. I am delighted at my good fortune to have found my pilgrim friends again after such a long, lonely day. I arrange to eat my pilgrim dinner with Gregor and Bogdan, my Polish buddies, where I will be able to indulge my wish to speak German on the Camino. Their German is impeccable given they are both University level German teachers. In the meantime, I will not miss a chance to join the Irish.

If there is such a thing as reincarnation, I would like to be reborn as an Irishman. In the summer of 2000, I had the opportunity to teach in Ireland, and over the years have had numerous Irish students. The Irish story is a rich tapestry of suffering and overcoming, so visible in their literature and music. They touch the poet and philosopher in me every bit as much as my German inheritance. Besides, they know how to party better than the Germans do, so I plop myself down in their midst, and they do not disappoint. Jokes abound, and between the laughter and the two beers I have been working on, I feel much better already. I can barely feel my ankle pain, but it may be that sitting down and having two beers has something to do with it.

It is now time to claim our beds and hopefully shower before dinner, and then attend the pilgrim Mass later this evening. Oddly, while I was one of the stragglers off the mountain, I am one of the first to claim a bed after the doors to the hostel open. The scene that awaits me is like nothing I have ever seen or imagined. As I enter this 1000-year-old Romanesque church, row after row of tightly packed bunk beds awaits me, and I am told up to 200 people will sleep in this room tonight. Since I am a lower bunk fundamentalist, I claim one right next to the front door, behind the boot racks, where hundreds of boots will be stacked for the night. Since the bathrooms and showers (three for men and three for women) are downstairs, I want to be as close as possible to them in case night time bathroom needs overtake me. While being close to bathrooms was helpful, it turns out sleeping next to the smelly boot rack was not such a good idea. But one cannot think of everything.

Albergue at Monastery of Roncesvalles

Waiting in line for a shower stall with dozens of men is a strange experience. Perhaps because we all pretty much smell the same, it is not as oppressive as one might expect. Everyone is on their best pilgrim behavior, and the process moves along rather efficiently. While I am limping somewhat, I feel amazingly better. I will have to remember this formula for future occasions. Two beers plus a shower equals instant renewal.

By 8 PM the pilgrim Mass is about to begin as around eighty of us file into the Augustinian Chapel. Virtually every seat is taken as we participate in the liturgy. While nowhere near as stiff and disconnected as my experience at Notre Dame, I still feel the whole experience lends itself more to observation, not so readily to identification with the story of God-with-us. This detachment seems true for most of my fellow worshipers also. The Eucharist itself becomes a moment of pain for me. The instructions given to us are quite plain and emphatic: no non-Catholic is allowed to partake!

Sadly, this strong official and explicit stance is very different from other times and places I have known. As I sit on my seat while others proceed to the front, I recall one of many alternative moments. In 1990 I was asked to give a Protestant theological response to a conference on John Paul II's encyclical on Mary called "Redemtoris Mater." This conference was held at Newman Theological College in Edmonton, Alberta, Canada. The Catholic Archbishop of Edmonton at the time specifically came to me before the conference closing Eucharist and extended the following invitation to me: "Bill, you are most welcome to fully participate." This is only one of many such invitations I have received over the years especially from Franciscan and Jesuit communities. Sadly, times have changed, and I no longer feel such a welcome even as I know how much this pains my Catholic friends. Surely this is not what Jesus had in mind when he invited all of us to the feast that is visible in his life.

The entire experience is redeemed at its conclusion, however, when the presiding priest invites all of us as pilgrims to come to the altar for a pilgrim blessing. Not only does he look us in the eye, every country of origin is named. He specifically prays for us, for the particular challenges we are facing as pilgrims, and for the personal concerns we are carrying. This beautiful pastoral blessing allows me to be held in my hopes and anxieties, and empowers me. We all quietly slip out of the chapel and head for the stone edifice which is to be our home for the night.

It is more than just a novelty to sleep side by side and in bunks with well over one hundred and fifty people. Lights are turned off promptly at 10 PM, and a surprising hush falls over the room. There is a sense of oneness as a human family that seeps into awareness at such a moment, in sharp contradiction to our modern sense of privacy and separateness. Yes, there is a fair bit of snoring and coughing going on, but not as overpowering as one would expect, likely because the room is so vast that our sounds dissipate.

In spite of my tiredness I keep waking up and by 2 AM I am wide awake. Not wanting to wake anyone by turning on my headlamp, I simply begin observing the traffic moving past my bed back and forth to the downstairs bathrooms. The traffic rate is about one pilgrim per minute according to my calculations. I watch this for at least half an hour and soon calculate that over a four hour period, approximately two hundred and forty trips to and from the bathroom will take place. Presuming everyone who goes downstairs eventually returns, this means up to one hundred and twenty pilgrims, or about 75% of us used the bathroom that night. I conclude from this that pilgrims either have weak bladders, or have had too much Spanish wine the night before. In my case both would be true.

By 5:30 AM the shuffling and rustling of backpacks begins, although my upper bunk neighbor, Michael, a young Danish physician, has already left the bunk around 4 AM never to return. It turns out his mattress was agonizingly soft and he somehow found another bed for the rest of the night. By 6 AM the lights come on and by 6:30 AM most pilgrims have left. In that short time span, unbeknownst to me, since I was in the bathroom, a man in the far end of the church has had severe angina. He has become largely nonresponsive and an ambulance has been called. With our hosts, the "hospitalieros" fully in charge, and nothing the rest of us can do, I step into the cold and dark to stretch, settle my pack into a snug, comfortable position, and begin my first full day in Spain.

Given the lack of sleep for days now, and the foot problems of yesterday, I am expecting a rough start, but surprisingly my foot pain is modest and my energy brisk. After a short portion of trail along the main highway, the path soon veers into a dense birch forest that slowly brightens with the rising sun. I am brought up short by a modest historical marker off to the side that identifies these woods as a hiding place for persecuted witches during the Middle Ages. My heart sticks in my throat as I read that up to eight women from the village immediately ahead were executed by burning and/or drowning right here in these woods. All of a sudden history reaches me with a kick in the gut. One or two other pilgrims gather around but none of us knows what to say. Overwhelming sadness and a whiff of terror surrounds me. I offer up a silent prayer: "forgive us, for we know not what we do."

A few minutes later I reach the town where numerous pilgrims are crowding into the only open café for breakfast. I order my first "Cafe con Leche," the survival drink for every pilgrim, and spot Gregor and

Bogdan and join them on the outdoor patio. We debrief our nighttime experience at the monastery, but I cannot bring myself to talk about the impact the murdered women realization has just had on me. It feels too fresh and intense somehow. We decide to walk together for a while, and a surprising sight awaits us a few steps from the café. Immediately adjacent is the church of St. Nicholas, a saint closely identified with the Camino and the protection of pilgrims. To get back on the path we must cross the church courtyard, and we see there a large sign describing with even more detail the persecution of the women identified in the woods.

The three of us are compelled to linger and are deeply touched by this very public and visible acknowledgment, and are especially gratified to see these events described as arising out of the narrow and prejudicial attitudes of the day. While these explanations do not always go far enough at owning the religious contribution to such persecution, it is a huge step in the right direction. The sheer fact that this disclosure is on church property is most significant. It is a reminder that even our sacred religious traditions can be twisted into dark pursuits. We leave this solemn church courtyard and settle into a brisk pace in a long caravan of over a dozen pilgrims, each of us quietly nursing his thoughts about what we have just seen.

CHAPTER 3

Hitting Walls

He That Is Down Need Fear No Fall

He that is down need fear no fall;
He that is low, no pride;
He that is humble, ever shall
Have God to be his Guide.
I am content with what I have,
Little be it or much;
And Lord, contentment still I crave,
Because Thou savest such.
Fullness to such a burden is,
That go on pilgrimage;
Here little, and hereafter bliss,
Is best from age to age.
John Bunyon, Pilgrim's Progress, 1678
Ralph Vaughan Williams

*G*regor, Bogdan, and I trudge on at a reasonably fast pace and become engrossed in conversation. We continue for two hours or so and by 10 AM the sun has fully risen and the heat of the day is building, prompting a change of shirts, and a switching from regular glasses to sunglasses. I place my pack on the ground and set my glasses on top while changing shirts, without realizing my glasses have slipped off the pack. Back on goes the pack, with my sunglasses on my nose, and off I march. Approximately 5 mi/8 km down the trail, a haunting awareness dawns. I never put my regular glasses back in the pack, so I stop and check, and they are gone!

Since I remember exactly where I left them, an excruciating dilemma erupts for me. Do I go back those 5 mi/8 km, find these glasses which are my prescription reading glasses, and then walk the same distance all over again? Do I forgo my connection with these my Polish walking companions, or do I let the $400 prescription glasses go? I make the split second decision to walk on leaving my glasses behind, and serve up the following rationalizations to myself: (1) I am enjoying my walking companions very much, and may never catch up with them again if I lose the pace now; (2) I could use new glasses anyway; (3) there is something to be learned here, such as needing to find new direction for my life, so I am supposed to lose my glasses in order to get the point.

All these rationalizations begin to take on water faster than a leaky ship, and before long they sink under the weight of their own silliness. The fact is, I feel badly about this decision, and soon begin to second-guess myself. Yes, I had to make a decision and did so quickly, but the decision soon begins to seem terribly foolish to me. I become insistent that it was a bad decision. I had to make an immediate decision, which I did, but now I don't want to live with it. As I walk on with my friends I begin to wonder even more intensively whether I have chosen properly. Then I begin to wonder on what basis I can even make such a judgment? This small choice is but one of countless decisions I make all the time, but what it reveals is the ambiguity that is hidden in so many decisions. It is true that this decision will have consequences for me just as an alternative decision would have. But since the future is not known to me I can only judge myself based on the factors that are present to me at the moment, namely, losing $400 glasses, versus an extra 10 mi/16 km of walking. Even now, with the value of hindsight,

I doubt I would have made a different choice, since my decision at the time was based on the entire context, including my emotional state at the time. None of this of course stops me from second-guessing or berating myself, even before the serious consequences which are about to follow.

Within an hour of this decision, my Polish friends have moved on ahead since their pace is faster than mine. I had not yet made the brilliant calculation that since I am fifty nine years old, and they are twenty to twenty five years younger, they can probably walk faster than I. The entire dilemma is accentuated by the fact that a very steep descent has begun from Viskarret to the river Arga. On this descent over very rough and rocky terrain, I see my young Danish bunk mate from Roncesvalles, Michael, sitting at the side of the path looking rather forlorn. He is a strapping six foot six athletic type, with muscles and energy galore, and has blazed past me several times today. Each time I end up passing him again as he sits at trail-side working on his feet. This time I stop and ask: "What is wrong, can I help"? I am shocked as he shows me his feet. He has worn both heels so bloody that an entire layer of skin is missing.

I happen to carry a full if modest supply of foot care items: gauze, alcohol swipes, "second skin," as well as bandages, which I make available to him. I feel very strange trying to help this medical resident with his wound care. It seems impossible to me that he can continue like this but he is determined to carry on. I help patch him up and walk with him a while, but with his long, youthful legs, he also moves past me into the woods ahead and disappears.

I am alone again, and perhaps because I am sinking into unintended contemplation and thus not concentrating effectively, or because the trail is supremely rough and rocky, or, heaven forbid, my sunglasses are too dark to see clearly in the heavy forest, I now seriously twist my weakened ankle for the third time and fall heavily on sharp rocks and land with a thud, flat on my chest. I am at first too stunned to understand what has just happened. I try to roll over, but my backpack won't let me roll on my back so I turn onto my right side and swear under my breath as the throbbing pain in my ankle finally reaches my brain. I notice my pants are torn on the left knee and there is blood visible. My right knee also hurts like hell. I can't get up and think: "this is it, I am done!"

After about ten minutes of letting the shock and pain subside, I slowly turn onto my left side and get up onto my hands and right knee which does not seem to be injured. From this position I use my poles, which are surprisingly still attached to my wrists, to help pull myself up and stand on my right foot, with my two poles used for balance. I look like a flamingo on one leg but at least I am out of the ditch. It occurs to me I need to check my bleeding knee, but I have to pull my pants down to do so. It reveals modest bleeding, but no knee damage beyond the bruising, so far as I can tell. I take off my pack and fish out what is left of my medical care kit and begin my own wound treatment, as I stand on one leg and one pole.

A couple of large bandages later, I pull up my pants, and slowly try to weight-bear on my gimpy leg. It is no go. The pain is just too sharp. I sit down and allow another fifteen minutes or so to go by, and slowly increase the weight on my left leg. It seems the ankle can now hold my weight so I likely do not have a break but only a more serious sprain. Ever so slowly I take short hopping steps, and find I can actually move without screaming in pain. My knee, while bruised, seems workable. I realize that if I put as much of my weight on my wrists as possible by using my poles, the ankle can hold me up and so I improvise a tight wrist support system with my two poles. Amazingly, if I half hop and half walk, I can actually move. My pace is exceedingly slow yet I force myself to keep moving and a full two hours later arrive limping at the town of Zubiri.

Entering Zubiri takes one over the medieval Peunte de la Rabia bridge, and the River Arga. This is the famous spot where according to legend, any animal crossing under the bridge will be cured of rabies. I do not believe I have rabies, but conclude that any hint or prospect of healing can't hurt, so I head down to rivers' edge as fast as my one and a half legs will carry me. I take off boots and socks, noticing how swollen my left ankle is, and wade well into the river where I sit on a large rock and allow the river to cool and hopefully restore my feet. The cold icy water has an amazing effect. I stay in the water for over an hour and find that the swelling has gone down significantly, allowing my ankle to become limber enough to walk on.

Healing Waters of River Arga (Zubiri)

While sitting in this glorious stream I find two new small prayer stones in the water. I take the opportunity to hold a stone in each hand as I offer up the joys and sorrows of the day. I have had so many strong thoughts and feelings just in these last few hours I cannot hold them all in. Today I have encountered not so much a sense of loss, but more a sense of futility and self-doubt. I berate myself for the lack of concentration and poor decision-making which has contributed to my physical distress today, yet at the same time I am amazed at my strength, courage, and resilience as I have fought through pain in order to make it this far.

As I sit in contemplation at river's edge, Michael appears, his feet newly bandaged at the local medical clinic. His face is less tense with pain, but I sense his sadness. He tells me his Camino is over because his feet are simply rubbed too raw and he will need many days of complete rest to recover. Tomorrow, he will take the first bus out and head to Madrid for a few days before his flight home. I will encounter this scene many times in the days and weeks ahead. Strong, vibrant, vital pilgrims, young and old, fall by the wayside as the limits of flesh and blood, of mind and spirit, overtake them. Michael certainly pushed himself to the edge of his limits and then beyond, and in the end no other choice was available to him.

Why at this moment in my own threshold of pain and extreme discomfort do I make a different choice? I have every reason to stop here in Zubiri. It is my third day in a row of serious ankle and ligament problems, along with a banged-up and bloody knee. I have painful and worsening heel spur complications. I am near complete exhaustion, so why at this very moment do I decide to leave Zubiri where there is room in the hostel, to walk on to Larrasoanna, another three mi/five km away?

The choice seems crazy, and even with much reflection in subsequent months I am hard pressed to explain it. Yes, I am driven by the daily distance requirements that the guidebooks suggest. Since I have only thirty three walking days available to me, I feel I have to keep up the pace, since I am already behind. Yes, I am in denial about the fact that I am no longer 40 years old. But perhaps the deepest reason is that the Camino activates one's deepest inner drive mechanism. I believe the Camino is a mirror for one's life, concentrated into a few short weeks. There are core yearnings and impulses that drive all of us in our lives, and for most of us, when this fire is lit, we seek to bring those desires to completion. For me that fire burns in two directions.

First of all, I want to enter into life as fully as I can and to make as much sense of what I experience as possible. That means not taking shortcuts into convenient "outs," or settling for easy solutions or answers. Cutting corners experientially, intellectually, physically, or spiritually cheapens the quest and dilutes it somehow. I am not going to dilute my Camino opportunity so I have to give it all that I have to give. Stopping early, even with all my legitimate reasons, would be giving in to excuses and I am having none of that.

Fire number two has to do with "coming home." Perhaps being an immigrant to two different countries in my life, with two separate immigration experiences to the United States, has forever saddled me with this kind of seeking. At its heart, however, this second fire is spiritual and not defined by time and space. I believe we all seek our spiritual home, and for me this is particularly strong in a mystical sense. Santiago beckons me as a surrogate spiritual destination, a kind of practice run for the real thing. I am seeking my spiritual home and no bum leg is going to stop me.

So off I go into the late afternoon sun, hobbling up the steep hill that leads out of Zubiri toward Larrasoana. Given the lateness of the day, I have the trail to myself, other than a pilgrim or two passing me. I hobble the whole way, but make it to my own surprise. Arrival in Larrasoana brings me into a rather undistinguished small town, where the main fifty bed Albergue is full. I make a mental note to myself to remember that little fact next time I undertake a late in the day extension of my walking. Thankfully, a second albergue in town with twenty four beds is still taking pilgrims, but the extra steps to get there, never mind climbing stairs to the second floor, is more than my legs want to take, but up the stairs I must go. I can feel the bane of all pilgrims, blisters, burning on my toes, and am afraid to look. Besides, I am too tired take off my boots so I just sit at the edge of my bed staring at them. It is ultimately hunger and thirst that arouses me from my stupor and I stumble downstairs to shower.

It is amazing how water renews and washes away weariness. What the water cannot wash away are my blisters, one on each foot, as I feared. It may be hard to believe, given all the ankle and ligament problems that have plagued me, but I have practiced good foot care as best I can tell. I wear expensive silk sock liners under high quality wool socks. I have well designed boots, broken in before I left Chicago. I rest and air out my feet every three hours or so, so why am I getting blisters?

Granted, the trail is surprisingly rough and rocky. They say that God, when creating the world and attempting to distribute all the stones, had the bag of them break over Israel and Palestine. I can now attest with good authority, that the bag first broke over Spain. There are stones of every shape and size on the Camino, and eventually one encounters every variety of stone. One's feet bear the brunt of this pounding and whether the stones are sharp or smooth, they all grind away at one's feet. While I have "second-skin" patches and Band-Aids with me, I have no actual blister treatment, such as needle and thread, nor any remaining disinfectant since I gave the last to Michael. I will need to figure this out quickly, since untreated blisters can translate into Camino shut down even more quickly than my ankle problems.

My shower restores me enough to do my daily ritual of clothes' washing. With only two extra pairs of anything from socks and shirts, the smelly, sweaty clothes of the day must be washed daily to have a clean set for the next morning. Any interruption of that ritual and you become an olfactory hazard to yourself and those around you. It is quite amusing to see the seriousness with which we pilgrims take this matter. We march to the little sinks and basins with our smelly socks and underwear, and gratefully share clothes pins as our tattered and faded garments flap in the breeze. My torn pants look noble somehow hanging on the line. I at least have the look of a serious pilgrim.

A look around the two hostels in the village reveals no familiar faces and again activates this intense sense of aloneness. I try not to mope about it and trek over to a restaurant to make a reservation for the seven 7 PM pilgrim meal. All I can think of is to find the closest bar for a much needed beer before dinner, and to my surprise I find four of the Irish six. A joyous welcome ensues but I quickly discover that they have had their own problems. Phyllis and Sharon have taken a taxi to a medical clinic on the outskirts of Pamplona where Sharon needs treatment for a severe allergic reaction to an insect bite. She has a huge swollen and inflamed arm and she cannot continue. Phyllis has serious blisters and needs her own intensive help.

The rest of the group asks about my status and I share my tale of woe, including my own blister problems. Sean and Sheila now reveal their Good Samaritan pilgrim heart. Once they hear that I do not have proper blister treatment know how, nor supplies, they insist on treating my blisters immediately, on the spot. Up on Sean's lap goes my first leg while Sheila sterilizes a needle and the toe in question. She expertly pulls needle and thread through the blister at which point the thread is cut and knotted, leaving the remaining thread inside the blister. A bandage is applied, and then the process is repeated with the other foot, only this time they have reversed roles, with Sean working the needle and thread.

To receive spontaneous care in this fashion from virtual strangers is a mind blowing experience. My normal barriers of not being a burden to others, taking care of things myself, resisting the grace of unmerited care, all come crashing down. I become aware how much ego is wrapped up in self-sufficiency. I have been worshiping at the altar of my own capacities, and in this simple act of care, my little temple comes crashing down. I leave their circle of care humbled and enlightened. Since we have reservations at different restaurants for a pilgrim meal,

I feel the sadness of saying goodbye, but have overwhelming gratitude for the gifts of care and the awareness that have been given.

Arrival at dinner at a lovely rustic Spanish Inn brings me into contact with a whole new group of travelers. Of the twelve of us sitting at one long table, I am by far the oldest. A quick realization comes to me: "No wonder everyone keeps passing me on the Camino. Most of my table mates are half my age!" On my right sit two women art teachers from London in their early forties. On my left is a mid-thirties male Scottish Buddhist from Glasgow. Further down sits a mixed group in their late twenties including three men, two Australians and a Belgian, and three women, one a radiant blonde from Finland. She is getting the bulk of the attention from the men, and I am both glad and perhaps a little bit envious that I am not in that game anymore.

A typical pilgrim three-course meal begins. We start with a generous and full plate of mixed salad, followed by the main course of fish. I have three little trout, with their tiny heads intact and eyes looking up at me. There is a side dish of pasta or potatoes, followed by a small desert of either pilgrim cake (almond), yogurt, or an ice cream cup. This pattern seldom varies, and the options are generally few, but the cost is always reasonable, tasty for the most part, and yes, the wine is more or less unlimited. What's not to like?

Within minutes of sitting down next to my Scottish neighbor, even before the salad arrives, he shares with me his purpose for the Camino. He is on a ritual purification journey after a breakup with his girlfriend. He has had addiction struggles in his life and believes it was one of the factors in the rupture. He is on an intense spiritual journey, he says, and is finding guidance from within Buddhist traditions. He offers me one more example of the power of the Camino to open one up, and to give voice and direction for all the lost and broken parts of ourselves. He shares all this freely and without reservation, even though he as of yet knows nothing about me. He knows nothing of my work or spiritual commitments, but is sharing heart to heart as one human being with another, in this instance, with someone twenty five years older than he, from a different culture and spiritual framework. Yet share we do, mutually and fully, with no foray into roles, rules, or litmus tests of authority or legitimacy. Just human to human connection.

By 9:30 PM our party is winding down as we all weave our way back to our various hostels or hotels. I notice that not everyone goes the austere path as I am, and I carefully file that little fact away for future consideration. By 10 PM I am washed and in bed with my twenty three other roommates, and this surprisingly includes six children, two of whom are younger than ten. These two, it turns out, are part of a family of four from England traveling with two donkeys and two dogs. They have been underway for several weeks now and are on a three-month trek to Santiago. With a twinge of sadness I think of my own family and some of our major treks, although none included donkeys or dogs, so I let the association fade, and fall asleep to snores and squeaky beds.

Awakening at 6 AM just to queue in line for a toilet and sink has limited spiritual merit, I believe. I am not grateful this morning, and I don't feel like asking for the gift of gratitude either. The sinks are dirty and I have no place to put or hang anything. I would be better off to stuff my exotic little super-drying towel into my underwear than to lay it on that sink, so that is what I do. No one speaks at this hour and we are probably all feeling as pissy as I am anyway. I leave as soon as possible, and spot the two tethered donkeys in a field in the early dawn light. No café is open at this hour, and sadly, no towns appear either, so I must trudge on with no coffee or breakfast. The sky is mostly cloudy this morning matching my mood it seems. After two hours or so I take my first break, with water my only refreshment. I still have a bit of bread and sausage from yesterday, but I resist the urge to devour it since that will have to be my lunch.

My discomfort over no food is more than compensated for by the fact that I can move at all, after the events of yesterday. My ankle, while painful and swollen, is operational, and the blisters are manageable right now. So I march on, alternating singing with meditative walking, and eventually draw alongside a gentleman my age. A quick greeting reveals he speaks English and a robust conversation picks up, culminated in his beginning to cite poems by Yeats for me. This he does effortlessly without interruption. He is a walking anthology of poetry. But once he launches into interpretation and analysis, I take my leave and move on. My mind is not in analytic mode today and furthermore, I seem not to need intense company right now.

By midmorning I am at the outskirts of Pamplona and am feeling overwhelmed by the intensity of the place. This is my first encounter with a city since I left Paris, and it feels overwhelming with traffic, pedestrians, hard pavement, and the concentration required not to miss Camino signs. But perhaps I am not meant to walk alone on this stretch into Pamplona after all as I unexpectedly meet a white-haired, gaunt looking pilgrim around my age who greets me in a German accent very familiar to me, "Swabian." My birthplace is Goppingen in Swabia and it turns out he hails from a village about 18 mi/30 km from where I was born. Not only does this trigger many ethnic and cultural associations for me, it turns out Herman walked out his front door three months ago and has been walking ever since. His suspenders and very loose walking shorts are now about three sizes too large, offering evidence of pilgrim weight loss, and are ample proof he belongs to a group of exotic pilgrims I will from henceforth call the "long walkers."

These are the elite pilgrims who walk out their front doors most anywhere in Europe and have just kept on walking, although in the case of the English or Irish, they need plane or train assistance to cross the English Channel. These are the marathon walkers of pilgrim lore and deserve their place of honor in any pilgrim Hall of Fame. The fact that most ancient pilgrims utilized this method only enhances their glory in my eyes. The only ones who exceed even this honor are those who do it twice in that they also walk back the way they came. When one meets one of them going back the other way, one wants to bow at their feet, one hardly knows what to say to them, they seem ethereal somehow.

It seems to take forever to reach the old city center of Pamplona, but the famous walls of the Citadel eventually appear and guide me up a steep slope and stairway to the old city gates. Only one step through the city gate and a surreal world appears. I am hit in the face by smells, long wooden fences set up in the narrow medieval streets, all of which creates a canyon like effect. Then it hits me! Of course! Yesterday was the conclusion of the annual "running of the Bulls," and the city has just begun to clean up. No wonder I am smelling piss, shit, beer, and other by-products of human revelry and general mayhem. This year's running of the bulls was especially gruesome with two runners killed and many scores injured. Maybe the day after is the worst day to try and gain appreciation of this cultural event, so I move through the old town as quickly as possible.

Having had virtually no food since yesterday evening is not helping me keep my stamina up, so I find a small store to purchase my usual lunch of bread, Spanish sausage, and beer, and step off the path and its Camino markings to a quieter square (San Nicholas) to eat. Even here the place is being cleaned up, with porta toilets being removed, pavement and sidewalks cleaned, but at least I have found a bench where I sit under a row of shade trees and remove my boots and socks. Perhaps on any other day, having my socks hanging to dry on a bench in city center would be offensive, but today I even belch my beer as loud as I can. Today no one can possibly raise a stink about me.

Leaving Pamplona by midafternoon confronts me with the heat of the day, but I feel the pressure of putting a few more miles/kilometers behind me, and set pace for Cizur Menor, about 4 mi/6 km down the road. The climb out of Pamplona is not steep but reveals my fatigue. The rough and uneven trail has made praying and meditating more difficult since I have to concentrate so much on the path. Singing is also a challenge, especially when climbing, since one can't sing when one is sucking air. Thus I tend to save my singing for flat stretches. For today, I simply stay within my thoughts. What occurs to me is how the Camino is a microcosm of life. It is a concentrated version of one's life jammed into a few weeks. It draws us forward with hope and promise, but with every turn surprises await. Because I take my higher and lower self with me wherever I go, even here all my challenges and capacities follow me.

Today, I am amazed at my resilience. How can my worn-down body, full of aches and pains, be so ready to walk all over again each morning? Where does this fierce drive come from to walk through the pain with no assurance there is some satisfaction awaiting me? On the other hand, I sense my self-criticalness gathering steam. I have been beating myself up for days now for losing my glasses, for not going back to retrieve them, never mind for not doing proper foot care to prevent the blisters I am now dealing with.

I am also feeling the pressure that comes with the realization that this pilgrimage is not repeatable, just as my life isn't, and therefore I have to do it right, whatever that may be. Oh, I may walk another meditative and reflective journey someday, but I won't walk this one again. There can be power in that awareness, a sharpening of my focus perhaps, and an invitation to embrace this intensification of what I am experiencing in the moment. But there is also a touch of sadness, because I need to let each moment go, knowing it is meant to be released, hopefully to become the soil of my life where new things can be allowed to grow.

In the midst of these thoughts, the final hill into Cizur Menor approaches. By now I am in major foot pain. There is ankle soreness and tendonitis, but the main culprits are new blisters I can feel. At the top of the hill I have a moment of confusion as I stand at a traffic circle looking for Camino signs and a very specific hostel, the Albergue Roncal, which has been highly recommended. Two French pilgrims next to me move off confidently in a specific direction and I hesitantly follow since I have no idea how far off the trail this hostel might be. But there, just around the corner, it appears.

After some of the stark, box-like dwellings of the past few nights, this hostel rises up from the street as an apparition of luxury and grandeur. I enter a courtyard of green, lush vegetation, where I am welcomed by Madame Roncal herself. After she registers me in, stamps my pilgrim passport, I take off my boots as is pilgrim etiquette, and am led deeper into a complex of attached rooms toward a separate small building. It is a cozy and quaint Coach House where I am offered a choice of one of eight beds. Three beds are bunks and two are singles, and since none of the single beds is taken, I claim one, throw my pack onto the floor, and flop onto the bed, too exhausted and hurting to move.

I lie there paralyzed for a while before I can even appreciate the rich wood paneling, the soft lace curtains billowing in the breeze, the firm mattress, and the calm and quiet of this place. It seems I have stumbled into an oasis far more serene than anything I could have imagined. While my feet are hurting like hell, the brief rest on the bed restores me enough to allow me to stumble for a shower and my clothes washing ritual. My tasks complete, I seek out anyone who can guide me to a watering hole where my beer remedy can be found, when Madame Roncal herself appears.

Perhaps because she observes my blister induced gait, or sees me grimace when I walk, she invites me and any of her other guests for foot treatment after dinner, if we so wish. I file her invitation away as I walk to dinner taking note of my ambivalence. After all, I have learned blister treatment from my Irish friends, and have enough supplies for now. What can she possibly offer me that I don't already know or have?

Arrival at the restaurant brings a pleasant surprise. The two young Canadian women, Sally and Michelle from my first night in Orisson, are seated in a corner and wave me over. So much has happened to all of us in just these first early days that we hardly know where to begin. Their most memorable moment thus far came on the day of intense fog just after leaving Orisson when they became lost looking for the famous statue of the Virgin Mary, the Virge D' Orisson. In the midst of wandering and feeling increasingly desperate and confused, the fog which surrounded them lifted momentarily, and there was the statue, virtually in front of them. Within moments the fog closes back in on them, but in the meantime they have their bearings again, and proceed to find their way. Now, many days later, they continue to puzzle over the mystery of this moment and what it might mean for them.

As we tell our tales, I become aware of one of the powers the Camino possesses. It generates unexpected spiritual moments of insight, of synchronicity, of challenging old meanings, even as it offers new possibilities of awareness or truth. But at this moment I am even more fascinated at how the Camino is a great leveler of difference(s). Even here in my encounter with these two Canadian women I observe how different we really are. We have significant differences in age, gender, race, professional roles, and religion. We supposedly have Canada in common, but even in this item we are quite different since I am from the West, and they are from the East, and as any student of Canada knows this is also a great divider.

The leveling action of the Camino is that we all end up hurting, aching, and limping, and seeking something. When we meet in that place of our common experience of limits and our seeking, a unifying energy appears between us that is palpable. I believe this is a major source of the Camino's great appeal. It does away with so many of the role, class, religious, and other distinctions we place on our common humanity. Perhaps it is the equanimity of this realization that helps me overcome my resistance to receiving the full hospitality that Madame Roncal is offering. By the time I return to the Albergue I am ready to say yes to her special gift of hospitality. And what a gift it is.

My foot treatment begins with a cold vinegar and salt water treatment for my feet. While my feet are soaking, this foot Angel tells stories of her twenty two years of hospitality out of this her family home. This lovely setting with fifty beds is full most every night. I can hardly begin to imagine how many lives she has touched in those years. Yet here I am getting direct, explicit attention with my feet in her lap. To begin with, sanitized syringes are injected into my blisters to drain off excess fluid. After further sanitization, Band-Aids are placed on each blister (now numbering three), and directions are given for further care steps in the days to come. She then removes the arch supports from each boot, as she grabs large feminine napkins, spreading them flat and taping them onto each insert, and placing each back in its respective boot. From now on, she insists, I must walk on feminine napkins for moisture control and additional cushioning. After three days maximum, new napkins must be obtained!

I begin to swallow hard. How am I supposed to find and purchase package after package of feminine napkins in Spain when I don't speak Spanish, and furthermore, I will at a minimum have to tolerate weird looks from cashiers and fellow shoppers, even if I figure out how to ask for them? My raised eyebrows do nothing to deter Madame Roncal. My boot laces are quickly removed and re-laced, only now so they also allow the foot to slide back slightly when going uphill, but hold the foot snugly in place by not slipping forward, when going downhill. Then comes her final diagnosis after my feet are carefully back in their boots: "Your boots are too small!!" She reminds me that I have not calculated foot swelling as a by-product of daily extended walking in the severe Spanish heat.

I take my feet back out of their rejected boots and take a close look at them. By golly, she is right! Beyond being pink and puffy, my feet are huge. If they had some hair on them they could have passed for Neanderthal feet. Why have I not noticed this before? I leave the care of my "sole" Doctor somewhat chagrined, but enlightened, and am determined to fix this problem which is threatening to bring my journey to a halt.

I sleep well for virtually the first time on the Camino, perhaps because there are only five of us in the room, or perhaps because I am very relieved that a solution to my foot problems might be at hand. By 6 AM I am awake, and out the door by 6:30 AM. It is cool and cloudy which makes for good brisk walking. The early morning light and calm conditions contribute to a mood of reflection and contemplation. I find an insight taking hold of me about the thresholds of our so-called "limit moments" that life serves up for us, and which are a daily experience for pilgrims on the Camino.

If my experience is common at all, pilgrims seem to be constantly facing these limit moments on the Camino. These boundary moments have to do with our pace of walking, the distances covered, the daily duration of walking, as well as our experiences of hunger, thirst, togetherness or aloneness. One is always crossing over into a new zone of challenge. The changing landscape is often a mirror for us, a living backdrop to ever-changing body sensations of comfort or discomfort, welcome or unwelcome thoughts and feelings. The physical landscapes can sometimes seamlessly flow into one another, perhaps matching perfectly our emotional states, whereas sometimes they profoundly contradict what we are experiencing internally.

On this morning, I begin with inner and outer harmony. I am rested and at peace, hopeful, and surrounded by calm. Nature's hush and gentle coolness matches my centered and energized self. Yet after a few hours of walking my first strong sense of fatigue begins to overtake me. I sink into myself to draw out more reserves of energy and try to keep myself moving. By this time, the gray, cloudy sky of midmorning matches my growing lethargy and fatigue. I begin to experience feelings of sadness and turmoil building within me. Yet one moment later, everything shifts.

As I turn a corner on the trail, a massive field of sunflowers suddenly appears. All the bright, sunny heads are looking my way, seeking the sun just barely poking through the clouds behind me. What a panorama of celebration! At this moment all the pilgrims around me, myself included, cannot help themselves from stopping and taking pictures, not just of the flowers, but of ourselves next to these wonders of creation. What prompts all of us to spontaneously stop and celebrate this feast of color and delight?

William S. Schmidt

Happy Sunflowers

It is true that just their bright sunny faces are enough to demand a smile from us, but as I see it, they also have a natural orientation to what they seek. They seek the sun, the light of their lives, and they are very determined in their seeking. They crane their stems so powerfully and consistently, to the source of their nourishment and their light. This field of flowers invites me to cross over into this joy which I now do in full measure. I find that the ever-changing Camino landscape never ceases to invite me into this crossing over. At times this crossing over acts as a confirmation or validation of where I am, with nature serving as a mirror revealing where I am in my state of being, and blessing it. At other times, however, this crossing over comes as a challenge which awakens me to something I am not yet attuned to, but am being asked to accept and embrace. My prayer stones also function this way. They remind me that both hardness and smoothness define my way and both are real and legitimate.

This mirror of nature can awaken me to aridity, where the hardness of the trail is so packed and compacted that nothing can penetrate. In those instances I am invited to consider the possibility that as responsive as I was to the sacred flowers of this morning, I can also be like the hardened trail I so often walk on. Most of the time I welcome the thresholds of delight, but I can also put up roadblocks to joy when

I am too attached to my misery. In those instances I am being invited to face the hard, packed soil of my heart, the well-worn paths where I allow nothing new to penetrate.

I am discovering that the Camino is all about healthy discomfort which many times even crosses over into pain. How many hills and valleys have I already crossed that brought with them an aching pain in ankles and calves, back and shoulders? My whole body strains on these long, steep slopes, with sweat pouring off me, my gasps for air the only sound I am making. How can this pain and discomfort be in any way useful for me? This pain forces a concentration out of me which I would otherwise probably avoid. The pain in my feet forces me to notice them. They now have my attention. This pain is not masochistic, but is the price I must be willing to pay to get to new horizons. This is not simply "no pain, no gain," but more like "no challenge, no overcoming, and therefore no new life."

This for me is one of the great learning's that the Camino offers, and which is also a core learning about life. Change is central to life and there is no new life without change. I avoid change because it is uncomfortable and often painful, even extremely so perhaps. Yet it comes. On the Camino we come to it. On the Camino, as in life, perhaps I must choose the discomfort and maybe even the pain because I trust that there is something beyond that next horizon, even though I may have no idea what that next something is.

Leaving these fields of sunflowers and the forests which surround them, now takes me toward an open panorama of high hills far in the distance. Dozens of windmills dot the hillsides and I see the pilgrim trail winding its way up and over at their highest point. I am grateful for this cool morning yet and am constantly stopping to either take on or take off my windbreaker as I alternately overheat, become chilled very quickly, only to repeat the cycle all over again. By the time I reach the summit called the Hill of Pardon (Alto del Perdon), I put on almost all my remaining additional layers since the wind is howling and I am freezing.

One last rise, and I am on top of the ridge where a large metal sculpture of a dozen or so life size pilgrims leaning into the wind awaits me. They all face west, their metal coats flying behind them, matching my look exactly. There are also about fifteen to twenty living pilgrims milling about taking pictures, resting, and sharing snacks. I recognize no one and am constantly surprised at the changing flow of humanity that swirls around the Camino. It is way too cold for my liking on this ridge, so I take only enough time to grab a handful of nuts out of my pack as I begin the steep descent that now awaits me.

Wind Buffeted Pilgrims

By now it is midmorning and I have been walking for over 7 mi/12 km and unfortunately I sense another blister forming. The trail is brutal here, with loose boulders that are very hard on my feet. I stop and check, and sure enough, I am adding another blister to my roster. Thankfully, the ones treated by Madame Roncal are holding up under their bandages, but given how fast this next one has appeared, I feel the urgency of getting my boot problem taken care of. Even more troubling is my growing recognition that my feet are not yet tough enough for what I am asking of them. I am going to need to ask them for forgiveness at some point, but not yet. For now they need to know who is boss around here.

CHAPTER 4

A Wholeness Stone

A Pilgrim's (Difficult) Credo

I am not in control,
I am not in a hurry,
I walk in Faith and Hope.
I greet everyone in Peace,
I bring back only what God gives me.

By noon, July 17, I have arrived at Peunta La Reina, a lovely medieval town with its famous six arch Romanesque pilgrim bridge over the river Arga. Since I purchased my lunch items as soon as I entered the town, I decide to settle down for a lunch break on a grassy knoll right next to the bridge. The shade of the bridge keeps the sun off me as I stretch out and fall asleep. I lose track of time as I lie there, and awake refreshed even though my heel spurs are painful, and my blisters sore, but it all seems bearable, at least while I'm sitting down. It is only mid-afternoon, and I make the split second decision to plow on to the next village called Cirauqui, 5 mi/8 km down the road. If all goes well I can walk this stretch in two hours allowing me to arrive by late afternoon, with time left to shower, wash my clothes, and even rest a bit before dinnertime.

Climbing the stairs to the top of the bridge brings me face-to-face with Sally and Michelle, my Canadian friends. They let me know they are staying here in Peunta La Reina, along with Gregor and Bogdan from Poland. My new German friend, Horst, whom I met earlier this morning at the sunflower field, is also in their company. They have already all checked into the local hostel, having arrived well before I did. A moment of indecision overtakes me. Do I change my mind and stay, so as to not lose contact with these fellow pilgrims, or do I push on and get some additional distance out of the way? I choose the latter, perhaps because in my last such dilemma, when choosing to stick with the group, it ended in the disaster of the lost glasses, and a bad fall. Besides, I am already a day behind my schedule, so this is a chance to make up some lost time.

The steep hill that awaits me as I head out of town has me quickly second guessing my decision. There is no shade anywhere in sight, and I keep forgetting how hot Spain gets in the mid-afternoon. Sweat is pouring off me now, but I have plenty of water, so I will likely not die of dehydration. The wind is also picking up again, and pushes against me, but I enter into walking meditation rhythms to keep my pace strong and steady, and hopefully keep my mind and heart clear.

I am jolted out of my trance—like walking by an unlikely stone lying in the middle of the path. It seems to jump out at me and compels me to pick it up. It is white, round, and smooth, and in complete contrast to the dark, jagged stones that make up this portion of the trail. It is likely a river stone, having been washed over and ground away at through the ages, to give it its oval shape and smoothness. It is a mystery to me how this unusual stone has arrived at this spot. What occurs to me is that I have found a third stone to accompany my joy and sorrow stones, only this one I will call my "Wholeness Stone."

This stone comes to represent for me the requirement to take the joy and sorrow themes of my life, and integrate them within myself in a harmonious and unified way. I am deeply touched by the power of this symbol of unification, and I sense I have found a very helpful addition to my practice of praying with stones. The question it asks of me is: "Am I willing to be changed, to be worn smooth by the joy and sorrow that enters my life?" What rough edges need to be knocked off me, and what will be the effects of all this inner and outer work?

The question is persistent and given all I undergo in my life, whether positive or negative, joyful or sorrowful, will it bear fruit? Will it find some coalescing of purpose, and can I live from this center? I am very energized by this additional avenue for my prayer life, and even though a windstorm has broken out on top of me (without rain), I lean into the wind, and feel the power in my legs and arms, even with the foot pain that seems to forever accompany me. I extend my arms as far out in front of me as I can, let the poles dig in, and propel myself forward through the dust.

Ahead of me is Cirauqui, a medieval hilltop village, with quaint and narrow winding streets. The last steps into the village are a strain, all uphill, but at the same time I feel the satisfaction of having walked 17 mi/25 km today, the last quarter of which are a leap ahead I was not expecting to accomplish. At the very top of the village is a lovely private hostel across the square from the thirteenth century church of San Roman. Everything is fresh and clean, and I actually enjoy trudging off to shower and wash my clothes. With about a half hour to spare before the pilgrim meal I decide to lay down on my bunk for a moment, and am startled when someone shakes me awake. It turns out to be our hostess, Maria. The meal which her husband has beautifully prepared is already underway and I am the only one missing. She had to climb the four flights of stairs to come and get me, and I feel slightly sheepish as I walk into the restaurant behind her as the meal is just underway.

We twenty pilgrim dinner guests are seated at three tables, and I take the last chair at one of them. At my table are a French couple my age from Brittany; two young Swiss walkers, and two gorgeous French women in their thirties who look as if they have just walked out of a fashion magazine. Since I did not see a helicopter pad in the town square, I conclude that they probably didn't just fly in, but it seems impossible that they walked. Between the designer outfits, subtle makeup, and great hair, there is no strain on their faces. Given a smattering of a few common words of French, English, and German, which we share between us, I gather that the French women are about one week into a two-week Camino "vacation." I start to realize there may be other ways to approach this trek. What I have embraced as an ascetic discipline of medieval proportions, they see as an excursion of fun and relaxation. They must think I am doing penance for some unspeakable sin, since all my pain and suffering talk goes right over their heads. They find me amusing it seems, and I likely remind them more of a clown than a saint, but either way a good time was had by all.

Pilgrim meals tend to linger, not because there is little else to do in most towns and hamlets, but because the comradery is so great. I am convinced that this is one of the great draws of the Camino, this built-in internationalism and the removal of normal social and cultural barriers. Connections are made quickly and the shared experiences of the Camino itself acts as a social, emotional, and spiritual magnet. The key is to find a common language, and tonight it was mainly German with a bit of English and a few words of French which get me through. But beyond the words, it is a certain feeling that seems to bind us to one another, and the word which best represents it is "respect." We respect what we are doing, and are eager to honor what the other is attempting, without necessarily knowing all the motivations or reasons behind our walking. Even if we think we know why we personally are walking the Camino, every one of us is in a process of discovery about why we are here, and this connects us all in some way, old and young, male and female, rich and poor.

On this night I linger until about 9 PM and am in bed by 10 PM when most hostels have lights out. I fall asleep quickly, and although there is rhythmic snoring among the twelve of us seemingly throughout the night, I sleep so well that I slept well past my desired wake-up time at 6 AM. I even slept through the noisy ritual of everyone rushing about packing, and by the time I awake a half hour later, the last stragglers are leaving. Another half an hour goes by and I am finally out the door, with only a small vending machine cappuccino to jump start me and get me on my way. Still slowly packing up around the hostel are the eight or so bicyclists who tend to leave later in order to arrive at their destinations later. They are generally only admitted to hostels after 6 PM when most walkers have already arrived with the walkers given priority for beds.

I begin walking alone this morning under partly cloudy skies with the sun not yet visible. It is cool and I am glad I am wearing long pants and sleeves. I find myself walking gently downhill over actual Roman roads and a still useable ancient Roman bridge. The large paving stones are uneven, with many gaps, but the whole experience is surreal. To be walking on 2000 years of history touches me deeply, and I think of the slaves that had to haul these stones from far away quarries with no equipment to speak of, with at most only rough implements and their bare hands to complete their excruciating work.

It occurs to me that one of the common features of our human experience through the ages is our experience of pain. It would of course be downright grotesque to compare the physical pains of these road builders with my Camino complaints. But I do find a valid question slowly surfaces for me as I walk this morning: "What are the most painful moments of my life?" This is a valid question for anyone to ask themselves, and for me a variety of memories hit me including moments of rejection, alienation, and loss. The most intensive pain factor for me at this time, is of course the loss of my marriage. In an odd way, however, all the pain memories coalesce into a kind of generalized pain best represented by a sense of homelessness. I feel the full force of these feelings and they are followed by my first modest tears of the Camino. I normally do not cry this way and find myself surprised by what is happening.

I intentionally seek not to control these feelings even as I am left with a deep ache in my gut. As I am swimming in these emotional currents I take the sorrow stone and the wholeness stone out of my pocket and hold them each in one hand. I feel spoken to in a distinct way as I do so. It is as if the Spirit has spoken to me through the stones reminding me that all this pain can be used for good through the power of God if I align myself with that power.

As I continue walking an analogy occurs to me. At the deepest parts of the oceans, the pressure of the water is so enormous that it pushes the tectonic plates of the Earth's crust down into the molten core of the Earth, where they are softened and reconstituted to emerge as the new land masses of islands and mountains. Even now the Pyrenees Mountains which I have just crossed, are growing several centimeters a year. Perhaps pain acts the same way in us. It takes us down into the core of our being and through the alchemy of our painful journeys, and the small deaths that accompany them, we ultimately are transformed into new life. Jesus' parable of the seed that must fall into the ground and die in order to bring forth new life, is a vivid scriptural analogy for this process.

My walking is strangely solitary today, perhaps simply because I was the last one out the door, but few others have passed me from whatever their starting point of the day has been. But perhaps I needed solitude today in order to sink more deeply into myself. The emotional work of the morning, on top of the brisk walking, has left me very tired by lunchtime, and thankfully the town of Estella appears, and I take a long two hour break to give my feet a sunbath, with blister-management included. Getting back underway at least somewhat refreshed, I take aim for Villamayor de Monjardin, a high hilltop village about 7 mi/11 km away. But first a wonderful surprise appears right in front of me as I am leaving Estella. It is a great compensation for all my pain reflections of the morning. It is the monastery Irache, where free wine is dispensed in a pilgrim wine fountain.

I curse the fact that I have no cup with me to capture this red gold. I would have gladly emptied my water bottle to turn my water into wine (my own small miracle moment), but the spigot dispensing wine is too large for my bottle, and it would be sinful to have it spill all over the place. Not to be deterred, I hold my open mouth under the tap and take big gulps as best I can. It spills all over my face and down my chin anyway, but no matter. I am having way too much fun with this once in a lifetime surprise.

Monastery of Irache (Free Wine)

A few gulps later, I stand up, turn around, and spot not ten feet/ three meters behind me two large, well-stocked vending machines with soft drinks, locked up behind wire mesh. I burst out laughing as I think: "these monks have a great sense of irony; they lock up the expensive, useless drinks, and force us to drink the free good stuff." I point this out to a small group of pilgrims who have just arrived, but they don't seem to think it is as funny as I do. Their thoughts seem written on their faces: "this guy has been here a bit too long!" I take this as my cue to pack up and get moving, while chuckling to myself and feeling happier than I have for days.

My bliss does not last long because the mid-afternoon sun is baking me dry, and my feet are killing me. Monjardin sits on a hill at least 500 feet above the valley floor, with the ruins of St. Stephen's Castle at its peak. I know a final climb awaits me, and as I begin my ascent I soon resort to grunting and groaning, but nevertheless keep breathing deeply to keep oxygen circulating, and finally arrive at the crest, only to realize that the village is on another higher hill beyond the one I have just climbed. My heart sinks as I realize I have probably another half an hour or so to go. Now I am really struggling since the pain has become very intense, yet I have no choice. There is only one way to get relief and that is to get to my destination.

A half an hour later I stumble upon one of the two hostels in the village, and simply collapse on the bench in front, only to discover it is still closed for another hour. I drag myself to the second hostel further up the hillside, and find that it too is still closed, as is everything else in this little hamlet. This siesta business may be good for the locals, but it makes for some challenging situations for pilgrims. There is not even a bar or café open, so with no beer or coffee available to me, I stumble back to the first hostel and plop myself on the ground at the front door.

In a fit of temporary insanity, I seriously entertain the thought of keeping going for another 6 mi/10 km to Los Arcos. It is as if my mind and my body are going in opposite directions and they are no longer effectively communicating with one another. What may have saved me from my folly is the sight of two strapping, athletic-type pilgrims, stumbling towards me as they round the corner. It turns out they are two Swiss "Iron Man" triathletes, in top condition, who have just finished three days of over 25 mi/40 km per day, in other words, one marathon a day. They have obviously overdone it, with one of them in agonizing tendonitis pain with a huge swollen foot. The sight of these well-conditioned athletes rendering themselves virtually immobile wakes me from my insanity and I make the decision to stay. I grimly note to myself that we all seem to have to learn the lessons of mind-body disconnect, whether we are fit or not fit.

An hour or so later our host appears and begins to register us and offer admittance to the cool interior of the primitive abode that will be our home for the night. Within another hour the place has filled up, and not a familiar face in sight. I keep being surprised at the pilgrim turn over, and it accentuates my sense of aloneness, but I try to make the best of it by getting to know my table and bedroom neighbors. This includes a couple in their late sixties from South Africa who are on their second Camino, with fascinating stories to tell.

We eventually meander to our sleeping quarters where a most unusual scene awaits me. There are sixteen of us in this small, old, and decrepit building, with ten of us sleeping on a raised platform all in a row, with no space whatsoever between us. We are all on old vinyl-covered mattresses, with the only way on or off the platform from the front, since the three remaining walls form the perimeter of our bed space. There are three bunk beds on the remaining wall with a narrow, one person wide corridor between the bunks and the raised platform, presuming you stand sideways. It is all very intimate to say the least. If that does not provide enough closeness, we have the benefit of sharing two old showers, one toilet, and one sink. We have reached another level of initiation it seems to pilgrim land.

I am grateful to be next to the wall, so I have only one neighbor to my left, a thirty year old Italian man walking with his sixty year old father. At my feet (literally) on the lower bunk is a young French woman who does not seem to mind that my feet are inches from her face, since the room narrows at that spot. The real problem turns out to be the backpacks which have no place other than on the tiny floor, so we have literally to crawl over them to get to our beds. Between our clothes, toiletry bags, bedding, and other personal items, the room is a mess and a jumble of arms, legs, and heads, trying to find things, not lose things, get comfortable (maybe), and get back up to wash or go to the bathroom; in short, general chaos, all of which is not normally associated with spiritual well-being.

Yet here we are, stretching our spiritual muscles toward sensitivity, patience, and general goodwill toward our fellow human beings. It is hot and noisy, and even after lights-out, the headlamps we all wear cut through the darkness like a laser and light show. Strange languages are heard softly whispering, and together with the rustling of bags, zippers opening and closing, the beginning of snoring, we create a symphony out of our rituals of settling into sleep. It feels wonderfully ancient, archetypal even, and in that spirit I too fall asleep.

Six AM means lights on, with several pilgrims already packed and ready to head out the door. I quickly rinse my face and join the early birds in the small kitchen for a bread and jam breakfast. There is no point heading into the sleeping quarters right now to pack, since it is too crowded to do so properly. In short order people begin to leave, and by 6:30 AM I too am out the door into the cool morning air. First light reveals a cloudless sky slowly turning light blue. Within a half an hour I am walking completely alone over gently rolling hills of grass and grain. The trail is smooth and made up largely of crushed gravel, and at this point of the day at least, not too hard on my feet.

My first indicator that something is wrong with the trail is the absence of footprints on the ground in front of me. I stop, turn around, and notice no footprints other than my own. There are tractor-tire tracks visible, which makes sense since I am on farmer's field paths, but I see no footprints. On a pilgrimage there are always footprints, so something is odd. I come to a split in the trail, and the absence of a marker indicating directions gives me my first real confirmation that I have missed the trail. I am still calm, but nervous. Retracing my steps for a few minutes reveals nothing helpful, and since I have the sun directly behind me, and I know I need to keep heading West, I decide to keep moving forward in a generally Western direction, hoping to find the pilgrim trail up ahead, or if not, find a road which will lead me into the town of Los Arcos, my next major destination.

What I discover, however, is that these farmers' tracks all go in circles, around endless hills, all looping back into one another. I have now been walking for an hour in this fashion and realize I am lost. I start to panic and conclude I cannot even retrace my steps any longer. I slow myself down, stop, and force myself to become calm. Yes, I am in the middle of nowhere; yes, it is early on a Sunday morning and I have seen no one since I left Monjardin one and a half hours ago. Yet,

I rationalize, if I keep going West, I am bound to run into someone or something helpful.

Sure enough, fifteen minutes later I see a middle-aged man walking way off in the distance. I dash off over fields toward him, and see he is actually on a path walking more or less in my direction. He is wearing earplugs and I motion him to stop. He is Spanish, and I know no Spanish, with the exception being the only phrase I taught myself back home as a joke: "Estoy Perdido;" "I'm lost!" I use the phrase liberally with him, until I am sure he thinks I am an idiot, and then remember to add the words "Peregrino" and "Los Arcos." He smiles, nods, and points in the general direction I have been walking. My relief and gratitude is overwhelming as we say goodbye, and all of a sudden I see way off to my left alongside a series of low hills, a small group of three people walking, and by their backpacks I know who they are. Pilgrims! Hallelujah! I once was lost, and now I am found.

I slowly work my way toward the sighted pilgrims by marching over farmers' fields and within fifteen minutes, have joined the pilgrim trail and spot my first blue scallop shell marker of the morning and feel the relief of being back on the path. As I walk I cannot help but draw some spiritual and life lessons from my little adventure. When no tracks are visible, chances are we are setting out more or less on our own. Sooner or later life asks us to enter uncharted territory, if only because our life is unique, and no one can walk on our own path but we ourselves. So, there is an inevitable solitariness and unknown quality to all our walking. At the same time, much of what we pursue in life, whether in loving, or working, or spiritual seeking, is not exclusive to only us, but there is always someone who has blazed at least a partial trail for us. The wisdom figures through the ages, the sages and saints, never mind our own mentors and models, all walked the trail before us and left some markers for us to consider for our lives. This allows us to at least orient ourselves in many of our life choices, even when other moments ask us to reject a certain path. Sooner or later, however, we will find ourselves in uncharted territory either by choice, or by accident, as happened to me today.

At some deep level, even as I was panicking today, I knew I needed to experience this. How could I presume to walk the entire 500 mile/800 kilometer Camino and never get lost? Even while I seemed lost, however, I realized that I was not without guidance. I had the sun; I had my inner sense of direction; I had a trust that a path would eventually appear, and above all I had the unexpected arrival of an "angel" in the guise of the Spanish stranger. I only became "lost" when I lost trust. In everyday life I tend to use the comforts and reassurances of things "going well" as my markers, my every day "scallop shells" that I am on the right path. But when those confirmations disappear how do I orient myself? Do I in fact have deeper levels of trust from which I can draw courage and direction? This is of course the eternal gift of Faith, the assurance of that which is not yet present or visible. The loss of my marriage is just such a challenge. I am not yet able to "trust" this loss in the sense that all will be well, or that it will somehow serve me toward further growth. For now, I am living in the void, but perhaps my experience this morning is a reminder to simply trust the void.

In spite of the strain of the morning with the lost time and extra mileage, I make it to Los Arcos by noon and after a short break of baguettes and sausage I plunge on for another 10 mi/16 km to Vianna, which includes two very steep stretches, completely taxing my endurance. By the time I am still 2 mi/3 km or more from my destination deep exhaustion has set in since I have now already walked 18 mi/29 km today. In this state I happen to come across a pilgrim resting at the side of the road. She is an older French woman, thin as a rail, with a club foot. We can barely understand each other, and I discover she has also set out from St. Jean, not many days before me, and here she is walking with incredible stamina and fortitude, and above all with this vibrant, happy spirit. I am not sure if it is my shame at my own irritability with my fatigued self, or being inspired by her example, but somehow this encounter propels me forward with new vigor toward Vianna.

Another preoccupation today includes the question whether to step away from pilgrim accommodations for a night and treat myself to the luxury of a hotel. Prior to the Camino I wrestled with the question of how 'pure' my Camino needed to be. Could I occasionally skip a hostel and still be a "real" pilgrim? What if I took public transportation for a portion? These are not just abstract questions or reserved for a neurotic perfectionist like myself. I experience many pilgrims with the same sort of questions, although perhaps they agonize over their choices less than I do. Before the Camino began I thought that I might treat myself to comfort and privacy once a week or so. So here I am, one week into the Camino, having just endured a night sleeping like sardines. Even more importantly, tomorrow, July 20, will be my thirty fifth wedding anniversary. If ever I needed comfort surely this is it.

By the time I stumble into Vianna with 20 mi/32 km on my odometer for the day, I am ready for luxury, and luxury I get. At the end of the street all the way through the historic medieval center of the town, appears the beautifully restored palace "Palacia de Pejudas," a hotel with many stars next to its name. As I stand gazing up at its ramparts, the glass doors magically open and give me entry. As far as I am concerned, the gates of heaven have just opened and the Lord God Almighty is whispering in my ear: "Well done, thou good and faithful servant, enter into the joy of your Master."

There is nothing like a week of deprivation and suffering to heighten the pleasure centers of the brain. Just stepping into the lobby leaves me gaping with delight. I am not sure if I am most taken with the grandeur and spaciousness of this place, or the fine art on the walls, or my fantasies of clean sheets and a private bathroom, but I do take a full turn inside the front door in complete awe before even proceeding to the registration desk. The arrival of smelly, stunned pilgrims must be normal for the staff because no one seems to give me a second glance, although there is a chance they may have been holding their noses behind my back. No matter, I am soon heading for my private room and it's glorious upscale bathroom. It does not disappoint. I use every possible bathroom feature I can, including all shower settings, soaker Jacuzzi tub, and bidet (recommended for swollen and blistered feet). The luxurious, plush bathrobe together with the wine from the refrigerator, makes for a royal transition to the dinner hour.

As I am changing into my evening clothes, I make a startling discovery. My only other long pair of pants is missing. A bout of head scratching takes me to the only conclusion possible: I forgot them at the hostel last night in Monjardin. With the crowded conditions in the place, I was probably rushed in my packing and forgot they were hanging to dry outside. I do not beat myself up over this omission, which is surprising. Maybe this Camino is softening my demanding inner voice. I slip on my only remaining pants, still torn and dirty as they are, to head down to the fancy restaurant chuckling to myself. If they don't like my attire I will go back and change into my walking shorts, the only other pair of pants I have left, and let them look at my skinny legs with the pilgrim tan, and see if they like that any better.

Eating alone in the fancy restaurant begins to take me deeper into myself, particularly my feelings of isolation. Every other table has two or more patrons at it, with no pilgrims in sight as far as I can tell. As solitary as the Camino can be, the evening social and dinnertime provides instant community and belonging, often at unexpected levels. I find myself missing this comradary, yet I need to face my own reality on this anniversary eve. A temptation presents itself at the table next to me in the form of three attractive women speaking Polish, who keep using the word "Chicago." I can't resist inquiring, and as they are reasonably fluent in German and English, I find out that two of them have friends and family there. They find my pilgrim identity intriguing and invite me to join them at their table. I am sorely tempted by these Polish maidens, but it would be a distraction, so I graciously decline by mumbling something about being tired and needing to get my rest. I take my own advice and don't linger over the meal, but retreat to my room for some important journaling time, and inner preparation for the hard day to come tomorrow.

During my restless night I cannot find a comfortable temperature setting, and am jumping up and down to either open or close the window (too noisy vs. too stuffy), or to turn on or off the air conditioner (too cold or too drafty). At no point do I find my way into restful sleep and eventually awake knowing I will be facing a challenging and emotional day. I give myself a final indulgent treat of fully utilizing the hotel buffet breakfast, and filling my pockets with rolls as I walk out the door. I feel no shame since I am after all a poor pilgrim. The cool 7 AM air fully wakes me as I saunter down the medieval streets with the horizon slowly brightening behind me.

My plan for the day is to revisit my recollections of my wedding day as a way of honoring those two special young people and the hopes for loving we brought to each other. I remember every detail of our wedding day and want to gather it all up in my heart. I have the fleeting thought that I may simply be setting myself up for unnecessary pain, but that does not deter me. I feel I need to do this to affirm the love I came to know both in giving and receiving over these many years. There is an attachment which lingers even over two years of separation, and I cannot honestly turn my back on what I feel. Trying to honor that love, while at the same time recognizing the challenges which split it asunder, is agonizing. Throughout the morning I float between surges of love memory and loss memory. But the raw reality remains. I am not envisioned as part of Margita's future, and having no future together makes it even more painful to remember the gifts the relationship brought.

By late morning I am so exhausted with this emotional work, never mind severe pain in my feet, that I decide to take a lengthy stop for lunch in Logrono, the major city just ahead. Even in the short time it takes me to reach Logrono, I am feeling horrible, with sneezing and achiness adding to my misery. I find a bench in a green square close to city center and decide to linger for a while to contemplate my state.

The realization slowly dawns on me that I am stuck in marital grief. It seems to have become my sole focus for the Camino even though I began with wider intentions. But today I surely need to make an exception since this is after all my wedding anniversary eve. But at the same time the question remains whether my preoccupation with marital loss is perhaps taking too much space in my entire life? One of questions emerging for me on the Camino concerns how to appropriately come to terms with the messy aspects of one's life. Preoccupation with pain, with loss in my case, can become a fixation, a kind of idolatry. I do want to enter into healthy self-assessment without losing myself in blame or guilt.

Here, on the eve of my wedding anniversary day, I am being called to release my attachment to something that was precious, yet was finite, and can no longer define my life. In the middle of this internal battle I feel the unifying stone in my hand. It invites me to hold the tension of these two life forces closer together. Sometimes life pushes love and loss very close to one another. Both are so real right now and to remain authentic I must embrace them both as part of my experience. I have loved deeply and been deeply loved, and I must feel the full weight of this love even as I release myself from it. I am being asked to honor, but not to hold. What hard and sacred work this has turned out to be, and I offer a prayer of gratitude for the way the Camino is supporting me in this work.

CHAPTER 5

A Wedding Anniversary

Peace

There is a peace
that passes understanding, (Philippians 3:6)
a peace
that needs not
control.
Though life is
uncertain and random
and chaos is ever present,
there is peace.
There is a peace
an intuitive knowing
that fits
like pieces of a jigsaw puzzle
into a coherent whole,
at peace that seeks and finds
Peace.

William S. Schmidt

> There is a peace
> longing to be present
> in all the world,
> Peace that desires
> nothing more
> than quiet
> forgiveness, acceptance
> and recognition
> of the sameness and differences
> that make us human.
> When peace and Peace
> connect, as if God's hand
> on the Sistine Chapel finally
> reaches Adam's,
> the world will breathe
> a sigh of relief,
> and the *thank you* will reverberate
> through
> eternity.
> Jennifer (Jinks) Hoffmann

*L*eaving Logrono in early afternoon on hard pavement and scorching heat is a grueling slog, but I also feel somewhat lighter given my new insights. The way has also been made lighter by a surprise encounter with my German friend Horst on the outskirts of Logrono. His slow and steady mode of walking is a perfect match for my state today. We agree to walk only as far as Navarrette today, another 8 mi/12 km distant, but perhaps reachable in two and a half hours.

As we approach the outskirts of town a woman named Anna with a small boy is standing next to her car, adjacent to the trail. She is advertising rooms in her private home at a fairly reasonable price. She is Ukrainian, but speaks German, hence Horst and I can understand her. Her husband of five years has left her, so she rents out her home to pilgrims to help support herself and her little boy Alexander. We quickly decline the offer, when she informs us it would involve up to four persons in a room. As sick and miserable as I am feeling right now, I know I need a private room and decide to opt for a second night in a hotel. Upon entering the historic Navarrette, Horst and I split up to see what is available, with Horst searching for pilgrim hostels, and I scouting out nearby hotels. We agree to meet in an hour to compare results. By the time we rendezvous Horst has discovered that the hostels are full or seriously inadequate somehow, while my research has revealed that the cheapest room available in the three hotels I visited is €70. I do not dare spend that much money two nights in a row if I don't want to completely blow my budget, so we go off to find Anna. Her home is situated at a high point in the town, and although new, is surrounded by several collapsing buildings, as often seems to be the case in rural Spain.

It is now late in the afternoon, and with Anna's chances for additional guests slim, she agrees to give each of us a private room for a modestly higher fee. I gladly oblige her since by now I am utterly exhausted with severe leg cramps in both calves, throbbing blisters, and sharp pain in the soles of my feet. Excruciating pain is no excuse for not finding an open bar with cold beer, so off I go hobbling and grimacing, but determined. Besides, it is my wedding anniversary day and I am going to drink a toast to myself, and if I am lucky, get drunk for the first time in my life. Horst senses how pensive I am and decides to explore the town on his own. I am relieved that he is giving me my personal space since I need to claim private time to reflect and to journal. Down the hill I go and find a nice cool bar where I am the only guest.

I soon realize I am way too tired and exhausted for any decent reflecting, so I quickly finish my beer and walk back up to the hill to Anna's. As I walk in her door I realize I have forgotten my wide-brimmed Canadian "Tilly" hat which is indispensable for a bald eagle like myself. Back down to the bar I trudge to find the missing hat. A thorough search through the entire bar reveals no hat. I cannot imagine anyone taking such a sweat-drenched monstrosity so it has to be back at Anna's. Back up the hill I go and this time I scour every part of the house. Again, no hat. By now I think I am going crazy.

It can only be in one of two places and I simply cannot manage without it in the scorching Spanish sun, so back down the hill I go. Back at the bar I look under every table and in every corner, when it hits me. The bathroom!! Sure enough, there is my hat, calm and cool, patiently waiting for me. Perhaps the sun has already scorched my brain even with the hat, because this memory lapse has created a terrible rift between my mind and my feet. The mind blames the feet for my misery, and the feet cannot believe how stupid this mind is for forgetting something as simple as a hat. I must now crawl back up the hill for the third time.

At this point I feel so physically and emotionally worn down, I can barely drag myself to my room, only to fall down on top of the bed where I fall asleep sweaty and dirty. I awake almost two hours later feeling tired, sore, and sick, with a heavy cold. Miraculously, however, between the sleep and the long hot shower, I am sufficiently restored enough to decide to take up Anna's offer to make a private pilgrim dinner for me. Horst has decided to eat elsewhere, and given my sneezing and general misery, along with my wedding day blues, he has made a very wise choice.

Anna's house has a small garage at its front which opens onto to a narrow lane. A small plastic table sits at the entrance of this garage, with a view overlooking the town and the valley below. She serves her pilgrim guests here, and tonight I am her only customer. The early evening air is soft and mild and the light golden, as I settle in with a bottle of wine for what I hope will be an evening of being at peace and somehow comforted, even in my misery.

Anna's Pilgrim menu begins well enough with the typical first course of salad and a small pasta dish. The main course arrives eventually and upon arrival all I can do is stare. What sits on my plate is unrecognizable as food, and a few pokes at it with a fork, reveals it has excellent bounciness. It looks like a huge overcooked Portabella mushroom, loaded with piles of overcooked spinach which I hate beyond any food item. On top of all this sits a mountain of melted cheese. It takes major effort to cut it, and the first bite leads to endless chewing, to no effect. I have never eaten rubber, but this has to be what it would be like. The taste is so disgusting I simply cannot swallow one bite. I smirk as I realize this is my wedding anniversary dinner. But what am I to do with this thing on my plate, with my host hovering nearby?

Anna is playing soccer with her son in the lane right in front of me. I cannot try and sneak the dish into the bathroom to attempt to flush it, because it would surely clog the toilet. Eating it is out of the question, and I do not have the courage to hand it back. After all, this may be her primary dish. Just then God intervenes. The soccer ball takes a big bounce, and careens madly down the hill with Anna and her son running after it and are soon out of sight. My moment of liberation has come. I grab the large napkin on the table and dump the blob into it. It is larger than a large softball, and nicely round. Directly across the lane is a decaying house with a large hole in the roof. I take aim and try to throw the entire mass into the hole. Wonder of wonders, it is a direct shot, and I cannot believe my accuracy. It had to be the hand of God guiding me.

Some ten minutes later, the happy duo return with their ball, and Anna is very impressed with how clean my plate is. I smile sweetly, pat my stomach contentedly, and happiness is felt all around. After she leaves I want to burst out laughing, a gut splitting laugh that I have to suppress to not draw attention to myself. This of course gives me cramps, which makes my situation all the more absurd, leading to more repressed laughter. As final wedding anniversaries go, this one surely has to rank as one of the most bizarre, and leaves no doubt as to God's sense of humor.

The next morning brings departure after an edible breakfast prepared by Anna with thankfully no left-overs. She also offers to pack a lunch for me, just as she had offered to wash my clothes yesterday, and brought me extra drinks when I first arrived, all of which I gratefully accepted, without of course asking about the price. Now as I am packing and getting ready to leave Anna hands me the bill. It reads as follows:

Room	€40
Dinner	€15
Soft Drinks (2)	€5
Breakfast	€10
Lunch	€10
Clothes Washing	€10
Total:	€90

My jaw drops. This is well over $120, more than I spent the previous day at a four-star hotel, and well beyond my pilgrim budget. I choose not to grumble or argue and grudgingly admit it was worth every penny. When tears are turned into laughter, how can one impose a price tag on it?

It does not take long after my departure from Navarrette for new problems to begin. Within the hour I experience cramps in my calves which seriously slow me down. There is also numbness in my right foot from my toes through the ball of my foot. Perhaps that will be the answer to my foot problems? Just pound my feet into numbness until they no longer feel anything, and everything will be just fine.

The cramping forces me into an early break, and when I sit the cramps subside which does not exactly motivate me to get back up again, but in time I do. Within minutes the cramps are back only now so severe that I am slowed to a crawl. I will never make it this way. I begin to seriously wonder what I can possibly do to salvage the situation I find myself in, and as I agonize over this question I pass a sign noting that I have passed the 125 mi/200 km mark. I am amazed to realize that I have already walked one quarter of the way to Santiago, yet it dawns on me that I have already used up one third of my time available, namely ten days. These numbers are not adding up and something will have to give.

As I contemplate my dilemma I think of yesterday's walking companion, Horst. He has shared with me that he has taken the bus on two occasions even as he is critical of those he calls "tourist pilgrims" who are driven from meal to meal, hotel to hotel, with a few hours of walking in between. But even he regulates the level of energy he will expend, and I suspect, probably makes the most reasonable choice available to him. Now, I too am confronted with my own limits and the tough choices that arise from these limits.

Sitting in a rest area adjacent to the trail literally unable to move, gives me opportunity to think about this factor of limits in my life. In normal everyday life I generally do not think actively of boundaries or limits and am simply not conscious of them. This would include the daily limits of my energy or resourcefulness, but also include the limits of my understanding, my compassion, my awareness, or any other aspect of my capacities. Only rarely do I consciously allow limits to directly impact my choices.

On the Camino, however, the theme of limits is not so easily avoided. One is quickly and inevitably confronted with limits and in many ways the entire experience is defined by this question. The first and most obvious limit the Camino forces into awareness concerns the limits of my body. How much will I demand of it? Every pilgrim must answer this question every day, and often every hour. Today, at this very moment, the question is screaming at me in the form of cramps that are not allowing me to walk.

My pain is so strong and intense right now, it is as if I am peering into an abyss. This is a place I rarely get to because I normally do not live at this threshold of pain. In this moment of being brought to a screeching halt, my sense of my own power, my competency, and even my freedom itself, are profoundly visible to me, but in their limit form. When my limits are not in doubt there is often no reason to consider them. Perhaps this is why we need such moments, because in such a place of radical limit is where our freedom is most in question and thus most visible. At this point of radical limit my momentum no longer carries me. I have to choose. Do I plunge into the pain again and attempt to break through the barrier of pain or do I not?

Today, on this pilgrimage, I face this question at virtually every level, the physical, emotional, and spiritual dimensions of my being. How will I meet this moment of challenge? Can I even still hope to do this? Do I still want to do this? Will I make it? What does making it actually look like? Have I not gotten enough benefit out of my experience and what more do I possibly hope to gain? At this moment when I cannot really even walk, only hobble, the only answer I receive for my question is: "You can try to walk if you force yourself, but be aware that you will pay high price for it."

In the middle of these ruminations Horst suddenly walks up behind me. I have not seen him since breakfast, and he is obviously taking his sweet old time since I was slower than a turtle myself today. I share my painful tale of woe with him but he interrupts me to declare: "you have an electrolyte problem and need some magnesium or potassium." "Here," he says, and pulls out his tube of magnesium tablets and has me dissolve them in my water bottle. I gratefully accept, and begin to realize that he may be onto something. Between my cold and fever, and the heat and strain of walking, I have seriously dehydrated myself.

We bid each other goodbye since I still need to rest and hopefully allow the healing remedy to take effect. There is also no reason for Horst to sit and watch me recover when he has his own challenges to meet. An hour or so later I decide to test things out, and surprisingly I am relatively cramp free. Even though all my other pains are still there, I can at least walk! Hallelujah! By now the heat of the day is fierce, and I decide not to tempt fate by extending my mileage, and choose to stop at Azofra, in midafternoon. I may have 'only' walked 15 mi/24 km today using many more hours for such a distance than I normally would, but perhaps I have come into a more conscious relationship with my body which I hope will serve me in the weeks ahead.

Given the small size of the village of Azofra (500 people), I have no difficulty finding the municipal hostel which is a new sixty bed facility with only two pilgrims per room, a real luxury. Surely I will sleep well tonight! There is a lovely shallow wading pool on the landscaped property, with pilgrims clustered around, splashing and laughing. All seem much younger than I and I recognize no one. My roommate is Fernando, a Spanish man in his thirties from Valencia who has been walking from his home on the Mediterranean coast of Spain. He has been walking since May and is in his third month with another month to go. His story prompts me to shut up about my aches and pains. His commitment represents a significant example of the range of pilgrim paths and motivations. His English is sparse, but I glean a spiritual hunger that is born out of his life which is in major transition, with the recent loss of a parent and the challenges of his own identity quest.

His story is becoming all too familiar to me on the Camino, yet his version is unique with all the features of his one unrepeatable life. While we have never met before, will probably never meet again, and have a wide gulf of language, culture, and age between us, we experience the kinship found among seekers for a spiritual home. We are street-walkers of the Spirit and are getting good at recognizing each other.

After cleanup I wander down to the patio/pool area and surprisingly Horst is sitting there. We greet each other like long lost brothers, even though we last saw each other only several hours ago. One learns very quickly on the Camino that each encounter is temporary and fleeting, and not repeatable. Most pilgrims one meets only once, and whether the encounter was sublime or mundane, one should not assume another.

When a reacquaintance does happen one must enter into it, because one may not get another. This life lesson is not lost on me and I am grateful for these moments of connection and reconnection.

Tomorrow, July 22, will be the feast day of Mary Magdalene and the village is having a festival beginning tonight. The streets are decked out with banners, and a musical stage is set up in the village square close to the hostel. We as pilgrims are invited to join the festivities which will begin around 8 PM, so Horst and I find a small bar for a bite to eat before the fun begins. In several spots in the village there are smoky fires of grape stumps burning, upon which huge ham roasts are cooking. Sweating men are working the fire pits and turning the rotisseries.

By 8 PM the village has come alive with games, music, children running wild, and old people walking slowly in groups of men and women. There seems to be an absence of young adults in the village, yet a good time seems to be had by all. With each hour the music gets a bit louder and more raucous, with teenagers now appearing and taking over the dancing. By 10 PM Horst and I are tired, and we and the other pilgrims settle in for the night. My room is very hot so the window must remain open. Fernandez is in bed although with the loud music blaring in the square just a street away, I cannot imagine he is sleeping. I do not even cover myself with the light silk liner I normally use as a bed covering since it is so very hot this night. I can't help but wonder why the music has gotten so loud. Surely the party will wind down by midnight.

At midnight it only gets louder. I cannot believe it and even with my earplugs in place, the pounding beat penetrates every pore of my body. One AM comes and goes; no let up. Two AM, the same thing. At 3 AM the 'tunes' are becoming familiar as the song cycle repeats itself. By 4 AM the sound is even louder since the party seems to have moved to our street directly in front of the hostel. At 4:30 AM I give up trying to sleep and get up and go to the only place where I can turn on the lights, namely the toilet, where I do blister treatment which I need to do anyway before I walk this morning.

The noise factor has so gotten to me so badly that even though the toilet next to me has overflowed, it does not matter. I need some place to go to try and get the pounding music out of my head. At 5 AM I lay down again with pounding rock tunes still swirling around me. At 5:30 AM I get up to pack and wait for the first light of dawn. My roommate left while I was washing up, and must have had equal distress. As I leave the building at 6:00 AM I see a large group of young drunk men dancing to boom box music directly in front of the gates of the hostel.

In a town of 500 there are not too many options for continuing a street party, but right in front of our door? That seems intentional to me and they are lucky I do not know any Spanish. Although given how drunk they are, maybe I am the lucky one by keeping my mouth shut. I now completely understand why certain governments have used loud music as a form of torture. It is an auditory pathway utilized to hammer you into submission, and hammered into oblivion is how I feel.

In that frame of mind, with no sleep, I stagger out of town dreading the day. My body feels hot even though the early dawn is very cool. This worries me in that I may still have a slight fever. I have no energy whatsoever, but even with no sleep, I should not feel this zapped. My feet are killing me, with each step sending pain up my leg. I sense I am getting into trouble and am desperately hoping it is not serious. Everyone is passing me, even a tiny seventy year old granny from France. No one this slow has ever passed me before, so I now know for sure I am in difficulty.

I know I am sick and am certain I have an elevated temperature. I may even have heatstroke for all I know. I decide at this moment to only go as far as Santo Domingo de Calzada today and stay as long as I need in order to recover. It is the next major town and 'only' 9 mi/14 km away. Just the decision to stop gives me an unexpected feeling of peace and tranquility. It even seems to restore some modest energy, allowing me to maintain a steady, if slow pace. Even so, every bone in my body seems to ache as I finally stumble into Santo Domingo de Calzada around noon. The shops thankfully are still open before Siesta begins, and I find a pharmacy for desperately needed iodine and bandages for foot care, as well as some much needed pain relievers. The first two modest hotels I check out are full and my heart sinks, since I cannot risk another sleepless night in a hostel, especially if I am ill.

My third stop at a very modest old hotel bears fruit. They have a room. Even though I can barely move, I head off to shower and then fall into bed and am asleep before my head hits the pillow. I awake a full three hours later feeling very sore and with my usual foot pain, but the flu achiness is gone. I offer a prayer of thanksgiving for the restorative power that sleep brings, and decide to take advantage of the opportunity that a larger town offers and do what I was told to do way back in Cizur Minur: go shoe shopping!

While the options for better shoes are limited, I settle on a pair of low cut hiking shoes, which above all are roomier than the fancy boots I bought in Chicago. I don't want to carry these expensive discards around with me, nor do I want to just get rid of them, so I try and follow the city map to find the post office to ship them back to Chicago. A $200 pair of boots cannot just be tossed, especially since I am already $400 lighter through the loss of my glasses.

As I wander along the winding streets getting more disoriented all the time, I am delighted to run into the group of six young pilgrims I met on my third night in Larrasoanna. The group includes tall, gangly John from Belgium. They have arrived in Santo Domingo de Calzada earlier today and have also succumbed to heat and exhaustion as I have, so much so, that three of them are calling it quits for this year and are heading to the beach. The other three have been shoe shopping as I have, and are proudly showing off their new clogs in the hope that their blister count will also go down. There is an ease among all of us, those that are leaving the trail as well as those who are staying, including even myself, who is somewhere in the middle. It is imperative that I take a time out from the Camino to get my bearings. We say goodbye and I feel the weight of these goodbyes since I know we will likely never see each other again, and while this letting go is a normal microcosm of life, on the Camino I am so much more conscious of its inevitability.

My sadness is accentuated as I end up eating alone in an outdoor street corner Bistro. This is often the price one pays for claiming the privacy and comfort of hotel accommodations in contrast to pilgrim hostels. In all of these daily choices I am learning about myself. As I move along the continuum of feelings between loneliness and the desire for connection, I recognize both my hunger for community and belonging, right alongside my need for privacy and solitude. It is difficult to get it right, and perhaps I am needing to learn to move more freely on this continuum and to trust both possibilities more fully. If they are both inevitable, perhaps the flexibility between them is the key.

William S. Schmidt

It is now early evening as I get up from my solitary table and meander down the street. There sitting at a sidewalk bar are Gregor and Bogdan, my Polish buddies. Our joyful hello reflects our mutual surprise and delight at this unexpected encounter. Talk about a quick shift from aloneness to connection. I sit down and share a glass of wine with them and recognize again that so much of our relational joy in life comes out of mutual recognition. We have become known to one another and revel in this knowing. Now walking on the opposite side of the street, is Horst, my most recent walking companion. He has never met my Polish friends, but with the common German language between us, we quickly find ourselves in a lively exchange about our experiences. My aloneness and isolation is quickly forgotten. It is dark when we break up our rendezvous, and all head off in different directions to our various accommodations. My joy is tempered by the knowledge that they are moving on tomorrow, but I am staying. Or am I?

CHAPTER 6

The Chicken Oracle

"Great suffering opens you in different way. Here, things happen *against your will,* which is what makes it suffering. And over time, you can learn to give up your defended state, again because you have no choice. *The situation is what it is,* although we will invariably go through the stages of denial, anger, bargaining, resignation, and (hopefully), acceptance. The suffering might feel wrong, terminal, absurd, unjust, impossible, physically painful, or just outside of your comfort zone. So you see why we must have a proper attitude toward suffering, because many things every day leave us out of control . . . . Remember always, however, that *if you do not transform your pain, you will surely transmit it to those around you . . . ."*

Richard Rohr, <u>The Naked Now</u>, 2009, p. 124-125.

*W*hile my night was restful and surprisingly restorative, I awake with a cloud of indecision over me. I know I need to change my pressured way of walking, but my limited time availability for the Camino has forced me into a drivenness in which I am constantly telling my body what to do instead of the process operating the other way around. Simply staying put in Santo Domingo de Calzada seems unfocused somehow, yet what else to do? I know from prior research that the monastery of Santo Domingo de Silos, made famous by the monks of "Chant" CD renown is only 40 mi/60 km south of Burgos, which is on the Camino trail. Burgos is about three days of walking away, but right now I do not know if I can force my body or my mind into plunging into that stretch. Since I know the monastery can be reached by bus the thought begins to form that perhaps a focused retreat time can bring me to a greater clarity of purpose than I have been able to find thus far. I certainly need to find more balance than I have been able to accomplish up to this point.

With this question on my mind I step out of my cheap hotel looking for a place to buy some breakfast when I spot a street cleaning worker with a severe limp pushing his wheelbarrow up the cobblestone street. He obviously works like this all day, probably without complaint, and here I am whining about all my aches, pains, and burdens. Feeling somewhat chagrined I take my few morsels back to my room, and as I eat, I gaze out the window and observe four Italian women 'pilgrims' walking out the front door of the hotel with walking sticks, scallop shells hanging around their well-dressed necks, and each with a rolling suitcase. No backpacks are in sight. I burst out laughing at the contradictions I see all around me, and recognize that I myself am caught up in these conflicts. These are surely fair weather pilgrims, who are likely sending their suitcases on ahead as they take a leisurely stroll along the countryside. But why the walking sticks? Yet who am I to judge what they are or are not gaining? Is my asceticism really more virtuous than their leisureliness?

In this climate of contradictions I head back outside to visit the famous cathedral of Santo Domingo de Calzada and its quirky legend. In this cathedral one finds surely one of the most unusual exhibits in all of Christendom. Directly inside the church at the main entrance is an elevated chicken coop containing two live white chickens. Known as the legend of The Hanged Pilgrim, it tells the story of a pilgrim couple on their way to Santiago with their teenage son. The innkeeper's daughter has her eye on the handsome but devout young fellow, who at his peril refutes her advances.

Enraged at his refusal, she hides a silver goblet in his satchel, and reports him for stealing it. The poor young man is subsequently caught, dragged back to town, and condemned to hang. As legend has it, the parents are unaware of the fate of their son, but as soon as they learn of it they rush back to find him hanging on the gallows, but miraculously still alive due to the intervention of Santo Domingo. They desperately rush to the house of the Sheriff who is about to begin his lavish dinner. Upon hearing their lament he laughingly reports that their son is no more alive than the chicken he is about to eat. At this moment the rooster on the plate stands up and crows loudly. The Sheriff knows a miracle when he sees one, and rushes back to the gallows to cut down the now fully pardoned and alive lad.

No stay in Santo Domingo de Calzada is complete without seeing the descendants of these highly honored live representations of the miracle. The church opens at 10 AM so I meander over to the Plaza and there waiting to get in are the three young German women from my very first night at Orisson. There is Hannah, the older ring-leader still in her medieval finest; Karsten with her nose rings and assertive punk attire, and Sabine, a hard to describe cross between the two. We are all excited to see each other and after a round of hugs come to realize we are all in the same state of uncertainty as to how to proceed with the pilgrimage. They seem even more 'done' with the Camino than I am, even though the younger two are only eighteen and nineteen years old respectively, with Hannah having recently turned the ripe old age of thirty.

We arrive at the unanimous decision to enter the cathedral together and go directly to the chickens and wait for them to rise and to speak to us, much as their ancestors did so many chicken generations ago. This somehow makes sense to me, and it cannot be any worse than any of the inner voices I have been listening to in recent weeks. Enter we do, and stand in a semi-circle around the raised coop, waiting to be inspired. A more unlikely looking group of chicken admirers has surely not frequented that spot in many a year. Perhaps this is why the chickens are rather subdued as we stand beneath them waiting for the Oracle. Or, perhaps they are more quiet because they feel the burden of our longing for guidance.

Nevertheless, they eventually stand, and a few squawks emanate from their holy beaks. I turn to my companions and exclaim: "I hope that was as helpful for you as it was for me!" We all nod our gratitude, but are strangely reluctant to offer our gems of insight to one another. We say a round of quick goodbyes, as the three of them seem determined to move on, and since I wish to linger in the church for a bit more serious reflection, we part ways, unsure if we will run into each other again.

I find a quiet spot in the cathedral to contemplate the growing recognition that I need to take a timeout to rework my relationship to this entire pilgrimage. I seem to have reached the limits of my body, but even more troubling is that my mind and my spirit are not in harmony either. My body is certainly protesting the unrelenting demands I am placing on it, but even more importantly, I feel I am losing the self who is doing the walking. My desire to make sense of what I am about on this pilgrimage is sputtering badly, and a time out is sorely needed to recalibrate. That seems to settle it for me. I will leave the Camino trail and take a bus to the monastery of Santo Domingo de Silos, and spend two nights there.

To get to Santo Domingo de Silos requires taking a bus to Burgos and then transferring on to de Silos. I know a bus is leaving for Burgos at noon, so I hurry back to my Hotel to check out, and rush on to the bus station. I arrive at the station, to discover sitting at the street side café, the trio of German women I have just said goodbye to barely an hour ago. We all begin laughing as we realize the chickens have told us all the same thing. We are all taking the same bus to Burgos, although they are undecided as to what comes next. A final round of Café con Leche's later, we board the bus. As I am boarding I turn around and see that Sabine is no longer behind me, and is actually getting on the bus next to ours. I try to get her attention, but Hannah and Karsten tell me that Sabina has changed her mind, literally as she was boarding, and has decided to travel back to Logrono where she has fallen in love with a German volunteer host at the hostel there. This lucky fellow works there, and she is going to follow her heart to see if that relationship can blossom. It turns out the chickens can be more specific in their guidance than I had ever imagined.

Two minutes later our bus lurches out of the station and onto the N 120, the major northern highway across Spain. Since this highway often follows the ancient Pilgrim trail, there are many sections where the two are directly next to one another. So it is as we pull out of the station of Santo Domingo de Calzada. As we move along, I see pilgrims walking right next to the road. There are dozens of them leaning into the wind and contending with the noise of the highway right next to them.

There in the pilgrim midst is Horst walking his nice, slow pace. I have a pang of regret, of failure even, that I am violating my unspoken pilgrim pledge to be true to the trail. I feel as if I am cheating somehow and become stuck in this emotional funk for virtually the entire trip. As I continue to observe our passing so many pilgrims, it occurs to me that the 50 mi/80 km I am covering in less than an hour on this bus would take me three hard days of walking. No wonder our modern life has no time for deeper reflection or soul-searching, and since we are generally operating at such a frenetic pace, our deeper selves never have time to reveal themselves.

Arrival in Burgos brings the shock of big city intensity after the relative quiet of the village and countryside. I say goodbye to my remaining two pilgrim companions, Hannah and Karsten, and feel sad as I see them disappear into the crowds. I have about two hours to kill before my bus leaves for Santo Domingo de Silos, so I head straight for the magnificent structure called the Catedral de Santo Maria. It's thirteenth century edifice is considered one of the largest and most beautiful cathedrals of Spain. It has been very closely connected to pilgrim traffic over the ages and its grandeur can in many ways be traced to its importance for pilgrims. It is a structure that has century upon century of adaptation, and layer upon layer of melding political and religious power. As I tour this vast church with its glittering gold, I find the historical and religious elements interesting, but they do not capture my heart, with two significant exceptions.

The first is a life size sculpture of the scourged Jesus bound to a pillar. Normally I have a strong aversion to images of a bloodied Jesus because of the theology that often stands behind it. This theology holds that God required the abuse of Jesus as a punishment and payment for our sins. I have no room for this belief since it completely undercuts the love of God, never mind God's radical solidarity with Jesus, as with us, as a broken and wounded humanity.

The difference I experience with this image is on the one hand the depiction of Jesus as bound, and on the other hand the gaze of this Jesus as he peers into my soul. This Jesus is bound to the post of his suffering as I am to mine. He cannot control the forces that have been unleashed upon him, yet his body remains soft and fluid as this suffering passes through him. This softness in his body speaks to me, and invites me to release the temptation toward rigidity and resistance, with bitterness and retaliation their manifestation. This Jesus shows me how to suffer, and draws me nearer to God, without necessarily having to know why I suffer. His gaze helps me with this because it is a gaze of infinite love based on mutual identification, not on some belief about his paying for my 'badness'.

Scourged Jesus

As I carry the impact of this encounter inside myself, I hear faint sounds of chimes and chanting in the distance and try to find their source. In the vast array of rooms and chapels that make up the Cathedral complex there is a huge inner courtyard into which I stumble. A contemporary chime/choral composition is playing. In this courtyard hundreds of empty chairs are set up facing a huge cross in the center. Large chains drape the cross and flow like a river onto the ground and into the seating areas. Hung suspended by pulleys and ropes are twenty five or thirty huge black ceramic cylinder-shaped bells, each around four to five feet tall. They hang at varying heights, some only a few feet off the ground, others up to fifty feet in the air. They are all mechanically connected to a soundtrack which is ringing the chimes even as chanting is heard over a speaker system. It is a haunting sight and sound event of deep lament. This work of art so powerfully engages my senses and my soul, and is clearly the most moving spiritual moment I have had thus far on the Camino.

It opens up for me the lament I carry inside myself, and is bringing all my pain closer to the surface. This includes the historical and relational pain of my life, but not in a way that feels morbid or masochistic. I feel held somehow, as if my experience is being mirrored back to me, rendering it more acceptable than before. I feel a strong identification with this Jesus who in the first instance was bound to the pillar of his suffering, but now here in the courtyard, has been freed from his cross and his chains. His narrative reveals to me that I can be both bound and free, and all aspects of his story seem to mirror my soul.

I am of course also deeply burdened by the hard truth that with my serious foot problems, my Camino may be ending all too prematurely for me. I have trouble pulling myself away from the chimes and a chants, but I have a bus to catch. As I leave the Cathedral I step onto the rough cobblestone path at its entrance and notice cracks in the pavement in front of me. I place both my joy and sorrow prayer stones in one of the cracks. A chapter has closed for me today, and I want my prayer stones to stabilize the path for someone else who might follow in my footsteps. I know I am entering a period of lament, and new stones will be given to me.

Leaving Burgos on the one daily bus to Santo Domingo de Silos takes me abruptly into very arid country. It is very hilly and rugged, essentially high desert, very fitting for the asceticism I am now living, yet the sky is strikingly blue, accented by the brown hills spreading from horizon to horizon. I arrive several hours later at the village of Silos, 90% of which is dominated by this ancient monastery. Monastic life began here as early as the seventh century, with the particular monastery which stands here having been founded by Saint Dominic in the year 1041. He served as Abbot until 1073, and the Benedictine life that resides here has existed for over a millennium, with only a few brief interruptions.

I have arrived just in time for Vespers (6 PM), and do not even bother looking for a room, but head straight for the Romanesque church where services are held. I find the simplicity and austerity of the church a welcome relief from the glitter and gold of Burgos. The chanting of the monks is like a gentle rain and even though I understand hardly any Latin, I have enough knowledge of Scripture to have a general idea of the text they are singing. Yet the words are largely unnecessary for me.

I left Burgos feeling the haunting emptiness of my losses and on a small, yet parallel way, the loss of the Camino as well, at least as I have envisioned it. The sense of loss I am feeling is not so much about success or failure, but about fullness and emptiness. My life has been emptied out of some of its richest elements, especially the loss of my marriage and our family structure, along with the hard reality that the life lived there is not repeatable. With rupture and alienation, even the memory of that lost life has become tainted, and at least for now, those memories are not able to be integrated into the composite picture of my life.

I enter Vespers feeling very alone, very lost, and very much in pain, although somehow held by the silence of this place. I am also very hungry, not having eaten since noon, and upon leaving the service need to first find a room, which I do directly across the street from the monastery. It seems I am the only guest in this boardinghouse, and I am obviously the only patron for dinner, forgetting that most Spaniards do not begin the evening meal until 9 PM or later.

Lonely or not, I linger as long as possible over dinner and nurse my flask of wine until after dark. Shortly before 10 PM the church bells announce the beginning of Compline, the end of the liturgical day. I rush over, and join the twenty or so fellow worshipers along with a roughly equivalent number of monks. The lights are all out in this vast space except for one bright light directed at the cross, which slowly dims as the service ends. At its conclusion we participants receive a holy water blessing as the monks process down the dark center aisle of the sanctuary as they chant. We all follow them as far as we are allowed, namely to the gates which close on their private living quarters. We hear their soaring voices slowly recede down the cloister corridors. It is as if a magnetic force has pulled us to follow, not so much to follow the monks themselves, but the peaceful vibrations they exude for which we seem so hungry. I linger for a bit in the darkness of the church feeling as if I am in a death vigil of sorts. I am calm, but with a calm that knows that pain is here with more on its way.

By now it is 11 PM and time for bed. After I finally take a belated bath since my shower is broken, I sit on the edge of my bed and feel overwhelmed with aloneness and begin to cry. These are my first true tears on the Camino. Perhaps I need the isolation of this place and distance from my Camino agenda to feel the full pain of my losses, and now finally, the catharsis can begin. I am glad for the tears because they not only bring relief, but also ground me more fully in my experience.

As I begin to fall asleep, the Spanish proclivity for intensity intrudes as an argument breaks out either directly below me in the hotel restaurant, or perhaps outside my window. I keep thinking it will settle down, but no such luck. This argument seems to be between a man and a woman or between two men and two women, I cannot tell for sure. Just as the argument is about to settle down, they seem to always keep coming back for more. Someone seems desperate to have the final word. I am too tired to get up and see what is going on, and maybe getting it all out of their system is not such a bad thing. The Spanish don't seem to be killing themselves at the same rate as Americans do, so maybe they are onto something. I just wish they would pick someplace else to do it.

Friday, July 24, dawns bright and cloudless and I decide the day will include as much rest as possible, with a full tour of the monastery, and, if possible, a phone call to Margita. I have wanted to be in touch for some time now since we have not talked in over a month. She herself has been in Europe for over a month and recently returned to Chicago. I know I hope for continued connection, if not perhaps some magical renewal. Up until this point on the Camino I have not been able to find a phone, or if I found one, the time difference made a call unworkable.

In this small village there is only one working pay phone in the public Plaza, with very precise calling card instructions, all in Spanish. Of course, the operator(s) only speak Spanish, as does every person in the village. I speak about fifteen words of Spanish by now, all of which I use liberally in various combinations, all to no avail. After almost two hours of futility, a dear woman in a tobacco shop who understands my pleas has mercy on me, and leaves her shop to walk to the village square with me to attempt to make the call for me. At last, success, as she hands me the phone.

I immediately sense the coldness and distance in Margita's voice, and my heart sinks. I should have known better than to call, since she has consistently declared her intention to end the marriage, and this after two years of separation. What happens next, however, completely surprises me. She informs me that she has sent another letter to my mother challenging my mother's behavior toward us over the years.

I suspect in every marriage that comes into difficulty, there are likely intractable issues that become unresolvable. This was one such issue for us. It has haunted us from the beginning, and in spite of several attempts at resolution including face-to-face encounters, no resolution ever materialized. The psychotherapist in me can offer many analyses of this stalemate, and its roots go deep into the mists of everyone's unconscious. Whatever their source, they are debilitating, and became so for us. What shocks me today, however, is its on-going reality, and what it sets off in me.

I have been stuck in the middle of the pain of these two women, and have tried to buffer, interpret, soothe, or soften each person's reaction to the other. As most any student of psychology knows, relational triangles are notoriously problematic. This one is no exception. At this moment I avoid my typical temptation to again jump into the triangle in the old way by justifying, protecting, or explaining, but instead simply affirm Margita's right to do whatever she feels she needs to do, and proceed to end the call. My second temptation immediately presents itself, however, in the guise of trying to reach my mother to buffer, or somehow explain yet again why Margita feels the way she does, and offer suggestions to my mother as to how she might respond. The absurdity of my fantasy intervention becomes immediately visible to me.

Perhaps for the first time in this long road of pain for all parties, a new path appears to me. I reach the sudden conclusion that I do not have to protect my mother, nor Margita, nor help either of them figure the other out, nor generate harmony. I just have to "be," namely, aware and awake in the middle of this wound that has touched everyone so deeply. Being in a wound means being aware of its presence and simply holding it prayerfully as one manifestation of God's wounded world. My sin in this regard, if I may use that powerful word, is that I wanted to deny that wound since I saw no basis for it. But the fact remains that it was and is there, and I needed to own it more honestly.

In this spirit of inner turmoil, I decide to climb a high hill behind the monastery, on top of which stands a large statue of Mary with her arms spread wide over the valley below. A stiff climb later, I find myself at the foot of a weather beaten Mary who has embraced her valley for many a year. The base of the statue is crumbling, and I see bumpy and weathered reddish stones have fallen from her statue. I pick one up and know I have found my next sorrow stone.

Mary over-looking Monastery of Santo Domingo de Silos

This Mary is an Earth mother and God mother rolled into one. She carries all our longings and universal hunger for nurture. Without nurture we die, and our birth mothers are the first vehicle of this gift which brings us into life. Our mothers are rooted in the earth of their bodies and nourish us there. They soon must hand us on to the wider world for additional nourishment for better or for worse. We, both mothers, and we their children, know this dependency of ours, and yet we are mightily ambivalent about it. Most of us are journeying somewhere on this continuum of need/dependence and its twin, separation/independence. Life is a stage upon which this drama is played out in countless ways, with our joys and sorrows reflecting how well or poorly this process is unfolding at any given time.

Mary of Nazareth can be understood in this sense. She is an archetype or an icon of this sacred eternal process of birthing and suffering on behalf of creation. We project onto her our deepest yearnings of being nurtured in our longings for the sacred. She is a representation of our need to be held in this ever present process. This Mary I am looking at today is not an idealized or cleaned up picture of that process. Her weather beaten and crumbling form is closer to where it is at for me. I see my aging 84 year old mother in her. A mother who transcended war and massive loss in Europe to birth five children on two different continents, yet was also overwhelmed by worlds she could not fully integrate.

I also see Margita in this Mary. I see a woman who birthed our three precious sons and lavished them with gifts of love. I see the woman who loved me truly and deeply, even if finitely. I see the woman who urgently seeks to realize the destiny of her life before she runs out of time, and who needs to do so without me. At this moment I give thanks for these Mary's I have known, and for their continuity with the life force that is their source and goal. I give thanks for all the Mary's, female and male, that suffer in order to give birth to the new and the next.

I am roused from these contemplations by bells ringing in the valley below. It is the call to Vespers and I cannot believe how quickly this day has flown. I am overwhelmed by all that has happened today and without even being able to fully understand why, have a sense that this day will turn out to be one of the most important of my Camino. I slowly return to the Valley and the Vespers service, ready to enter the evening on its own terms, and for what awaits me tomorrow, as I return to Burgos and hopefully the Camino trail.

My evening finds me oscillating between the peace that comes from being released from a trap I have so often fallen into, alternating with waves of anger and frustration that I am in this situation in the first place. I am glad for the focus on prayer that evening Vespers and Compline services offer me, because it grounds me in the midst of this inner battle.

I awake early the next morning to catch my 8 AM bus back to Burgos. There is no bus stop that I can find, and were it not for two senior citizens waiting at a street corner, I would have been wandering around looking for the stop and perhaps missing the bus altogether. This bus stops in every village between Silos and Burgos, and especially where there are no villages, so this relatively short trip takes all of three hours. The only event of note is our passing a flock of vultures picking away at a large carcass they have almost picked clean. I immediately find myself identifying with the carcass being picked apart and ground into dust. But soon I come to recognize that I am also a vulture picking away at the dead tissue of my life. There is a place for vultures, since they are part of God's clean-up crew along with ants, flies, and many other assorted creatures. I may actually need to be in vulture mode for a while, as long as I know when the carcass of my life has been cleaned up and it is time to move on.

I finally arrive in Burgos late morning, and this being the feast day of Saint James himself, I consider going back to the Cathedral to revisit the musical exhibit I so savored just two days ago. I actually walk back to the Cathedral and am about to enter when I realize I am resisting the trail. The section leading West from Burgos is considered the most mentally and spiritually, if not physically, challenging section of the entire Camino. Here are one enters the Meseta, the vast high plain that stretches over 100 mi/160 km and takes up to a week of walking in a hot, treeless vastness that seems not to end. It is into this emptiness I must now step and where I must now be tested.

CHAPTER 7

Angels in the Wilderness

> I believe my vocation is essentially that of a Pilgrim
> and an exile in life, that I have no proper place in the
> world, but that for that reason I am in some sense to be
> the friend and brother of people everywhere, especially
> those who are exiles and pilgrims like myself . . . . My life
> is in many ways simple, but it is also a mystery which I do
> not attempt to really understand, as though I were led by
> the hand in the night where I see nothing, but can fully
> depend on the Love and Protection of Him who guides
> me.

> Thomas Merton, <u>Cold War Letters</u>, 2006, p. 129-130.

I know instinctively that all I have experienced thus far on the
Camino is preparatory for the challenges to come. Yes, I have
had to face my physical limits thus far, and have certainly faced
my life issues head on, but now I will be driven deeper into myself.
The full power of the Camino to open me up and take me apart is now
upon me. I find myself having to consciously say yes to this challenging
Meseta phase as I strap on my pack tightly, adjust my walking poles,
turn West, and begin to walk.

There are no pilgrims in sight as I leave the center of Burgos toward
the suburbs, and at first I cannot find the yellow arrows to mark my
way, but a friendly local resident with broken English walks with me
for a bit, confirming my general direction and eventually pointing out
my first Camino marker in two days. Off I go, and although I do not

have the confidence or spring in my step which I had at the start only twelve days ago, I am well-paced, and feel ready to take it an hour at a time, feet and lungs willing.

The path begins a long a beautiful river walk with shaded lanes, through a well treed park and finally out of the city. The path soon becomes hard packed gravel, but my lighter new shoes from Santo Domingo de Calzada are handling it well. My Chicago boots as well as my sandals are still swinging on the outside of my pack since I have not yet found a way to send them home, and I do not simply want to trash an expensive pair of boots. I must be quite a sight with all of these boots and shoes flopping outside of my backpack. I probably look like a traveling shoe salesman, but no matter, I will dispose of them somehow since I surely don't need the extra weight.

The trail gently winds through the countryside, although by now I have lost whatever shade I had. I begin to consider water rationing, because I have only one water bottle left, having lost the other somewhere along the way. An hour and a half later I am still walking completely alone, and feel the isolation building up inside me once again, when a short, stocky Pilgrim, a bit younger than I blasts past me, without an acknowledgment or hello of any sorts, never mind a "Buen Camino." I think to myself, maybe solitude is better than company of that type. I realize that I often initiate greetings of some sort, and know that to be part of my character, but perhaps that does not give me the right to expect it of others, although I still was annoyed at his indifference to a fellow pilgrim.

The first option for stopping for the night appears at the village of Villabilla, and I seriously consider it since the village has my name in it, but realize that only an hour and a half of walking does not a day make. So I trudge on, even though the heat is seriously building now that it is mid-afternoon. Again, I make no grand plans as I was prone to do at the start of the Camino, but simply head for the next village, Tariados. My energy is good, although heel spur pain is building. Another hour later I enter the village to the delightful sight of a farmer selling his fresh fruits and vegetables from the back of his truck. I delight in my good fortune and load up on refreshing treats.

I am tempted to go to the bar across the street for a beer given the heat, but think the better of it and walk a few streets further to the small pilgrim hostel/Albergue. Lo and behold, they have shade trees along with a picnic table, and the two pilgrims seated there have no objection if I join them. I introduce myself and discover they are Nina from Germany, and Jean-Claude from France. We combine our meager ingredients, and together they amount to a feast of bread, cheeses, sausages, and sundry fruits and vegetables. It is not quite on a par with Jesus' miracle of the loaves and fishes, but it hints at the power of sharing.

I discover that Nina has walked all the way from St. Jean Pied de Port in two fewer days than I, and all this with no use of buses. This is truly an impressive feat, but now her body has given out on her, and she must quit. She has hit her wall. Jean-Claude is a "long-walker" who walked out his front door at Puy in southern France over three weeks ago. He tells us he has only two more days to walk before he calls it quits for this year's Camino. Now on his third Camino, he will be back next year for the final stretch. He is part of a small, but growing group of pilgrims, I have dubbed "serial walkers," who walk long stretches of the Camino on an almost annual basis.

These two lunch companions are the first pilgrims I have encountered and conversed with since my monastic time out, and I am struck immediately by the varied patterns of journeying. I take note of that fact as I remind myself to walk the Camino in my way, attending to my rhythms of body, mind, and spirit. In that mode I get up, gather my remaining food, and pack up for my trek to Rabe de las Calzados, only 2 mi/3 km away. I am given a goodbye gift of a large tomato by my lunch mates, which I will save for my lunch tomorrow.

Just before I am about to depart I notice a boot rack standing beside the door of the Albergue, and make my decision to leave my fancy boots here, hopefully for some other pilgrim whose shoes have worn out. I remove my boots from my pack very slowly and respectfully, and appreciate the symbolism of giving up the way of walking that these boots represent. This way was not necessarily a bad way. These boots I am leaving behind helped me to train and prepare, they even brought me a third of the way. But now a new way must be found, and the old must be released. In this spirit I say goodbye to my boots and head out into the blistering heat.

In this scorching heat I become quickly grateful that Rabe de las Calzados is a relatively short distance away. As hot as I am, I find myself wanting to sing which I do with full gusto. There is no one around to inhibit me and today I am singing out of a sense of freedom and the quiet joy that I am truly back on track. What tomorrow will bring I do not know, but today I sing a song of joy. I have a repertoire of songs I sing, almost on a rotating basis. I do have my favorites, however, and today it is my own adaptation of a song the Mormon Tabernacle choir sings which has three simple verses that include the phrases: (1) I "have" peace like a River; (2) I "have" joy like a River; and (3) I "have" love like a River.

I do not believe we ever truly "have" these states of being, as if they are somehow our possessions. I do, however, believe we should seek them, and so today I am singing of my quest for peace, joy, and love, by singing the phrases: "I **seek** peace/joy/love like a River." Such singing lifts my spirits and energizes me. It even seems to change my sense of time and space, because before I know it, I am at the outskirts of the village of Rabe de las Calzados, where my pre-departure pilgrim research recommended a stay at a private hostel run by Michelle, a Camino legend.

It turns out that Michelle is not just a Camino legend, she is the chief bed bug enforcer of the entire Camino. Entrance to the small foyer where pilgrims are registered requires an immediate placement of all personal items into large black plastic bags which are then hung onto hooks. This makes the packing and unpacking of backpacks extremely awkward, and essentially something we can only do on an outside patio. Granted, this is her private home, and I do not know what experiences are behind her harsh attitude. She seems jaded, and perhaps suffering from pilgrim burnout, so I have compassion for this woman who has done so much for the development of the modern Camino. Her lovely home used to house large numbers of pilgrims, which she now limits to one small room into which ten of us will be squeezed on five bunk beds.

The regimented manner of our welcome is eased as evening arrives, as we gather around the lovely pilgrim meal which Michelle and her husband have prepared for us. We are an interesting group, all of whom are strangers to me. The group includes another two French women who are on a two week "Camino vacation," and have also just stepped out of a fashion magazine, not unlike the French women I met a week ago in Ciraque; a young Italian couple who just married three weeks ago and who are on their honeymoon; a forties aged Brazilian attorney and politician; a young male Spanish engineer, and an angry looking Spanish male attorney around my age. I am the only English speaker and so the evening proceeds largely in Spanish and French, although with the occasional English sentence thrown in to help me out. Surprisingly, I feel relatively involved in the conversation.

What emerges is a fascinating history of the Camino through the eyes of Michelle who has no doubt seen it all. She has hosted pilgrims off and on for over twenty years, and while she affirms the diversity of the Camino, she is frustrated by the so-called "caliber" of many pilgrims including those with physical and psychological ailments. I remind her, however, that this reality is no different outside the Camino, and that we all bring our burdens with us onto the trail. Furthermore, these personal challenges of ours are perhaps the reason why many of us are on the Camino in the first place. My table mates for the most part nod in agreement, that this melting pot of humanity with all its visible problems and potentials is a big part of the appeal of the Camino. Michelle, however, remains a Camino purist and is not convinced. We end the evening amicably, and are grateful for the warmth of her hearth, even if it has become a bit jaded.

We head to our cramped but clean room, where I settle into a bed next to, of course, the young couple from Italy on their honeymoon. I was not too concerned that I would become an unwilling witness to amorous activity going on next to me, but I must admit my curiosity got the better of me and I bring myself to ask: "So, how does this work, being on your honeymoon on the Camino, sleeping in cramped hostels?" Without missing a beat they reply, "Oh, we have to sleep in a hotel every third night or we couldn't stand it!" With a wink I tell them I hope they have been keeping accurate track of what day in the cycle this is. Soon the rest of the room gets wind of our banter, and after a few jokes, we all settle down for the night.

Perhaps sleeping next to a honeymooning couple was not the best spot for my psychological equilibrium, but I have a restless night, and am the first one awake well before 6 AM. I wait until 6 AM and then quietly get up and begin to pack in the dark. Trying to pack in the dark inside a large black plastic bag is crazy, so I go outside using my headlamp for light to finish packing, then go back inside to wash up, and grab an orange for my "on the road" breakfast. It is only 6:15 AM and I am the first one out the door on an extremely cold morning. The

High Plains have their temperature extremes, and as cold as I am now, I know I will be roasting in a few short hours. I am quickly in climbing mode on a rolling, dry prairie. Within the hour I am stopped by two civil defense officers who are patrolling in a four-wheel drive vehicle. Who or what they hope to catch out here in the middle of nowhere, at this time of day, I have no idea, but my English answers to their Spanish questions seems to satisfy them, and they move on looking for more criminals in their pilgrim disguises.

Much as I try to divert my mind, I cannot seem to stop processing Margita material. Just like the rolling hills around me, I have rolling anger, rolling grief, rolling betrayal, rolling yearning, all rolling around in and through me. My spiritual bag of tricks is no match for this juggernaut of mental pain and poison. I try singing, reciting Scripture, meditating, holding my prayer stones, all to no avail. I realize I am constantly climbing out of valleys on the trail today, which seems to match the inner valleys I am constantly at the bottom of. The more I focus on my surroundings, however, they speak to me and help me to recalibrate my inner stuckness.

I notice how desolate everything is around me. Everything is brown, the track is rough and stony, and the heat is intense even by mid-morning. I recognize that there is a natural death phase going on around me, even the birds having gone silent or missing. I am in that same place internally, and my mind is struggling to accept this reality. I am undergoing a loss of life as I have known it, with sorrow and powerlessness all part of the dying, and leaning into these feelings gives me a more conscious engagement with them, and while I still feel their power, they seem no longer to overwhelm me as they did just moments ago. I find the same dynamic is at play in my walking these hills. When I consciously lean into a hill I find that my center of gravity adjusts to the slope, and my legs seem to become much more powerful, and I climb more efficiently.

As the day unfolds I feel reasonably fresh, and even though heel ligament pain develops within the hour, I feel fairly certain that I can make it to Hontanas, 15mi/ 25 km away. Barely an hour later a mirage of trees appears on the horizon. For days now I have not seen one cloud in the sky, nor hardly a tree either, so how can there be a growth of huge trees off in the distance? Perhaps I have gotten sunstroke or received some other visual impairment?

The closer I get I realize it is not a trick of my mind, but an actual cluster of huge poplar trees surrounding an Albergue called San Bol sitting in the middle. This Albergue of San Bol is one step up from an abandoned hut, with no running water, no showers, no toilet, no electricity, but a true oasis of giant trees around a fast, cold, running stream, with a large and deep holding tank of the coldest water. Although the Albergue is off the trail by several hundred paces, I immediately make the small detour and stop for lunch.

The temptation to stay for the night is strong, but my other responsible voice has determined I should walk at least 14 mi/22 km a day in my first days back after my monastic break, to get at least get a modest pace going. Now, on only my second day back on the Camino, I am considering not going any further even though it is barely noon. My plan has been to walk at least two more hours today. Surprisingly, the healing pull of the oasis wins out, and what a gift it becomes. It turns out that the peace I am so missing is not to be found by keeping "up to speed." It is not to be found by meeting some arbitrary inner or outer obligations, but by embracing the natural gifts this spot offers. But first I have to stop.

I begin my oasis experience by bathing my feet in the cold, icy stream, and discover its' amazing gift of soothing and rest. I lay down in the grass under the large Poplar trees and watch the dance of leaves, branches, and blue sky as the trees move in rhythm with the wind. The timelessness of it somehow transports me out of my mode of being snagged by anger or injustice, and even the agenda of needing to fix and repair my life. These trees, surely over fifty years old, have survived the raw conditions of heat, drought, wind, and cold; everything the Meseta can possibly throw at them. Yet here they are, dancing in the wind.

The sound of the stream babbling away adds to the effect of washing away care, hardness, and brittleness. All the combined gifts of this refuge takes me into a restful sleep within natures lullaby. I completely lose track of time and remain asleep under the trees. Once awake, I come to realize how powerful a gift I have just been given. Perhaps the biggest gift is to be freed from time bound agendas, and maybe even from the agendas themselves. Of course, there is always an agenda in life waiting to be completed, so my lesson for today may have to be repeated tomorrow. Yes, there are things that need fixing in my life, but my San Bol lesson is to let go, and let the eternal flow of God, who brings us into balance and sustains our truth-seeking, to do God's Sacred work. Perhaps I no longer have to determine all the details of the how, the where, the when, or even the why.

San Bol Albergue

I spend the entire afternoon lying next to the stream, drinking in its healing waters, sensing my soul and spirit reviving in ways that go beyond what even my monastic interlude provided. My sojourn in the monastery began with the mind, and only faintly reached the body. This healing stop of San Bol has begun with the body which has now embraced the mind. By 5 PM the dozen or so pilgrims who fit into the place have arrived, and have claimed their spots, with a few stragglers deciding to sleep under the stars which is not a bad choice either.

A thin wisp of a woman in her late forties appears and approaches me as I sit at poolside. She is wearing a long flowing sundress, with matching long flowing hair, and carries a large, glass jar under her arm. Her name is Jacqueline, is French, and is spending her summer dispensing paper cut-out Angels to pilgrims from her jar.

Her method is ingenious. She is driving the Camino backwards from Santiago (after having walked it herself several times), and is going backwards so not to run into the same pilgrims over and over again. She has quit a twenty year teaching position, and has made this her mission in life, to bless pilgrims with angels. She opens her jar and asks me to reach in and pick an angel. I do so, and pull out an orange-colored angel called "Paz" (Peace). I am amazed at this sacred gift here beside the healing waters of San Bol. We converse a bit longer, and then she must move on: there are many more pilgrims to bless today.

Perhaps twenty minutes pass, and to my great surprise I see Jacqueline returning to the Albergue and walking toward me. She has been given the message, she says, to return and give me a second angel. This time she reaches into the jar and pulls out a light blue angel called "Mimo," (Nurture). I am stunned and don't know what to make of it other than to receive. I feel both gratitude and puzzlement at this double gift. She has no time to waste and after a quick hug goodbye she is on her way again. I believe she was floating slightly as she left.

The surprises of San Bol are not over. Judith, our volunteer hostess, is a massage therapist/energy worker from Hungary. My father's family has a 200 year history as ethnic Germans in Hungary and I have been there several times. So Judith and I have much to talk about. She is about to make a Hungarian meal of goulash, my favorite, which was a staple dish in our home. The "nurture Angel" did not take long to get to work. Several of us as pilgrims pitch in to prepare the meal, all of this of course, in primitive conditions. The simplicity and comradery works together beautifully to create a feast of food and fellowship. During dinner, Judith announces that she will give chair massages after dinner to whomever desires one, and I waste no time volunteering.

I am the first in line for massage treatment, and Judith has barely begun to work on my back, when she utters her diagnosis. She notices I have left side weakness which she declares is related to issues with the feminine and connectivity. The right side, she notes, is stronger which is connected to planning and life direction. All of this is happening on the outdoor patio where we have our meals and gathering place. I am sitting in a chair in the middle of a circle with Judith working on me, and the others all gathered around loosely observing and interacting. In essence, I have ended up in the middle of an unexpected group therapy session.

So, I plunge right in, and validate Judith's diagnosis and go on to share how my very first day on the Camino as well as the days thereafter, have all had left side pain and symptoms, from a twisted left ankle, falling, cramps, heel Spurs, tendinitis, and so forth. I offer a brief commentary on my marital issues and everyone nods and murmurs some words of understanding.

The whole episode unfolds as the most natural thing in the world. This includes all my problems. They are just not that big a deal for this group, but simply the way things are. I find their neutrality and minimalism strangely refreshing and savor the relief that comes with accepting a diagnosis. The evening continues in this vein and rich conversations flow. A tiny, wiry German woman named Ke arrives, and it turns out she will be taking over from Judith as hospitaliero here in San Bol in two days. She has finished her fourth walking Camino, the last one, theVia de la Plata, well over 600 mi/1000 km long, all the way from Seville. She is a treasure of Camino lore, and understands its power well. We talk at length about the inevitable crisis that the Camino creates, one which throws you back into yourself where all of one's inner demons reside. For most people the crisis arrives at the beginning, and is usually prompted by the physical limits that inevitably impose themselves.

For Ke, however, the crisis came at the end she tells me, and involved questions surrounding how to move into her future. This growth discovery occurred for her in a less-traversed portion of the Camino which leads beyond Santiago, namely, to Finesterre, the so-called "end of the earth." She suggests that if the journey to Santiago is a ritual of cleansing and letting go, then the journey to Finesterre is a movement into the next phase of life, into what lies ahead, not what is being left behind. I quietly take note of her wisdom, and sense a seed has been planted.

Since we are in the middle of the emptiness of the Meseta, with nowhere to go and nothing else to do, the dozen of us form an instant community. We linger as dusk appears when Judith announces a late evening Spanish treat will be served. This flaming alcoholic drink will be prepared around 11 PM by which time it will be pitch black, so that we can properly observe the Milky Way over our heads. The Milky Way has long been associated with the Camino. The term 'Compostella' actually means "field of stars,'" with the stars not only forming a canopy over our heads, but actually pointing the way to Santiago. Their brightness is breathtaking, something city dwellers never get to appreciate.

Eleven PM arrives and the flaming drink is served. Our treat is a smooth Spanish liqueur in which the Brandy is still burning on top for an additional twenty minutes or so, and which can best be described as a Sangria with a kick. While I am sure that the ambience of the evening was additionally lubricated by the drink, I also have the distinct sense that this mode of human sharing around the fire, late into the night, is deeply rooted in human evolutionary experience. We likely first came to our sociability in the dark around a fire, hence it feels so natural for all of us, even archetypal. Most everyone lingers well past midnight when we finally migrate to our beds, having first washed our faces in the stream fed pool.

Dawn brings the usual rustling of plastic bags and backpacks, the alarm clock of every hostel. A light "help yourself" breakfast has already been set out, and after a quick bite I proceed with two very different activities. The first is to find a replacement joy stone since I have been without one since Burgos. I know the perfect spot to find it, namely, the healing stream that is at the heart of this oasis. I spot my rock immediately in the water. It's shape is that of a flat triangle, and since it is a shale stone, flakes have broken off to reveal an actual smiling face on its surface. It is an actual "happy rock," which the Earth has produced. I cannot believe my good fortune and eagerly clutch it and realize this stone is for keeps and must accompany me for the duration of my journey.

My final act before getting ready to leave San Bol is in some ways unique to San Bol, but in other ways a part of the entire Camino. It involves "toilets," understood in the broadest possible way. Going to the toilet in San Bol means grabbing your roll of toilet paper, and heading for a line of bushes one hundred meters or so in the distance. Thankfully, this cluster of bushes is downstream from "the stream," which is the source of all of San Bol's cooking and cleaning water.

This line of bushes provides only modest visual protection from the building, and the toilet area itself is a totally open field upon which countless people have made their deposits. Unfortunately, no one has yet thought of digging a hole, so anywhere will do. This creates the effect of walking in a minefield, and may explain the odd gait of recent San Bol visitors. Having no hole and no stool upon which to sit, means one must squat, which I believe is a dying art in modern Western culture. My squatting technique certainly has room for improvement.

Had I known this skill was needed on the Camino I would have at least practiced while still at home, but alas, I did not. The rest must be left to everyone's imagination.

As I maneuver across this field I also find myself speculating that there is a severe shortage of plumbers among the Pilgrim population. No plumber would tolerate these conditions for long. While San Bol is probably unique in its Camino toilet culture, there is plenty of "side-of-the-road" toilet action going on throughout the Camino. Most of the time there are simply no other options. While most of us probably start the Camino dearly holding onto all of our urban and modern modesty, by the end we throw much of it to the winds, and simply respond to nature's call. Human, all too human, is our discovery.

My departure out of San Bol is bittersweet. High thin clouds filter the early morning sun into radiant shades of red and purple. The beauty is stunning and the healing gifts of yesterday remain real and true. Yet I cannot linger here, and must head back into desolate country and the challenges of this day. I have been strongly encouraged by Ke to stop at the Hermitage of San Nicolas some 18 mi/25 km away. It is a twelfth century Romanesque church in its original form, which hosts only eight to ten pilgrims per night, plus two hosts/hospitalieros. While everyone sleeps inside this one-room sanctuary, much like Roncesvalles, it is on a much more intimate scale. Its unique feature, however, is its practice of the foot-washing ritual as described in the Gospels. This practice forms the core of the spiritual expression of this hostel. I am undecided about whether to make this my goal for the day, since I have learned the hard way not to get too fixated about my destinations.

As I walk with the intense morning sun on my back, I find myself reflecting on deeper questions about myself. I find myself frustrated with the all too familiar "who am I?" question, since it seems to take me into a dead end, or at best a circular loop where I focus on roles, functions, or choices I have actualized. In a sense I am tired of this question, perhaps because I am tired of myself as a function, an operationalized apparatus that performs its duties admirably.

When I change the question, however, to "Who am I **with** myself?" the question becomes more interesting, and I see deeper layers of self-relatedness emerging. I see the harder to own hurting or angry me, the more acceptable sad me, the lonely me, as well as the gentle and peaceful me. All of these states reveal the deeper attitudes I carry about myself, and the relationship I have to these expressions of myself. This seems to be where the real work of self-love must take place.

Three hours of steady walking in the growing heat brings me to the outskirts of Castrojeriz, a sleepy, historic pilgrim town of around 1000 inhabitants. The guidebooks describe it as "permanently occupied with Siesta," and since it is now noon, and Siesta is officially underway, I can make no argument with this conclusion. No store is open, and since I have not seen a store for two days, I must content myself with a three day old Danish bun for lunch, along with some nuts I always keep in emergency reserve. There is no reason to linger here, so off I march, but as I leave the last houses of the village, a fascinating sight meets me as I turn the corner.

A shepherd and his two dogs are herding a large group of sheep directly toward me. There are houses on either side of the roadway so there is no escape, and before I know it, I am surrounded by dozens of sheep bleating away and kicking up a huge cloud of dust. They brush up against my legs, their wool rough against my skin. This river of life flows around me and I stand transfixed by the energy and power of the flock. I feel absolutely no fear, even though I suppose they could have knocked me over had they tried. The subtle communication between shepherd, dogs and sheep is remarkable as they move through the village.

Surrounded by Sheep

As they slowly move on by, I reflect on the common use of shepherd and sheep imagery in the New Testament. My very deepest understandings of ministry and ministerial identity is shaped by this image, but I become aware of how ambivalent the image remains for me. On the one hand, the close connection between shepherd and sheep is remarkable and reveals a mutual recognition and participation of one with the other, which fits my sense of Christ's participation with us as shepherd of our souls. I seek this kind of resonance with the persons I meet in ministry, and for me such grace is the supreme model of such radical solidarity, however much I might fall short of this in my own finite efforts.

At the same time, however, I find being in the middle of a flock suffocating, and in this case, actually choking as I gasp for air in the middle of this dust cloud. This flock of sheep also cuts me off from my path, which is how any herd mentality operates when it has a hold of us. To the extent that the shepherd is about safety and nurture, the image informs me, but when it comes to growth in responsibility and authenticity, the image loses its usefulness. If safety or protection alone ultimately defines our spiritual life, then fear management becomes its primary impulse.

The spiritual life, however, is also about authentic self-realization, and for this freedom is required. For this the shepherd must morph into wilderness-guide and many contemporary shepherds do not have this model in their repertoire. For me, Jesus represents both the one who protects, but also the one who has been to the wilderness and who has been fully informed and shaped by it. I love this Jesus because as I am in my own wilderness I know I have a friend who meets me there.

It is with these internal musings that I stare out at the wilderness out ahead of me as I leave Castrojeriz. There is a killer ascent staring me in the face since I have to climb back up to the top of the Meseta. The landscape is as dry and desolate as any I have ever seen. There is no breeze stirring and in this heat even the birds are silent. I resolutely put one foot in front of the other as I climb, with sweat pouring off me and wondering if this monster hill will ever end. Some hills are very deceptive because there is a farther rise beyond the horizon which is visible at any given time, and this is one such hill. I finally break out on top, with one final steep climb yet to go, and can only bend over with panting breath and quivering legs as I get there. From this vantage point I can see for miles in all directions, including the valley below. I see no one anywhere, with the exception of two pilgrim bikers who are just beginning at the bottom of the hill. As I anticipated, the hill is too steep for them and they come to a grinding stop halfway up, and must get off their bikes and push them the rest of the way. It will be a while until they catch up with me.

Catch up they do, and perhaps since I have encountered more bikers in recent days, a joke about bikers begins to form in my mind. Since the ritual of foot washing is a Christian ritual first initiated by Jesus, depicting servanthood and blessing through the washing of the dirty feet of wanderers and pilgrims, what ritual might Jesus have initiated had he been ministering to a bunch of bikers instead of walkers? What body parts would have needed washing, since the bikers' feet never touch the ground?

At first I am mildly amused by this thought, but after a while I find it so funny that I burst out laughing. It becomes so funny that I begin to howl and then double over with laughter, and even have to stop walking for a bit. I am soon crying tears of laughter and cannot stop. It is of course possible that I had mild sunstroke, but the tenacity of this joke is amazing. I simply cannot shake it; it is like a bad song that takes over one's mind, and no matter what one does, one cannot stop humming it. So it is with this joke. It just keeps looping through my head.

A few minutes later, I conclude that it is not funny at all, and is actually kind of sick. I begin to berate myself for my sick sense of humor, but another minute later think my joke is the funniest thing I have ever come up with. So it goes, back and forth for longer than I care to admit, until finally I am rescued from my heat diseased mind by the sight of a new valley up ahead, and off in the far distance I see the solitary ancient church of San Nicolas. Instantly my laughter subsides as I walk down the hill to meet an unexpected new challenge.

CHAPTER 8

Resisting Grace

"Attend . . . until the day breaks and the morning star rises . . ." II
Peter 1:19
Then, let us follow toward our destination.
Travel light and lean
Upon your staff, a friend, our common dream.
Hopeful pilgrims ~
Be Love,
Glimpse God
In your midst ~ in the smallest things,

In the cracks,
Between the pages,
In each other's eyes.
Forget disguise ~
Receive ~
Give Presence along this dusty, rutted, detoured road.
Sandals worn or barefoot
Remember ~ remind ~ speak ~
Be Peace.
Martha Bartholomew, <u>By Hand Unseen</u>, 2010, p.41.

*A*rriving in front of the imposing 1000 year old church of San Nicholas is a surreal experience. It is the only building in sight, and is a windowless structure except for a small window over the altar. As I arrive around 3 PM it is locked, with no one around except for four Italian and two Spanish pilgrims waiting to get in. As I stand there my ambivalence about staying is strong. Not only is it not yet open, there is no shade to speak of. Here I am, sitting in the blazing sun, waiting. I recognize no one, and given I am in a group of non-German or English speakers, I will likely have another dinner experience where I will barely be able to converse. But then the real source of my ambivalence surfaces: I am nervous about this foot washing business. It feels invasive somehow, and why would I enter into this ritual with strangers I cannot even talk to?

My ambivalence is so strong I actually decide to walk on, intending to walk an additional two kilometers to the next village of Itero, or, if I am up to it, even five more kilometers to Boadilla. I in fact get up, put on my boots, strap on my pack, take a few steps, then stop again. I am totally confused. I have been strongly encouraged to stay here. There are only ten beds which are always full, and here I would have one of them! Not only that, I seem to be willing to risk further injury and the possibility of full hostels down the road. As I stand in the middle of the path, undecided, a moment of sanity kicks in, and I make the spontaneous decision to stay.

Within minutes of my decision, the two English speaking Spanish hospitalieros, Javiar and Carlos, arrive and open the doors admitting us to the wonderfully cool and serene interior. Within minutes a middle-aged German woman, Brigitte, arrives, along with two young Slovakian women. Our community for the night is complete. Admission to the interior of the church reveals a completely open space, with a high wooden ceiling, thick stone walls, with the only variation to the open space a raised altar on one end, beneath a small stained-glass window. Ten empty chairs are arranged in a circle on this platform. Our five bunk beds are all in a row along one wall, and in the center of the room are four long tables with straight backed chairs. This open Romanesque structure will be our kitchen, living room, and bedroom.

Because the front door is directly on the pilgrim path, several pilgrim stragglers come walking by looking for water, a bit of rest, and perhaps feeling a bit envious that this Albergue is full. As I sit outside on a bench at the front door resting and greeting pilgrims as they trek on by, a young woman on a very modest looking bike with a basket on the front rides up. She looks rather odd compared with the vast majority of "bicycle-pilgrims" one sees in droves on the Camino. Whether male or female, they are invariably on fancy trekking bikes, in full sports regalia, and on a speed and adventure mission. This person clearly is not. She stops in front of me, and as she opens her mouth, I realize she is Irish.

Her name is Joan, and she decides to take a brief ten minute break, although she never chooses to get off her bike. In these ten minutes I learn that she comes from a very devout Catholic family which includes several priests, and a very faith-devoted father. She has rejected the Church and its traditions, yet she claims she is spiritually seeking, and the Camino pilgrimage is one of her attempts to address her spiritual hunger. She will turn 30 she tells me on the Camino, and believes something profound is underway for her. I share little of myself in those few minutes, yet somehow a level of connection occurs which always surprises me, although is becoming so familiar. The Camino seems to work on us as pilgrims and we come to recognize this in each other even across generations, genders, and belief systems.

Joan rides off, and as I continue to mull over our encounter, I am roused by the hospitalieros who announce that our evening will begin in a few moments with our foot washing ceremony, to be followed by our pilgrim meal. I feel immediately anxious, without really knowing why, although I feel some relief knowing that I have already showered and cleaned up. Thank goodness my feet are already clean, I think.

As we ten pilgrims take our places on the platform next to the altar, I immediately recognize the folly of my conclusion about clean feet. It is not about clean or dirty feet, it is about my heart, my mind, my soul. As we sit in our circle I look down at my feet and at the feet of those around me, and realize how pathetic a sight we are. Most of our feet are red and puffy. Many have Band-Aids over blisters, and a few seem to have toe nails missing (I will lose two, before my Camino is over).

Our hosts approach us wearing modest red and white vestments, carrying a large bowl of water. They place the bowl on the ground in front of the first pilgrim, and if we are not already barefoot, we remove one of our sandals, which for me was the left foot, the one so in need of healing. Carlos and Javiar take turns with each pilgrim, with one taking our designated foot, placing it in the bowl, and gently washing it. He then kisses our foot as his colleague reads a personal prayer and blessing, using our full name and in our native tongue.

As my turn comes, tears begin to roll down my cheeks, and slowly drip onto my shirt as I hear my name called and my blessing given. To have one's burdened and disgusting feet washed and kissed is overwhelming. It is a profound act of grace to be so embraced in one's vulnerability and woundedness, yet I am simultaneously aware of how powerfully I resist this grace. At one and the same time I have the awareness of how completely and deeply my very life depends upon such grace, that I could not exist without it. Yet at the same time, I resist this gift and feel unworthy of it. This awareness floods me with joy and sorrow in equal measure.

This moment of heightened spiritual awareness shines into my murky soul and reveals me to myself even as it reveals the God force that resides there. The grace that is present in all my vulnerability and frailty is the truth that breaks me open. The top of my head feels like it has blown off and the rest of the ritual becomes a blur. I sense others have been deeply touched in their own way. We linger quietly for a while within our individual reflections, and then slowly reengage the group by expressing our gratitude to our two hosts, and to each other. In this spirit we slowly wend our way to the tables for our evening meal.

My recollection is that the meal is a quieter affair than most pilgrim meals tend to be. My sense is we all have some inner processing to do, and I certainly need to do so. By 9 PM I am claiming personal space to journal, as is Brigitte, the German woman who sits next to me as we write. Within the hour I am on my bunk gazing at the thousand year old stone wall next to me, and feeling a profound sense of continuity with the countless pilgrims who have found their rest in this sanctuary. What pains have they all carried? What sorrows accompanied their journeys? What hopes and joys were in their hearts? Did they find grace sufficient for their path? Did the Spirit of God meet them as the Sacred Spirit found me? I offer up a prayer for the souls of these my brothers and sisters who have preceded me, as well as for those yet to come. In this prayer mode, I fall asleep.

Morning arrives fresh, crisp, and clear which means good walking weather for now. Everyone is eager to be off, but we insist on making sure we have a group photo before departure, something that has not happened before on my Camino. There was obviously something powerful going on for all of us and we want to capture it anyway we can. I head off with Rinaldo, a Spanish man in his forties, and we banter briefly, but soon settle into a silent walking rhythm. I seem to need a faster pace today, so I say my goodbye and move on.

San Nicolas Foot Washing Pilgrims

I am hoping that the hamlet of Itero just ahead will have an open shop so I can find some breakfast, but no such luck. As I enter the tiny village, just around the first corner and across the town square, I find Brigitta sitting at a fountain eating her breakfast yogurt with her fingers. I tell her of my breakfast plight and she graciously offers to share her yogurt with me. I decline, and think to myself that I will need a few more foot washing rituals to completely turn the corner when it comes to my receptivity to grace.

I do have some mixed nuts with me for just such a situation, and they serve the purpose for now. The morning is too fresh and I am too primed for walking to linger and talk, so I wish her well, and move on. This village marks the boundary of the historical kingdoms of

Castilla and Leon, and I immediately sense I am leaving the more arid High Plains of the Meseta, and entering a rich agricultural area with many small rivers and canals. The monotony of the Meseta is soon interrupted by a lush canal which accompanies me directly on my right for over two hours.

A final crossing of the canal at Fromista includes a fast moving stream roaring downhill into the valley below. It is a welcome sight after days of virtual desert. I have high hopes for a nice lunch in Fromista, and I gratefully find a large grocery store where I pick up some fresh Spanish sausage, butter, juice, and a child's toothpaste tube since adult sizes are too large and heavy. All I need now is some fresh bread for my picnic. But no matter how hard I look, even with several detours, I cannot find a bakery. By now my butter is melting and running into my backpack, so I am left with no choice but to throw it into the garbage. My lovely fantasy picnic becomes reduced to chewing on my sausage between swallows of juice as I walk. Yum!!

Before leaving Fromista I decide on a new foot care strategy, namely, switching from my hiking shoes to walking sandals, and alternating back and forth, depending on the terrain. The path ahead looks flat and reasonably smooth, and walking with sandals cannot be much worse on my feet than what I have been doing to them thus far. My guidebook notes that the upcoming portion of the trail has been constructed as a modern pilgrim pathway, meaning it is flat, boring, and devoid of any character. The guidebook recommends one take a longer, more remote route along the river. I should have realized that words like "remote" and "longer" do not necessarily mean "easier." This alternative route becomes a grueling long stretch of sun, heat, and the very occasional tree. In addition, no pilgrim even comes into view in over two hours of walking. Suddenly, literally out of the blue, a bike rolls up behind me startling me out of my heat induced stupor. It is Joan, my brief Irish acquaintance from yesterday. We are both surprised to run into anyone out here, it is so desolate, never mind encountering someone already met.

This time Joan gets off her bike and we walk together for an hour or so. We begin by sharing our essential stories. I offer the narrative of my pending divorce; she, the fear of being doomed to solitariness. Two recent boyfriend endings have deepened this fear for her. Our conversation then moves from the personal to the universal: the Big Bang theory, angels, eternal judgment, i.e. will we have to give an account for our lives, what is spirituality actually?

I find this level of spiritual inquiry to be fairly typical on the Camino, especially among young people and this inspires me about the future. They are not content with dogma of any sort, or belief for its own sake, but truly seek spiritual input as it meets and informs life. They demand experiential integrity for faith, and Joan is one of its ambassadors. After an hour of intense talking and walking, I have been on my feet for well over three hours, and I badly need to rest, so we say our goodbyes and she rides on.

During my fifteen minutes of resting, I note how this young woman, half my age, is also my peer on the Camino. Here, I am not "the expert," but the wounded traveler whose only "expertise" is my direct life experience. She lives similar dilemmas to my own, and we meet there. On the road to Emmaus as depicted in the Gospels, the disciples share their heart based experience of Jesus with each other, and in this sharing their "eyes are opened" and the sacred appears to them. Joan and I are also on that Emmaus Road, only now in Spain, many centuries later, and in the sharing of our vulnerability, the sacred reveals itself to us again as it eternally pledges to do.

I plow on, again alone, with only one solitary Pilgrim passing me all afternoon. The terrain is more or less flat, which allows for easier singing. I go through my repertoire of hymns, and as I vocalize or hum through my favorites, one of them usually pops up as the anthem of the hour. At this moment it seems to be: "It Is Well With My Soul." I know it by heart, and so I sing with gusto. I have done enough singing over the years to know the difference between singing from one's throat versus singing from one's gut. Gut singing means moving your diaphragm, and singing from that place gives it extra power, even when singing softly. So I sing from my deepest gut, and sense the inner alignment that this brings, and I express my gratitude to God for the incredible gift of song.

Late afternoon brings me to the outskirts of Villasirga, a well-utilized pilgrim stop since the twelfth century, when it became a command center for the Templar Knights. They built the magnificent thirteenth century Church of St. Mary the White which I see directly in front of me. At this point I have been walking 20 mi/32 km today, close to my longest one-day distance yet, and even though I am very tired, I can tell my body is responding much better to the challenges I am imposing on it. True, my feet are killing me, but my shoe switching method seems to be tricking them into walking extra distances. I am pleased that I have been able to fool them in this way.

At some point during the day I seem to have made the decision to claim some solitary space and stay in a hotel for the night. The "noble" and more spiritual reason I am presuming for myself is to claim some quiet time to reflect on the power of last evening's foot washing events. My less conscious but more neurotic reason is to find an Internet link. I am still tripping over the events set in motion by Margita's phone call while I was at Silos. In addition, I also feel guilty that I have not e-mailed the people I promised to send occasional messages from the Camino as proof that I am still alive. I embarked on my pilgrimage with fantasies of sending a "Camino update" from time to time to a select group of family and friends. It is so difficult to find Internet access in rural Spain, or when finding it being so totally exhausted that I can hardly think straight, never mind send coherent e-mails, I have essentially given up on the idea, but today I will give it another try.

My first hotel option has a non-functioning Internet, so I move on to the next one. This hotel is full as is the one after that. At this point I am fed up with myself. I have walked over 20 mi/32 km today in searing heat, and I am now stumbling around this village on some vague mission to please family and friends, if not a soon-to-be ex-wife. My neurotic need to please has never been this clear to me. This stark recognition seems to free me from my compulsion and I return to the first hotel, where there is, thankfully, still a comfortable room available.

By now I am famished and dying for a beer. To my pleasant surprise this hotel has a lovely garden restaurant in the back, and this being Spain, no one is eating at 6 PM, so I have the place to myself. I order a beer which turns out to be the biggest beer stein I have ever attempted. Given how I feel, this stein does not stand a chance. Next, I order a ham omelet. It arrives on a plate half the size of my table, and on it is an omelet the size of a small pillow, between two enormous hunks of bread. It is surely an order for four people and I look around thinking someone has played a trick on me. The young woman serving me, and her mother who is the cook, look puzzled at my surprise. We speak no language in common, so I can only smile back and pat my stomach as a sign all will be well, although I am not so sure.

I valiantly work at this mountain of food and an hour later have given up. I take a small portion with me to save for the next day, and unfortunately have to leave the rest. As I am eating, I realize that in the village square directly across from where I am sitting, is the Pilgrim Albergue here in Villasirga. Strangely, however, there is no activity going on for some reason. I wander over and see a large "Closed" sign on the door because of a bed bug infestation. It now dawns on me why I have seen no pilgrims in town and why I am likely the only pilgrim around. This thought actually amuses me as I realize I will have to keep my own company tonight. I actually smile to myself as I walk around looking for a bar and my evening glass of Spanish red wine.

As I leave the locked and bug infested Albergue a solitary young pilgrim with a huge backpack arrives and asks what is up with the locked door. I pass on the bad news, and let him know there is a hotel with rooms across the way. The hotel is not a financial option for him, and I see the fatigue in his eyes as he hitches up his pack for another 4 mi/7 km of walking to Carrion de los Condes, the next village, where they have two large hostels, and he will hopefully be able to find a spot. Yet his plight is not unusual in that many pilgrims have pushed themselves to a limit only to find they have to suck up energy from somewhere, to go a distance they did not expect.

The spiritual parallel to this is not lost on me, and I contemplate how life has thrown me onto paths that turned out to be much longer or harder than I had "planned" for. I can only laugh at the absurdity of my belief that I can control my "plans," or know what will be required of me. I must admit it is much easier to be impressed with my little spiritual insight sitting at a bar with mild Spanish air swirling around me watching the evening sun go down. My young friend in the valley below who is straining to put one foot in front of the other right now, is not finding enlightenment so easy to come by, I suspect.

As quiet as my hotel turns out to be, I do not sleep very well this night. I keep thinking about my home situation and what awaits me there. Do I even have a home, and what does home mean for me at this point in my life? Can I learn to be truly at home wherever I am? As

I lay awake, I find I am at least more at peace with this question than I normally allow myself to be. Spiritual awareness tells us that there is a peace that passes all understanding, and that this peace is available to us even in the midst of our most difficult trials and tribulations. Yes this is one of the great challenges of the spiritual journey, to stay centered in that peace.

As I reflect more fully on this question I become aware that there is a true center to my being and that this center is not necessarily subject to all the storms swirling about me. At the center of my being, and in my deepest reality there is a calm, the calm in the "center of the storm" that makes up my life. This center is not so much a place, but a path, a way. When the claim is made about Jesus that he is "the Way," I believe it speaks about the particular way in which Jesus embraced the full reality of his life. He seemed to meet everything and everyone he encountered with a desire to find and actualize God's purpose within that person or situation. He sought to place his life and all he encountered in the service of God's sacred intentions. These intentions may not always be easy to discern, but they are discoverable.

In that Jesus' mode, perhaps everything can be faced as it is. It can be met fully, without fear, and one can look for the sacred impulses that move within all things, even when those impulses are faint, and hidden perhaps behind many veils. Jesus had an eye and an ear for those faint sacred vibrations, even when they are hidden behind the greatest darkness. As a follower of Jesus I also want to be on that way of serving that sacred impulse at the heart of all things. Maybe that is where my true home should be: to be at home on the Way!

With these musings filling my mind for much of the night, I eventually get up at 7 AM, pack, and slowly leave the hotel. In the quiet of the morning, with the sun just beginning to settle on my shoulder, I see my long shadow stretching out before me. This is another regular feature of the Camino. Because pilgrims walk from East to West, we always have the sun at our backs in the morning, which is why the backs of our legs are always more tanned than the front. As the sun first begins to shine on us, our shadows are enormously long. As the morning proceeds and the sun rises over our heads, our shadows recede.

Morning Shadows

   This daily pattern generates an insight for me into my own nature and the process of self-discovery. As we first gain self-awareness, even sacred awareness, our personal shadow appears in the light of such "truth." With enlightenment, what has remained hidden becomes visible often in ways we first tend to reject. Our shadow can loom very large when we first see it. With continued walking in the light, however, our shadow shrinks, coming into closer integration and ownership with the rest of who we are. In sunny Spain one enacts this ritual every morning and today particularly I take note of its deeper implications.

   In what seems like a very fast hour and a half later, I arrive at Carrion de los Condes where shops have opened and a lovely street café welcomes me for breakfast. My usual Café con Leche helps wash down two fresh croissants. Across the street I spot Brigitte, my "fingers in the yogurt" friend from San Nicholas. She is with a French woman and they walk over to join me for breakfast, reporting that they have stayed at a Benedictine convent for the night, and have just left after morning prayers. They report how the prayer service has touched them deeply.

The monastic echo they discovered for themselves seems to be able to reach across the centuries and has touched them, even as it nourished me only a week ago.

As we are in the middle of this deeper sharing, the three of us decide to embark together in our walking to extend our conversation. Soon our French companion needs to slow down, however, so Brigitte and I take our leave, and since she and I have a similar pace, we walk together for several more hours. Perhaps prompted by the spiritual sharing at breakfast, our dialog takes on a more personal tone. I learn that she is widowed for five years now, and has entered a new relationship which is proving to be challenging for her. Her life as a social worker has been quite rewarding, but a restlessness has overtaken her and she is moving in new professional directions which perhaps include private practice counseling and programs for women.

While I hear such stories often in my role as a counselor, on the Camino I am not in my counselor role and do not hear them that way. I hear them as human stories that inevitably touch mine somehow. As counselors we are of course required to be impacted by another's story which is at the heart of genuine empathy. But we do not allow ourselves to jump into our own parallel narratives, lest we get lost in them and become disengaged from the others' story through our own subjective material. On the Camino it is different, and I freely share my own story, and I find she does not receive it in her own "counselor" mode, but as a story which also touches her more mutually. This easy mutuality is surely one of the great gifts of the Camino.

All morning we have been walking into an increasingly stiff wind, which by 11:30 AM makes walking and talking difficult. I have also been walking for three hours straight, and very much need to rest my feet. And so I take my leave from Brigitte to rest at a picnic area beside the trail. Brigitte only walks in sandals, and her feet are obviously tougher than mine, but by now I have learned to take myself seriously. Thankfully, the picnic area has the first shade of the day, and I decide to fully stretch out on top of one of the massive stone tables which are amazingly cool and refreshing. On the Camino one is forever pounding away on stones of every size and shape imaginable. This stone is very different in that it lifts and holds me up as if I am being carried. I soak up the restorative power of this stone and its incredible strength, and imagine myself to be laid out on some ancient, sacred altar. This is not an altar of sacrifice, but an altar of blessing, with the Earth presenting me to its maker as one of God's precious gifts.

My rest period stretches to an hour or more, and with some reluctance I climb off my stone perch and back onto the hot, windy trail. In the entire hour of lying there, only one pilgrim passes by, namely our French friend from this morning. The Meseta's isolation is certainly consistent, just like its heat and wind. But now, back on the trail, in the midst of this solitude, I come across a group of ten or twelve young people led by a young priest, sitting on a bridge over a dry riverbed. They are singing, accompanied by guitars and handing out refreshments to passing pilgrims. Their ample supply tells me they have not seen much traffic today. Their youthful vitality and joy at serving pilgrims is a sweet acknowledgment of our efforts. I linger for a bit and converse with them in appreciation for their hospitality, but have to turn down their offer of additional soft drinks or water. I have enough water with me, and don't need any extra weight. Even kindnesses can bog us down, and sometimes need to be graciously declined.

Within a few minutes a rare and somewhat disorienting sight awaits me. Another pilgrim has appeared, only he is walking toward me and I become momentarily confused. Have I gotten heatstroke, or am I going in the wrong direction? I am about to meet Andre from Paris who is walking back home after having first walked from Paris to Santiago likely already having walked 1000 mi/1600 km or so. What makes him stand out for me, beyond even that weather-beaten look that long distance pilgrims all share, is the fact that he is walking the entire way in plastic "Croc" sandals. I ask him twice to be sure I hear him correctly, that he has in fact walked the entire distance in these so-called shoes, and he nods and confirms that he has no foot complaints. If the manufacturer of these shoes ever needs a new marketing strategy, Andre is their man. For a man who has been walking for well over three months now, he is one effervescent guy with happy feet.

It is hard to say if Andre's story inspires or shames me, and perhaps it does both. Whatever the reason, I make the decision to not stop at Calzadilla, my original target for the day at the 16 mi/27 km mark, but to stretch myself on out to Ledigos, another 4 mi/7 km further. This would make it very long day, close to my distance yesterday. What I discover again in this extension of my day, is that there is something about the stretching of my goal which impacts my mind to change its perception of time and space. This simple shift of the boundaries of my expectations, makes this additional mileage seem much longer than a full days walking. Those final 4mi/7 km simply do not want to end.

It is true that I am tired, but I have enough energy reserves to do the walking, so I cannot attribute my experience of endlessness to fatigue alone. It seems, rather, that my expectations for the day became locked into my mind, and create a rigidity of belief about what I can and cannot do. My goals and expectations it seems, are not fluid at all, but quite rigid based on what I feel I should or should not be able to do. I begin to wonder where else I might "decide" well ahead of time what the limits of an experience should be? Do I perhaps prematurely cut myself off from other horizons because I already think I know ahead of time what my capability might be, or that I can truly know in advance what the supposed "best" outcome is?

My relief is great as I turn a final corner on the trail to see Ledigos materialize before me. The Albergue in this town is large with a huge courtyard and multiple room and bed options. There are rooms with double beds in addition to dorms, and I put in a bid for one of the private rooms, but am turned down because I need to be traveling with someone else in order to qualify. It seems as if I will have a group experience after all tonight.

Suddenly, my host has another thought. There is one single room with bath, on the very top floor of the hostel, and I am welcome to use it. For a brief moment I wonder if this is an unnecessary indulgence that may not be good for my spiritual health, but I get over that thought quickly. I overcome this thought by figuring I will offer up enough pain in the coming weeks to atone for any over indulgence I might be guilty of. I feel even more wonderfully sinful when I am told that this floor is generally for overflow pilgrims, and will not be utilized tonight other than by me, so I will have the entire floor to myself. I can hardly believe my good fortune. There will be no snoring or 5 AM packing noise tomorrow, unless I am the one doing it.

I drop off my things in my room and head back to the courtyard where pilgrims are gathering and I spot the two French women from five nights ago in Rabe, who look as fresh and radiant as they did days ago. I have no idea how they pull that off, especially when I look at myself and see that I am slipping back very quickly on the evolutionary scale toward Neanderthalness. I have become a hairy beast, all red and puffy, a true experiment in regressive genetics.

My morbidity about myself is interrupted by a big, rousing hello from John, the tall lanky Belgian, from my first Camino days in Roncesvalles and our surprising reencounter in Santa Domingo. Of the six young pilgrims with whom he started almost three weeks ago, he is the only one left on the Camino. This choice seems to have been made easier by having found a companion, a French Basque woman with whom he is cooking dinner. "Would you like to join us for our meal"? I gladly say yes, and we are soon joined by the two French women, who are followed by an older Dutch couple, and again, the international Camino forum is off and running. Our ample potato and sausage main course is washed down by a steady stream of red wine. John is clearly in love, and believes he has hit the jackpot. But while he slips away for a bathroom break, his companion complains to me about his excessive drinking. I sense trouble in paradise, and if my experience is any indicator, most of us end up being expelled from our paradise sooner or later. But I do not let my pessimism get in the way of celebrating this new connection between them and the camaraderie of our spontaneous gathering.

I take my leave since I have not yet showered or washed my clothes, and proceed to do so. I hand wash my clothes thoroughly as I do every day, and upon returning to my room discover that I have mistakenly washed my clean clothes, and not my dirty ones. Perhaps John is not the only one who drank too much today. No matter, I must trudge back downstairs to wash all over again, and by the time I am done, my room is full of wet laundry waiting to dry. Of course, I have nothing clean to wear in the interim, and am struck by how consistently the Camino gives humility lessons. One can only chuckle at the Camino's little reversals.

CHAPTER 9

The Temptation of Leonard Cohen

Anthem

The birds they sang
At the break of day
Start again
I heard them say
Don't dwell on what
Has passed away
Or what is yet to be.
Every heart to love will come
But like a refugee.
Ring the bells that still can ring
Forget your perfect offering.
There is a crack in everything.
That's how the light gets in.
Leonard Cohen, 1992

*B*eing the sole sleeper on an entire floor makes for restful sleep but also no wakeup cues. In the silence of my private quarters, I wake up after 8 AM, a full two hours after most pilgrims are awake and well out the door. I spot a few stragglers in the courtyard below tightening their packs on their backs, so I pack in haste, and stow my still damp clothes as best I can. I shudder with cold as I put on the wettest ones, not wanting them to get moldy in the backpack. Besides, they will dry quickly enough if there is anywhere near the wind I had yesterday.

The vast horizon of the Spanish highlands welcomes me as I leave the village of Ledigos and begin the slow climb to Terradillos de Templarios. This ancient Templar stronghold marks the halfway point of the Camino, and I can't believe that in less than an hour I will already have finished half of my journey. This is followed immediately by the realization that I have *only* finished half the Camino. Halfway moments are like that. They are poignant in that one knows what pain, sacrifices, and joys are already faced, but that knowledge removes all illusions about what lies ahead. At this moment I carry deep gratitude for what has been given and for what has been asked of me, but at the same time I face trepidation wondering if I am up to the challenge of what lies ahead.

My intention for the first part of my day is to walk to the small village of Moratinos for a visit with Rebecca, a long-time Camino advocate and historian. She and her partner, both retired journalists, are a treasure of knowledge about the Camino. I am following up my e-mail contact with her of many months ago, hoping for a visit, if she happens to be at home. Although the village is tiny, I still have trouble finding their house, but with the help of a villager or two, I do find them.

Barking dogs welcome me, and in time Rebecca and her partner appear, and invite me in for coffee. We talk Camino lore and I sense their deep commitment to the pilgrimage, so much so, that they have built this home to be close to it. She is American, and he is British, but even with their strong Camino attachment, I also sense their isolation here in the Spanish hinterland, and the difficulty of managing life in a little Spanish outpost so far from social services. Her partner is ill, and he needs regular visits to far off clinics. I enjoy my visit, and learn much about the modern history of the Camino, but after an hour

I become restless, and need to be underway. Her partner insists on accompanying me for a while and since I have no obvious reason to say no, he and I and his three-legged dog with cancer, head off over the bare hills.

Any worries I have about being slowed down are quickly set aside when I realize that the three-legged dog is faster than both of us, just as my ill companion is faster than I am. The longer we walk the more engaging it becomes, as we find ourselves talking in depth about Kierkegaard and his understanding of finitude. Where else but in remote Spanish hill country can you stumble into a sophisticated Kierkegaardian dialog with a three legged dog hanging on every word?

My companions accompany me for well over 3 mi/5 km when we finally say our goodbyes. Of course, he and the dog have to walk all the way back, while I have perhaps another two hours to walk in order to reach Sahagun, where I intend to catch a train into Leon. I have been mulling over the possibility of skipping a portion of the trail for days now, ever since San Bol, when I was strongly encouraged to make the trek from Santiago to Finisterre.

On this particular morning my decision to skip the 40 mi/60 km from Sahagun to Leon comes rather easily, considering how badly I agonized over the missed section into Burgos. The ease and clarity of my decision this time boils down to the realization that I will probably experience a more meaningful culmination of my pilgrimage in Finesterre, and not in Santiago. Finesterre, "the end of the earth," has in practice been the true end of the pilgrimage reaching back into pre-Christian eras. Several people have encouraged me to go there, even if I need to take the bus from Santiago to Finesterre to do so.

I will need to make up those extra days somewhere, however, and skipping this portion by taking the train today from Sahagun to Leon is probably the best section to skip, since the final 6 mi/10 km heading into Leon are said to be especially grueling as one treks through endless suburbs on hot pavement. I will take my chances that my spiritual maturation will not suffer too greatly if I forgo that stretch.

My final hour of walking into Sahagun brings the first clouds in almost a week onto the horizon. I sense a change, not only in the weather, but also in myself. My encounters with the limits of my body these last weeks have brought me into a deeper relationship with myself for which I am in gratitude. My relationship to my own pain of the heart has become softer, less avoidant, acceptable even. It is now the fabric of my life, just as the gravel under my feet and the wind and sun on my face are the current real context of my life. As I sit at the station eating a quick lunch before the trains arrival, I sense a new chapter is about to begin.

The elegant, smooth train is an odd juxtaposition for a now trail hardened pilgrim. As I find a spot in the crowded train, everyone looks very comfortable, well-fed, and extremely civilized somehow. I on the other hand, feel my wildness, my closeness to the earth and the raw conditions of life. I also sense how much more open I have become to the inner and outer forces that modern life has been able to filter out for the most part through comfort and distraction. I have become aware that there is a certain numbing affect to civilization, one which I am generally willing to indulge, but right now I hope to resist this pending lure of the city which awaits me. Or can I?

Leon approaches so quickly I almost miss the stop, and thankfully have my wits about me just enough to grab my pack and poles as I race for the exit. As I spill out onto the crowded platform I am overwhelmed by the noise, smells, and the general commotion of the city. I find an open bench just outside the station and sit down to get my bearings. Where to go? Perhaps I need a spiritual buffer from the overpowering city and what better option could there be, than to stay in the convent Santa Maria, a 140 bed hostel run by Benedictine nuns right in the heart of the old city?

A relatively short twenty minute walk brings me to the huge oak doors that mark the entrance into the convent and a small courtyard where pilgrims are lining up to register. A rather cold and gruff woman checks me in, and directs me up the stairs to the men's dormitory. This room turns out to be a densely packed, low ceiling room full of bunk beds, most of which are already claimed. I grab one of the few lower bunks remaining and notice how already in early afternoon the room feels hot and stuffy. The women pilgrims have an equivalently sized room at the other end of a long hallway. Between the two large rooms are the bathrooms, which at least for the male population, include only three showers, three toilets, and two sinks, for up to seventy men. This will get very interesting.

I see no one I recognize, male or female, and choose to leave the tight confines of the convent and explore Leon. I am especially keen to visit the cathedral which contains 125 magnificent stained glass windows and is known to be one of the great cathedrals of Spain. As I wander the narrow streets of old Leon, I sense my resistance to becoming a tourist, even for a day. My city temptations multiply a hundred fold when I come across a poster advertising a Leonard Cohen concert in Leon, tomorrow of all days. I have been dying to go to one of his concerts on his "New World Tour" and sadly missed his stop in Chicago. Now, here he is in Leon, tomorrow. The ticket kiosk is just around the corner, so I inquire about availability, and wonders of wonders, there are tickets. They are affordable, and the venue is within walking distance from where I am staying. All I have to do is stay in Leon one more day.

What a dilemma! I take my ambivalence out into the street and find a quiet bar where I order a beer and contemplate my options. Leonard Cohen's music has been cathartic for me in the long months of my separation and divorce process, so there is likely to be some therapeutic benefit if I go. On the other hand, it would carry a heavy dose of entertainment, with crowds, adoring fans, never mind spending a perhaps wasted day and night sitting around in Leon.

Both impulses, to stay or to go, have equal strength and I feel no closer to resolving the dilemma, so I decide to become very practical and look at my schedule and mileage options. To my great surprise I realize that I have only thirteen days left with 200 mi/330 km still to go. At a rate of 16 mi/25 km per day, I know I can reach Santiago in that time, but will have no days left for Finisterre, even with the leap by train I took from Sahagun to Leon this morning. Not only do I not have the luxury of sitting around Leon for a day, I have to make up two more days in order to leave enough time for Finisterre. To my great chagrin I realize I will need to skip another 35 mi/50 km section, or let Finisterre go. I take this discovery hard which shows how attached I still am to being the ideal pilgrim. As flexible a person as I think I am, I realize I must still mature a bit more to be able to finally transcend my ideals.

Perfection in any endeavor is a relentless taskmaster and the spiritual arena is often the worst place for such offense. Perfection creates an instant dualism of right-wrong, good-bad, pure-impure, and so on. Even after all the setbacks and challenges of these first three weeks, with all the hidden blessings they have bestowed, I am still snagged by the temptation of my mind to lay an artificial script of the ideal onto the real. The ideal is an artificial goal, all bright and shiny, but inauthentic in that it wants to avoid the limits of the here and now, of time and space. My pilgrim journey has brought to this inner tension of mine close enough to the surface that I can finally see it clearly, and perhaps I can begin to make different choices about it in the future. I find a fresh freedom in this awareness.

Now even the Leonard Cohen possibility can re-enter the mix. What to do about this concert? The answer comes easily and freely to me. Leonard Cohen has to go, and I will leave Leon early in the morning, and take a bus for 35 mi/50 km from Leon to Astorga. I know deep in my heart that Finisterre is calling out to me, and I must honor that tug. Every other choice now will find its proper place from that awareness. I now feel free to take the bus tomorrow without becoming a "lesser" pilgrim because of it. After less than an hour on the bus tomorrow, I will be walking again, and will still be inhabiting my familiar body, mind, and spirit, and will encounter the joys and sorrows of that day in the reality of the moment. I feel buoyant in the realization that I can be present to all these dilemma moments, and with a renewed spring in my step, head off to the Cathedral of Leon, to savor my final hours in the city without guilt or second guessing.

As impressive as Leon's Cathedral is, it does not touch my spirit on this day. Perhaps it has to do with the crowds, or the scaffolding covering many of the windows, but the Gothic grandeur is not a good match for my conversion into a more "here and now" spirituality. I find I am not willing to get trapped in a tourist-like purely observational mode, so I bid my farewell to the cathedral, and head off to find a place to eat.

Even my eating habits on the Camino have changed, and I order only a large salad (with wine of course), with no meat. This is my fourth day in a row without meat, and for a meat loving German like myself this is truly odd. My body does not want to expend the extra energy digesting heavy things, so salad is it. I can tell I have lost weight on the Camino since my pants are getting very loose, and I will have to be careful that I do not lose them completely at some inopportune moment.

Returning to the convent takes me into what is now a full house of 130 pilgrims, none of whom I recognize. I feel my aloneness and otherness, and especially my advanced age compared to my fellow pilgrims. We are all squeezed together in exceptionally crowded conditions. The bunk above me has now been claimed, and as I introduce myself I discover that he is an American from Washington. It is very odd that he is the first American I have met after three weeks of walking, when others tell me of all the Americans they have encountered. What strikes me even more strangely as we talk is our age span. It turns out he is nineteen years of age which makes me over three times as old. I feel ancient all of a sudden and become aware that I am perhaps the oldest man in the room. Rather than feel badly about it, I feel rather satisfied, if not a bit euphoric. This is an amazing thing I am attempting which not many men my age would tackle. In that somewhat smug state of mind I head downstairs to the chapel where the pilgrim vespers service is about to begin.

Of the 130 or so pilgrims at this Albergue, over half have showed up for this prayer and blessing service, a rather high number of participants. Before we actually enter the chapel where the nuns await us, our "host" nun welcomes us and offers an initial meditation before the Vespers service itself will begin. In this large antechamber most of us sit on the floor, while others remain standing in a large circle. Our host launches into a sermon which begins with sin and goes downhill from there. I am aghast at the spiritual harshness I am witnessing. Here is a room of almost one hundred largely young people, pilgrims no less, eager for a message of "God-with-us" in some fashion. Instead, we are beaten over the head with a scrupulosity and pettiness about our wrong doings. The good news of the gospel has been buried under the weight of her moralization. My heart grows heavier by the moment as I see the message of Jesus, the living icon of the love of God, lost in the tide of our badness which has just washed over us.

This is not just an outdated religious model, but actually dangerous for one's spiritual health. It is a religious style that insists on our badness as our starting point, rather than our yearning for the sacred. The human hunger for God is missed and it is likely many souls are not fed on this night. To her credit, our nun does end her sermonette with a lovely personalized blessing, but by then most of her audience has drifted off by not offering her much attention.

Of course, sin is part of our human condition, our fear response to our conditions of finitude, and as such is deeply connected to our hunger and search for God. Understood as vulnerability, as brokenness, as incompletion, as missing the mark, we should be invited to embrace our sin in the light of a love that already waits for us there. In that love we find our refuge and a balm for every wound, past, present, and future. I feel pain for this nun and we her audience, because I believe in her heart she knows this, but her current presuppositions give her no permission to go there directly, freely, and consistently.

The sermon over, we are directed into the lovely chapel where twenty or so Benedictine sisters await us. They are all in their seventies and eighties, racially white, with the exception of three young African sisters. Their chants and readings are rich and full, but I am still too snagged by the earlier sermon to take much of it in. Perhaps my fellow pilgrims have been less burdened than I, and have drawn nourishment from the mystical riches these nuns and their community represent. For me, however, this cloister experience has been disappointing and I must find peace with my disappointment.

Given how crowded our sleeping quarters are, I remain outside in the courtyard as the evening shadows lengthen. While there, I befriend a pigeon with a missing leg. He is shunned by his fellow pigeons so I spend the rest of the evening feeding him peanuts. He and I are both alone, so we form a bond of sorts for one night, and give each other a bit of cross species comfort.

Nightfall arrives with a strict 10 PM curfew so everyone rushes indoors and the great bathroom queue begins. I believe I end up approximately tenth in the shower queue, eighth in the toilet queue, and fifteenth in the sink queue. I never imagined the male species could be so patient. Perhaps more spiritual input has rubbed off on all of us than I imagined. As I stand there waiting I realize that of all of the details the guidebooks offer about every hostel, none give a bed-to-bathroom ratio.

If I were writing a guidebook I would make that a primary factor in my five point lodging rating scale. On that basis, this Benedictine hostel with a ratio of twenty five people to one toilet, would get only one star, the worst hostel on the entire Camino. Conversely, the best hostel in Spain is in San Bol, where the ratio is one-to-one. While it is true that the hostel at San Bol accommodates only ten people, every guest can go to the toilet anywhere, anytime they like, therefore fully deserving it's full five star rating.

The Spanish have an interesting proclivity of keeping windows closed at night. When in a large room with few people this is somewhat tolerable. When, however, one is in a tight room with many people, it becomes downright ridiculous, if not dangerous. So it is this night. That heat and stuffiness builds up relentlessly until someone finally props a door open to the outside in the middle of the night to let in some breeze. Until then, I am perpetually bathed in sweat. And perhaps because of the heat, the snoring is horrendous.

What I notice, however, is that on this night at least, the snoring is in rhythm, with an actual cadence. When the person to my right takes a snoring pause, my neighbor to my left picks up where the other left off. They each seem to cue their own respective chorus of neighbors who then snore in sequence with them. On one occasion when returning from the bathroom in the middle of the night, the rhythm is so strong, I stop next to my bed and begin conducting this unholy choir in two/four time. They actually seem to be following my directions, although I would have been highly embarrassed had someone turned on the light at that moment to see my waving arms. Once back in bed, the magic of Kleenex in my ears allows me to catch at least a few hours of sleep in the midst of this carnival of sound.

As early as 5 AM the rustling of people packing next to me drags me out of my fitful slumber. By 6 AM I too am out the door, and even so I am one of the last to leave. Everyone seems desperate to get out of there, and who can blame them? I step onto the cobbled street in the dark, and I'm grateful I more or less remember the way back to the bus station through the maze of old Leon. I can't believe it was only yesterday I arrived here, and my scant eighteen hours in Leon have left a strong impression on me. But I feel very ready to leave, Leonard Cohen included. There is a spring in my step as I find the station in only half an hour. This leaves me a full hour to savor a lovely breakfast before my bus departs for Astorga.

Another hour later I arrive at Astorga, about 35 mi/55 km west of Leon. I have no pilgrim guilt on this bus trip, and I have made peace with the choices I have had to make. I am also learning to settle into better rhythms of walking and reflection rather than simply racing toward some goal. At this moment this means lingering with another cup of coffee before finding the trail. I do so in a wonderful plaza next to the cathedral in Astorga and its famous Bishop's Palace with its Gothic turrets.

As I scan my pilgrim guide I realize that within a few short hours I will begin climbing the hills which lead to an upcoming mountain range. If all goes well, I will arrive at the highest point of the Camino, the Cruz de Ferro, sometime tomorrow. It is perhaps the spiritual heart of the Camino, where throughout the ages pilgrims have carried stones from their homes to place them around a tall, thin iron cross. This huge mound of stones and the stories they represent has through the centuries become a hill as big as a large house.

I too am carrying a stone from my home, namely, a heart-shaped rock that Margita gave me as a gift many years ago. The loving inscription on it has faded, as have the sentiments that inspired it, yet the stone represents the substantiality of our lives together that must now be laid to rest. I will leave this stone at this sacred spot of the Cruz de Ferro and today needs to be a day of prayer and preparation for this profound ritual of release and renewal.

But first I have to get there, which means putting one foot in front of the other, so I must get up and leave this lovely café where I have been cocooning. I do eventually get up and snugly strap on my pack with its precious stone. As I leave the café I am struck by how quiet and peaceful this place is even at 9 AM, but perhaps the busyness of Leon has left me with sensory overload, and I am being restored to a more meditative level of stimulation. The trail is easy to find, and I am pleased that I have no need to linger here and sightsee even if it is a beautiful historic old town. I sense a new challenge for my journey awaits me.

CHAPTER 10

The Cross of Ferro

"Above all, do not lose your desire to walk; every day
I walk myself into a state of well-being, and walk away
from every illness; I have walked myself into my best
thoughts, and I know of no thought so burdensome that
one cannot walk away from it . . . . If one just keeps on
walking, everything will be all right."

Soren Kierkegaard, In a Letter, 1847

In no time at all after leaving Astorga, I realize the trail and
topography is changing. The former grasslands, with occasional
planted trees at trail-side, are being replaced by shrubs and
small, stunted trees which cover low rolling hills, with mountains in
the distance. I am buoyed by this return of green vegetation after the
forever stretch of brown fields. As lovely as this shift in my visual field
is for me, the reality of my body is a different matter. I am surprised at
how quickly my foot pain has returned this morning. My right foot has
severe cramps with continuing numbness in the ball of the foot. The
left foot has sharp, intermittent heel pain. The only good news is that I
am able to walk through this pain, which seems to be here to stay. I no
longer wish the pain away, but simply hope that my pain tolerance will
match whatever level of pain is served up.

Within three hours I have arrived in Santa Catalina, which has the
first overnight accommodation possibility out of Astorga. It is shortly
after 12 noon, and far too early to stop, however, so I swallow hard,
and decide to double my mileage for the day and head on to Rabanal

with looming mountains ahead of me. The final approach to Rabanal involves a stiff climb and by 3 PM, I have put on a total of 15 mi/22 km on my odometer for the day, and I am very ready to stop. The first Albergue as I enter the town has 24 tightly packed beds in one dormitory which seems far too claustrophobic for me after last night in Leon. The next Albergue is only 1 km away at the other end of town, but up a steep hill. After a challenging full-day hike even one additional kilometer feels daunting and I seriously question whether I should attempt it. But attempt it I do, and each step feels as if I am climbing up the side of a cliff. I arrive there only to realize my luck has run out. The place does not open for two more hours so back down the hill I trudge.

In an instant my luck changes again as directly adjacent to the first Albergue, is a small hotel with lovely renovated private rooms, with bath, for only €30. The owner has one room left which I eagerly take. I cannot believe my good fortune and head back downstairs to the street bar for the biggest beer they have. I join a table with two pilgrims, an athletic-looking man in his late thirties, and a fresh-faced teenage girl. They are both Spaniards, but speak fluent English. Maria, is only fifteen, and traveling the Camino alone. She is precocious and bubbly, mature beyond her years, and I can only speculate that Spanish parents must raise their daughters with much less fear than American parents do. She certainly seems responsible and self-aware, and is managing the Camino beautifully as best I can tell.

Israel, our other table mate, is a corporate executive whose life has hit a wall. He made a snap decision to walk the Camino a few scant weeks ago, and has only been walking for a week. However, he was putting in 28mi/40 km a day until terrible tendinitis pain brought him to a screeching halt here in Rabanal two days ago. He can now barely walk, the pain is so bad. Surprisingly, all this is happening to a man with solid athletic credentials, who supposedly knows his body well. It seems the Camino finds a way through all of our so-called strengths, into our vulnerable core no matter who we are.

We are joined a bit later by Christopher, a thirty year old Belgian voice teacher and children's choir conductor. It is hard to pinpoint what makes certain groups jell and others not, but this quartet of ours becomes Comedy Central. I have to give most of the credit to Christopher, who with his long shoulder-length stringy hair, bad teeth, and goofy smile, is our ringleader. His laughter is so contagious and his stories so outrageous that the rest of us also throw our inhibitions to the winds.

When I laugh hard, I am inclined to cry tears, and on this day I am crying buckets. We four are somehow able to tap into the absurdity of our lives and the absurdity of this thing we call the Camino. There is a style of humor that cuts and hurtfully exposes the vulnerability of others. Then there is a humor that welcomes others, and pulls down walls. The second type was our experience, and we reveled in it. Eventually our laughter emptied us out, or perhaps it was simply our stomach muscles giving protest, I am not sure which, but slowly our group disbands to take care of our respective errands. I have clothes to wash and a shower to take, but before departing I arrange to meet Israel for dinner later that evening.

Israel and I are not exactly strangers to one another after our riotous afternoon at the bar, but we know nothing of each other's stories. Perhaps the initial lowering of barriers through our shared humor allowed us to set aside the usual tests most of us place on personal sharing. I for one tend to have clear walls when it comes to such sharing, which is a combination of a therapists' self-discipline around self-disclosure, along with a strong sense of privacy and self-reliance. On the Camino my pattern seems completely reversed, and my quick and easy sharing with Israel, as with so many others, occurs at such deeply personal levels, it is as if I have experienced a conversion of sorts. This is part of the magic and mystery of the Camino.

I find myself easily sharing about my marriage, my children, life challenges, and so forth. He reciprocates, and I am particularly struck by the spiritual conversion that is underway for him. Israel is sending daily e-mail journal entries to his co-workers back at the office by using his smart phone. He includes pictures in these daily logs, and his narrative is so compelling, several recipients report crying as they read his stories. Now that he is injured, and perhaps at the end of his Camino, the inner and outer challenges this poses for his identity and self-understanding are enormous. Here is this business executive, on an "unchosen" spiritual/physical quest, which he is sharing in real time with co-workers hundreds of miles away, who are vicariously drawn into their own spiritual journeys, however faintly they are aware of them. As our evening of sharing ends, I can only reflect in on the amazing work of the Spirit within and through our stories, and in his case, with the assistance of technology that allows his story to be known widely.

A restful night later, I awaken slowly in the extreme quiet of my room. I set no alarm clock last night, and most of the time I do not need one since my fellow pilgrims seem fully capable of waking me at any point during the night. On this morning it feels good to wake up naturally, but when I realize it is well after 7 AM I jump out of bed. I have a heavy day ahead of me as I head for the Cruz de Ferro, and I need to get underway.

In light of the lateness of the hour, I do not have breakfast but manage to slurp down a Café con Leche, and grab a bun as I head out the door. I notice immediately that the weather has taken a strong turn. It is heavily overcast and I wonder what this will mean for this sure-to-be intense day. As I head up the steep street I hear my name called, and turn and see Israel hobbling up the street after me. He has seen me walking by through the Albergue window, and wants to say goodbye. I am deeply touched by this gesture of friendship from a man who has great pain even in simple walking.

What could I possibly have given him yesterday through our dialog that has prompted him to offer such an action of gratitude? I am very humbled by this and am utterly aware how little this actually has to do with me, but is a work of the Spirit which brings people together in time of need. I take my leave after our goodbye and offer a silent prayer of blessing for him. Even if his Camino has ended, he has already reached Santiago in his heart, and for that I am grateful.

Within the hour it has begun to drizzle and perhaps because of my preoccupation with the emotions that this day will surely bring, I seem to have missed the trail turn-off, but can see from my map that the pilgrim trail will again cross the paved country lane I am walking on somewhere up ahead. I let myself relax, and about a mile further the trail reappears. As I step onto the narrow earth-packed trail the darkest clouds lift for an instant and a rainbow appears. I am stunned by its beauty in the middle of the heavy gray sky, and by the time I get my pack off to dig out my camera, the rainbow has faded and is only faintly visible. No matter, I take a picture anyway, and feel deeply moved by this gift. I receive it as an omen of sorts, that this ancient harbinger of God's promise applies to me as well. I know full well, however, that this promise is only anticipatory, and I will have many storms to pass through first.

As anticipated, the first storm hits within fifteen minutes, although it starts out as light, then steady rain. I put on my poncho and stay dry from my neck down to my thighs, but the rest of me becomes quickly soaked. With every step I become more emotional and feel the weight of the heart-shaped stone in my pack. It represents the love given and received, which I must now release back to the God who first called it forth.

All love is of God even if in our human frailty we lose the wholeness of that love. This is where the real pain of my divorce appears. Yes, there is the pain of loss, of hurt, of anger, and of the collapse of trust. But the greatest loss of all is the loss of love, and it is the weight of this loss I am feeling. By now I am crying, and the wind and rain has picked up and is blowing the rain into my face. The tears and the rain are now washing each other off in cycles.

By now the full storm has broken out over my head and I am buffeted on all sides. My two poles are the only thing that keep me secure on the trail. It is a moment of vivid déjà vu. Ten years ago on our twenty fifth wedding anniversary, Margita and I were hiking in the Dolomite Mountains in northern Italy, when well above the tree line, a fierce hail and thunderstorm broke open over our heads. It was a life threatening moment since we had no visibility, no shelter, and the trail became a river of rushing hail in the midst of lightning strikes.

Even then we took it as an omen for our marriage, and whereas at the time we clung together and survived, the years following pulled us apart and threw us onto separate paths. Now here I am being battered again, alone this time, but still carrying in my heart and on my back the love that I know I must release. The pain of letting go is so fierce I find myself wishing desperately for another way, a glimmer of hope, some reprieve, some miracle. In my core I know that these are fantasies, yet they come nonetheless. I dread the arrival at the mound, the Cross of Ferro, because it is for me the burial moment of my marriage.

The storm itself passes yet the steady rain remains, and with the rising elevation, the loose, slippery rocks, and the emotional furnace inside, I am having to summon every fiber of my being to move forward, to do what I know I must do. I have no sense of time, nor hardly any sense of my surroundings, but at some point the climbing slows, and a huge mound appears out of the fog. At first glance I miss seeing the cross perched on its thin wooden pole in the center of the mound. It seems so small, how can it possibly hold all our pain?

Cross of Ferro

Then I realize, the cross does not hold us, we hold it with our pain. Our pain is the deep rock into which the cross is planted, and it is there in our pain where God works out our salvation. As I step to the edge of the mound I am not sure how to proceed. No one is on the mound, so what am I to do? Do I simply put my rock on the perimeter? No, I realize, my pain must be put at the foot of the cross, and there are tracks that lead up to the center from all directions. The rocks and stones are in the millions, all shapes and sizes, from pebbles to big boulders. I see many notes and letters which fill the cracks and spaces as I make my way to the top.

The rain is still steady as I remove my poncho and backpack, and dig to the very bottom to find my green heart-shaped stone. This precious gift from Margita must now be given back. I kiss the stone on both sides and know it needs to be in a secure spot which I find by tucking it next to a much larger white rock. I stand up and in a flash realize I want to take a picture. But how will my stone be visible in the midst of these millions of stones? I quickly place my poles around it to mark it off from the others, and find the camera, all the while getting soaked in the steady rain.

Heart Stone Left Behind

Unbeknownst to me while I am active in my ritual of release, three other people have climbed the mound after me. They are complete strangers and not one word is exchanged among us. We all seem moved by one Spirit to pray, and wordlessly reach our hands out to one another and stand in a circle around the cross holding hands. I offer a silent prayer of gratitude for Margita, for our family now broken, and finally for myself. My co-supplicants and I release hands, look at each other through tears, and silently turn to pick up our packs. I have never seen these people before, nor do I see them ever again, yet we became the most intense prayer circle I have ever experienced.

I slowly and carefully make my way down the mound and take shelter with a dozen or so other pilgrims under a covered patio. Everyone is quiet and subdued, deep in their own thoughts, as we gaze at the mound. I am literally fixated as I gaze and try to contemplate what has just happened. I am numb to be sure, but I know all at a deep level that something very important has been accomplished. I feel a weight has been lifted, but how will I make use of the power of this ritual? Will I allow it to take me to a new freedom of heart through the sorrow? Can I trust the wisdom of the gift of release that has been given or will I try and pick up the stone again?

With these musings rumbling in my mind, I reenter the trail and within minutes the rain eases back to drizzle and soon ceases, the clouds lifting for a bit. All pilgrims have disappeared as often happens on the Camino, and given the reprieve in the weather, I break for lunch on a high bluff, deep valleys and mountains flowing in all directions. Black swirling clouds roll in looking very ominous. I accelerate my lunch, donning my wet socks and boots, securing my pack for what will be a long afternoon slog.

From here, I have at least three additional hours of marching ahead of me, all downhill, in very rough terrain. Large drops of rain announce what awaits me, and within moments become steady rain. I stop briefly in a primitive Albergue at Manjarin, essentially an abandoned village, where a crusty old host is offering hot coffee for a donation. Rain drips everywhere through tarps that serve as the roof, and I wonder how pilgrims can possibly sleep in this place. I can't worry about them, however, because I have to keep my wits about me on this trail. It is among the roughest descents I have attempted even as an experienced hiker. The path is not really a path, but loose shale interspersed with large boulders. Being so wet, the shale is like a skating rink and highly treacherous. It takes great concentration and, again, I am saved by good shoes and my trusty poles.

The rain has now become a deluge and is accompanied by lightning and thunder with corresponding wind. I should not be so exposed to lightning on a mountainside like this, but I have no choice but to keep walking and trying to get down this mountain as fast as I can. My concentration is so strong I no longer even notice the pain in my feet. I finally have a recipe for foot pain management. Keep the danger level at a fever pitch and the pain disappears.

The rain and wind wrap themselves around me and I am oblivious to how wet I am. It all fits together somehow: the rain, the tears, the release of attachments through my stone, the danger, are all mixed together. I know the risks that come with relationship breakdown: the temptation toward bitterness, the desire to blame, the cheap dumping of anger, and above all, a general hardening of heart. These are all real inner storms that have every bit as much danger as the outer storm and slippery physical path I am on. I have prayed to be sheltered from these real inner possibilities, and am relieved and grateful that they have been avoided so far. The key, I am discovering, is to enter the pain and to say yes to it, to welcome it even.

Because pain is a form of energy it must keep flowing. Moving the pain along involves choice and for me that means directing it toward my growth. I know that if I hoard it as a basis for self-justification or self-righteousness, I will become addicted to it. I will need it to prop up and legitimate my victimhood, my wounded self. So I choose not to walk this easy but false path, just as I have chosen the difficult physical path I walk. Hence I do not mind the outer storm or its danger. The outer reality perfectly mirrors my inner work, and I recognize the vigilance this requires, both inner and outer. I am in awe that the universe mirrors my soul so profoundly. This connection lifts fear from me even though the inner and outer danger are both still very real. My spirit actually feels light and free in spite of all the pain. My feet seem to mimic this because my steps are fast and sure even though I am skipping over slippery rock.

The final hour into Molinaseca has one more extremely steep and slippery portion, but the rain has eased and then ceases. Low hanging clouds obscure the town until I am virtually on top of it. I arrive at a most beautiful medieval bridge leading me over the Rio Maruelo and on into Molinaseca. At the top of the bridge I peer down into the town and below me at River's edge is a lovely restaurant with patio, although largely deserted due to the heavy overcast conditions. To my great surprise I spot Gregor, my Polish friend from weeks ago standing there. I can't believe my eyes. I have seen virtually none of my early companions since Santo Domingo de Calzada, and especially no one from my first day on the Camino. I shout down to him from the bridge, and he recognizes me as we gesture to each other to wait as I make my way down to rivers' edge. We have a typically joyful pilgrim reunion, arising from a certain permanent brotherhood and sisterhood that we have all somehow bestowed on one another.

We catch up briefly, but he and his current walking companion, a young German, are about to leave for Ponferrada, a few kilometers down the path. Had I been two minutes later I would have missed him, a great example of the serendipitous moments the Camino generates. I am tempted to join them, but by now I am completely exhausted by my 17 mi/27 km trek under terrible conditions, never mind the emotional ringer I have been through today. Besides, I may need some solitude now even though I am ambivalent about my choice. So I decline to accompany them, and make the decision to find a hotel right here at river's edge.

They trudge off, and I cross the street to the first hotel option I see and find it far too expensive even for a modestly well off Pilgrim such as myself. I move up the street to a second hotel, and although it is somewhat less expensive, it still seems extravagant. I decide to try for a third alternative, and just as I step back onto the street, without warning, the heavens open up with a deluge that matches anything I have experienced today. I run back to the previous hotel as fast as I can with my pack bouncing wildly on my back.

They still have space, and I experience a sudden release of tension. Relief floods over me as I am shown my room and by now can think of only one thing: to peel off these completely soaked clothes, step into a hot shower, and stay there until the water runs out. The hotel must have had a huge water heater, because the hot water never does run out and my payment for the room probably only covered my water extravagance. My aching muscles now finally soothed, I fall into bed and am asleep before my head hits the pillow.

I awaken well after 5 PM, a full two hours later. The rain is still pounding on my window, and my thoughts immediately go to the pilgrims that I know are still out there on the path. In particular I think of the older couple from South Africa I first met a week or so ago. I passed them this afternoon on the downhill portion after the Cruz de Ferro, and saw them seriously laboring. How have they possibly made it down in this weather? I can only offer up a prayer of solidarity and strength for them.

Thirst and hunger drives me out of my room, and as I hit the street, the rain abruptly lets up, so I slow down, and begin to explore the town, stopping at the first bar I see for necessary liquid refreshments. By now people have returned to the streets and to my surprise I hear firecrackers and fireworks exploding nearby. I find I have walked into a Spanish wedding. The bride and groom are arriving in the back seat of a sporty BMW and the crowd gathers to welcome them. The atmosphere is festive, not extravagant, helped along by the firecrackers exploding all around us. I am warmed by this joyful moment, even though it also tugs at my heart. This was once us, although without the firecrackers, or the BMW for that matter.

Another hour of wandering, and I am famished and look for a suitable restaurant. Many restaurants have pilgrim meals advertised and I poke my head into two or three to see which one has an ambience that matches my mood: subdued and reflective. I enter one that seems to match my state of mind, and take a seat at a small table in a back room. There are five or six empty tables in the room, along with one large round table with six or so pilgrims already enjoying their dinner. I recognize no one, and am quite content with my quiet corner.

I have barely taken my first sip of wine and in walks Christopher, the Belgian music teacher, trailed by four attractive young women. He introduces me to the women, all South Americans. Two are from Chile and two from Venezuela, with the two Chileans children of German immigrants, like myself. They also speak German and are studying in Germany for a year. They insist that I join them all for dinner, and before long an Italian couple that Christopher knows has arrived, which raises our dinner crowd to a group of eight. So much for my quiet and reflective dinner.

As was the case the last time I was with Christopher, some unknown factor sparks uncontrolled laughter. Whatever it is, whether Christopher's goofy looks, or my being his set-up man, but the four South American women cannot stop laughing at our jokes and antics. When a crazy looking thirty year old music teacher, and a near sixty year old bald, brainy professor can keep four attractive young women enthralled, one does not stop. Our Italian couple adds their share of levity and were it not for the 10 PM curfew they are all under, we would have partied until closing time. I am amazed at how I received the opposite of what I thought I needed his evening. Instead of calm and collected, I got wild and wacky, but more than anything, I was shown to stay open to what comes my way. As my day ends, I shake my head in wonder.

I am not the first pilgrim who had too much to drink for dinner, and I will certainly not be the last, but for me it was a first. I awake with a heavy and throbbing head, and it would not be unfair to say

I had a hangover. This makes it awfully difficult to get up by 7 AM, which is already late, and a rare Camino luxury. Today it is 8 AM before I finally manage to roll out of bed. Nevertheless, I surprise myself that I am able to make it out the door by 8:30 AM, and become even more surprised when I cannot find one store or café open in the entire town.

Then it dawns on me that it is Sunday morning, a true dead time in Spain. This means no breakfast for me, and also no coffee to wash away the hangover. It might even mean no lunch either since I have no food with me and will likely not find any on the way. That thought sobers me up in a hurry and I begin to wonder about the entire evening. Was it really as funny as I thought? The universe made so much sense last night, but by this morning I seem to have lost the great truths that revealed themselves to us in such abundance. Feeling somewhat humbled, I grunt my way out of town under a heavy, gray sky.

CHAPTER 11

Reflections on Loving

It has been told that in the 10th century there lived a man who gave his whole life to pilgrimage. He walks thousands of kilometers until finally, in his old age, his legs told him "Enough!", and he retired to a monastery hidden in the mountains to get a well deserved rest.

The old man, though he never sought such, earned the reputation of being one of the wisest men, if not the wisest man in the known world. As a result, many young pilgrims from far and wide began to come to him in search of counsel.

It is told that one day a young Pilgrim arrived at that monastery. Despite his youth, he had completed the majority of the known pilgrimages. He approached the elder and asked him, "Master, what must I do to be a true Pilgrim?" The weathered man looked him in the eye and felt compassion for him. "Son, if you truly want to be an authentic Pilgrim, return home to your family, your neighbors, your friends and enemies and listen to them, serve them, forgive them and love them. In that way you will become a true Pilgrim."

They say that the young man dropped his gaze, turned and left that place without saying a word, deeply saddened because while he would have been perfectly able to hike thousands of kilometers more with a heavy load on his shoulders, he was incapable of carrying out the task that the wise old man had entrusted him.

www.lafuentedelperegrino.org

*M*y timing in departing Molinaseca could not have been worse because as I pass the last house in town I find myself behind a group of twenty five middle aged Spanish day hikers. They take up the entire trail and are spread out all the way up the steep hill we are climbing. They are happy and chatty and walk in clusters of two to four people. They walk too slowly for me to simply straggle behind them all morning, but to pass them may be impossible since they block the entire trail, with no backpacks to slow them down, while I have nineteen pounds on my back.

I eventually lose patience being hemmed in and try and out walk them. It takes forever for me to pass the entire group which seems to have multiplied as I walk. Finding and sustaining a higher gear is such a challenge that I exhaust myself. But if I stop now they will overtake me and my efforts will have been in vain. So I plow on and am finally ahead of the entire pack of them about an hour later. I have been climbing the entire way while trying to overtake them, and finally, after well over an hour of intense climbing, I reach the crest of a high hill at which point gravity helps me out and pulls me down all the way into Ponferrada.

The only thing that saves me from starvation on this Sunday is that Ponferrada is a noteworthy tourist town, with the magnificent restored castle of the Templar Knights as one of its treasures. There is a small café open across from the castle which offers the first available food of the day, and I indulge in as large a lunch as I can manage. I also grab a sandwich for the road. Maybe now I can now make it to the end of the day. As tempting as it is to linger and explore the castle as well as the old town, I know I cannot be true to my pilgrim commitments in light of my limited time and energies, so I choose not to wander around sightseeing. I savor the atmosphere of the town anyway as I trudge on through and imagine the rich pilgrim history of this place, including the tragic history of the Templars which ended with their complete annihilation in 1312.

As crowded as the trail has been this morning because of the Spanish hiking club, my afternoon is the exact opposite. I see no pilgrim for hours, and am reminded again of how strong the tension is between solitude and connection on the Camino, and how quickly it flips back and forth. This tension is also very real for me in my daily life. It is a particularly strong theme for me now as I am heading for divorce. Marriage can buffer a person from this tension and it certainly did so for me. It protected me from isolation, even when the marriage was in its more distant phases. There always seemed to be some dimension of partnership available to me, sometimes as confidant, sometimes as lover, sometimes as best friend, sometimes as co-parent, sometimes as co-worker. These connectors are now gone and I hear no echo of myself in the self of another.

The Camino activates this tension around connections very regularly in us as pilgrims, because, in sharing our stories with each other, we find companionship for an instant through the shared narrative. But then we all move on, and are left again with our aloneness, and feel the void in our inner space. This is a key source of the Camino's spiritual power, namely, that we experience our human dilemmas in a very concentrated way on this trek. On the Camino I am reminded on a daily basis of my sheer and utter aloneness, right alongside the deep joy that comes in meeting others in their unique selves, as I am met in mine.

If one is interested in encountering uniqueness, there is no better place to do so than on the Camino. The most unique characters often turn out to be the "long-walkers," those who walk out their front door, and who have been at it for three months or more in many cases. I, who have only been walking for three weeks, can only begin to imagine the impact such an extended journey is having on them. I am not sure if they were eccentric before they left, but they sure seem eccentric now.

One can easily spot them with their lined, haggard faces, pants that are too large, held up only by suspenders, and a general wildness of hair. Sitting on a bench about two hours out of Ponferrada I spot Wolfgang, a young Austrian from Salzburg. I met him two nights ago in Molinaseca, at the restaurant where I was partying with Christopher and his flock. Wolfgang was sitting at an adjoining table with Heinz, an older Pilgrim around my age from Vienna who has also been walking for over three months now. As I greeted them that evening I wondered if I might run into them again.

Now, two days later, I find Wolfgang sitting on a roadside bench taking a smoking break. He decides to get up and join me since I am intent on walking right now. As is so typical of pilgrim encounters, we immediately launch into our personal stories. I tell him of my marriage, separation, and pending divorce. He launches into his own tale of woe which actually begins quite happily. He and his girlfriend decided many months ago to walk to Santiago together all the way from Salzburg. They left their homes in Salzburg and walked through the rest of Austria, traversed all of Switzerland, and were more than halfway through France when his girlfriend announced that she needs a break from the trek.

They agreed to meet again three weeks later in St. Jean Pied de Port, my own starting point. Wolfgang continued to walk, and in three weeks arrived in St. Jean, only to discover that his girlfriend has also arrived, but, in the interim, she has ditched him and hooked up with a new pilgrim boyfriend. Wolfgang is bemoaning this loss, and trying to figure out what happened. I have empathy for him, but also wonder at the speed of this pilgrim exchange program. But then again, perhaps two months on the road with Wolfgang gave her all the data she needed to make her decision about him. Such is the concentrated power of the Camino.

Even though my legs are longer than his, Wolfgang is thirty years younger and walks at quite a hefty pace. I keep up for a while but after an hour or so I need to slow down, if not take a break. We bid our farewells, and off he marches on his short legs. I have made good headway today, given my racing to overtake the hiking club this morning, and now attempting to keep up with my Austrian friend. I also realize how easily I can overdo it, as my poor legs are now telling me. I therefore make the decision to stay the night in Cacabelos and not add on the extra 4 mi/7 km to Villafranca. Even so I have put in 16 mi/25 km today and that is more than sufficient for a soon to be senior citizen.

Cocabela is an ancient Pilgrim town with typical narrow winding streets. The Albergue is at the other end of town as is the case in many Camino villages. This makes for an easy departure out of town in the mornings, but also means that when arriving late in the afternoon, those final stretches through town on hard pavement seem far worse than triple the mileage on the open trail. Being tired at the end of long days also means one is less inclined to absorb the architecture and history of a place as one slogs through town looking for an Albergue. In this instance I absorb just enough of the towns' unique features to consider going back after dinner and having a look around later, but for now I simply put my head down and grind my way through its streets.

I find the Albergue easily enough, and I am pleasantly surprised at its layout. It is a municipal hostel of seventy beds in chalet style rooms with two beds in each room. The entire structure is constructed as a semi-circle around a lovely eighteenth century church. The complex is inside a walled compound, with the back wall of the chalets marking the compound perimeter. The entire site is tiled, with clean, mosaic tiles, giving the place a very relaxed Mediterranean feel. Rooms are assigned on order of arrival, and since I am given a card which says pilgrim number thirty five, I quickly calculate the place is now half full.

The room I am assigned is tiny but clean, and within the hour my roommate arrives. He is a young South Korean who speaks no English. We are left to smile at one another, but that becomes awkward after a few minutes. Given how small the room is I head for the patio and decide to e-mail my sons and Margita. Internet cafés are hard to find in rural Spain and most Albergues, if they have Internet, may have only one or two slow computers to service all pilgrims. I have given up trying to communicate regularly with anyone back home but no one is using the single computer right now, so I grab my chance.

I send Margita and my sons a brief summary of my whereabouts and my general condition, but am seriously disappointed that there has been no message from her in weeks. As disappointed as I am, I am not surprised. After all, she wants a divorce so why would she seek me out? My feelings of disappointment confront me with the real issue facing me, namely, my deep, unresolved attachment to her. We have known each other since we were young children, beginning with her move to Calgary, Alberta, Canada with her family when she was twelve, and I was fifteen. I had a crush on her throughout my adolescence, but given the rules of our conservative Baptist upbringing, we had no dating experiences as such in our teens, except in a group context.

My attraction toward her and this unspoken sense of connection never wavered, but it was only when I was about to leave to Calgary for theological seminary in South Dakota at the age of twenty one, that these feelings and yearnings were fully expressed. We became "committed" to each other that year, but not without ambivalence, especially on her part. I chose to more or less ignore this ambivalence, and essentially convinced myself that it would fade. These three "committed" years prior to our marriage in 1974, were all long distance years given that I was studying 1500 miles/2400 kilometers away. Even though there were hundreds of letters exchanged during those years, there was little opportunity for deeper exploration of what we were both seeking and bringing into the relationship. Now, thirty five years later, the full force of these omissions and the disconnects which grew out of them has brought us to this place, and I still don't seem able to accept it.

This is the temptation I was sensing at the Cruz de Ferro when I intuited that the real danger for me is to pick up the stone again and carry it with me in the form of chronic sorrow, or a permanent longing for an unreachable other. While on the one hand, I can be commended for my wonderful faithfulness and durability, but if I believe I deserve such praise, I must also be willing to face my own blindness, denial, and general unwillingness to face unpleasant truths.

While I am mulling over all these thoughts, the place has filled up and I do not know anyone, with the exception of the older South African couple I last saw straining against the storm that descended upon us on our way into Molinaseca. I am relieved to see them alive, and they share with me how terrifying it became for them on that mountain side. I can tell they are running out of steam on the Camino and will perhaps have to rely on other modes of transportation if they hope to make it to Santiago.

I find after my internet disappointment that I am not in the mood for a long conversation with them, nor necessarily wanting to get to know some of the "new" pilgrims milling about. So after my quick shower and clothes washing ritual, I head back into town for dinner. Many restaurants on the Camino trail have a pilgrim menu which is served generally by 7 PM in contrast to most Spaniards who do not begin to eat dinner until 9 PM, when most of us pilgrims are heading back to our quarters. As I arrive at the restaurant, two German women greet me who are already seated, as are a handful of other pilgrims, any of whom would have likely been quite happy to have me join them. But this night I decide to dine alone, since I have much to sort through. I have my journal beside me, and it will be my dialogue partner tonight as I take stock of my state of heart and mind. Sometimes, too many outer voices can mask the harder to hear inner voices, and I have plenty of inner material to address.

Returning to the Albergue by 9:30 PM finds most everyone in their rooms, including my Korean roommate sitting on his bed in our little cubicle. He knows no more English this evening then he did this afternoon, and I have also neglected my Korean lessons so we are no further ahead. We are as friendly as one can get under the circumstances, as we step around each other's packs and paraphernalia. He offers me a cookie from his pack, and I offer some nuts out of mine in return.

I should not have been concerned about too much silence between us, because the ceiling is open above us in our cubicle all the way to the roof. Since this is true of all other sleeping quarters, I can hear not only what is being said in the rooms on either side of us, but I can hear what is happening all the way up and down the row of cubicles. If anything, the sound seems amplified as it moves along the open ceiling. This will get very interesting tonight.

Sure enough, I can hear so well, it is as if I have landed in the middle of a grand sound chamber. While I do not necessarily hear distinct words, the sense of constant whispering makes one listen harder in case one **could** make out the words. As the night deepens, we move from the soft rushing sound of whispers, to the cacophony of snoring, only now as if it is coming from the bottom of a well. The remoteness of these distant but distinct snores is intensified by the snoring of my Korean neighbor who sends his sound waves directly into my ear. After an hour or so, all the fun has gone out of my sound experiment, and I resort to my Kleenex in the ear remedy since I have long ago lost my ear plugs. Thankfully, my improvised sound protection allows me to find my way into sleep.

As ominous as my prospects for decent sleep are, I sleep reasonably well, and awake at 7 AM to find my roommate already gone. Perhaps I too joined the chorus of snorers, and he left early out of frustration, but I have no way of knowing or of apologizing if I did, so I drop my mini guilt trip. I take my time to get washed and packed and am not underway until 7:45 AM. I find it hard to believe, but I cross paths with no other pilgrims the entire 4 mi/7 km into Villafranca, where I stop for breakfast. Here there are a few straggler pilgrims like myself sitting at cafés sipping their morning Cafe con Leche.

Nevertheless, the question of where everyone disappears on the trail is one of the great abiding mysteries of the Camino. It is as if the earth swallows them up, only to deposit them at the next café up the road. Perhaps it is simply that the distances are so great, and everyone is so spread out, that we don't often run into one another. Either that, or there is a booming taxi and bus service going on, which I have unfortunately not been informed about.

The trail is heavily wooded and lovely as I leave Villafranca, and follows a quiet secondary road on one side, and a rocky, fast-moving stream on the other. The stream serenades me as I walk. Today will be another physically challenging day since I am heading toward the wild mountains of Galacia. O'Cebreio is the first town I will reach in Galacia, a full 20 mi/32 km from Villafranca, with two strenuous climbs awaiting me. I know I do not have that kind of mileage left in my legs or my lungs today, so I will need to find a place to stay somewhere else along the way. I am sure my body will give me the necessary cues.

For now I am settling into a rather deep contemplation as I follow the stream. I am drawn into a meditation on my history of loving, focused heavily on my marriage of course, but also casting an even wider net, which includes my immediate family, extended family, and the broader circle of friends, colleagues, and the wider world of those to whom I minister.

My first conclusion about myself as I gather my impressions about loving is how inadequate my loving seems to me. As a Christian, I have been steeped in the overarching belief that God is love, and that my loving is sourced by that love. For the Christian the model of such loving is Jesus, a high bar if there ever was one. No wonder I feel so inadequate, a failure even. In Christian circles this tendency to focus on our shortcomings is accelerated by a dualism that crept into our understanding of love, namely, that it must be fully selfless and self-negating. God's love, understood as agape, is seen as fully free from self-enhancement and its highest form is sacrifice. Here the verdict is mixed for me. I have a reasonable record of self-sacrifice, but it always seems mixed with self-interest. I could of course always have sacrificed a bit more in virtually any relationship I can think of, but would my loving therefore have been more true or pure?

What occurs to me as I walk is that all our loving is always contextual and situated in a specific time and place. There is also no re-do. We love one moment at a time, and always face the limit(s) of every situation, and can legitimately question what love looks like in that specific situation. What is loving in one context or situation can be oppressive in another.

I ask myself what it is that I actually bring into my moments of loving. Do I bring compassion? Tenderness? Affection? Understanding? Presence? I could say yes to all of the above, and it is hard to disagree with any item on my list. But when I ask myself what is the point or purpose of any and all of these ingredients to loving, a deeper truth begins to emerge. What occurs to me is that they need to be in the service of freedom and wholeness for the other, namely, the freedom to be! If my attitudes and actions are toward the enhancement of the others' freedom and wholeness, I can truly say I am in continuity with the love that God has for that person.

I find this insight liberating and in some ways it lifts a burden from my shoulders. I find I can embrace God's invitation to me to move into fuller loving, into a more conscious embrace of what loving might mean in the middle of all the messy, ambiguous situations in which we all find ourselves. I am called to be an advocate of the freedom and wholeness of another in their authentic self-actualizations, and because this is a sacred calling, I know I will be nourished and guided in that process, even if I have not always been able to sustain that goal. I know that God fully supports and sustains me in my efforts to grow in this regard. Perhaps there is even a form of loving involved in accepting Margita's desire to leave me?

I am roused from these reflections by the sudden recognition that the quiet two lane road next to me has become a congested mess of traffic. I cannot figure out where this endless line of trucks and cars has come from, until I look up and see that the four-lane superhighway hundreds of feet above me on a vast bridge spanning the valley below is empty of traffic. Obviously, all that bridge traffic has been diverted to the valley right here next to me. At first I am only annoyed that my peace and quiet has been disturbed by roaring motors and smoky fumes, until I realize that the pilgrim trail requires me to actually cross this road on foot.

I can only stand at roadside and stare for ten minutes as I contemplate my dilemma. This road is winding around hills, and has no shoulder to speak of that I could walk along to see if a safer spot to cross might materialize. Besides, the large trailer trucks would sideswipe me in an instant since they have no extra room to get out of my way given no guardrails on my side of the road. I don't even know where this highway leads, so crossing over the roadway and taking the pilgrim trial on the other side is my only alternative. I have heard that pilgrims are involved in traffic accidents on the Camino with some frequency, and in spite of this knowledge, I feel I have no choice but to cross. I watch the traffic for a while, and realize there is an occasional gap if a truck moves a bit more slowly up the hill, but that gap is unfortunately not always matched by a space in traffic moving the other way. If all else fails, I will have to stop in the middle of the road while another opening materializes.

I have had several near death misses in my life, but they came upon me unexpectedly, and not of my choosing particularly. This is a near death moment I am choosing, and I hope that like the cat with nine lives, I have a few more lives left to use up. I curse myself for not having kept better track of which number of lives I have used up by now, but I know it is getting close to nine. I am playing with fire here, and am putting a lot of faith into 59 year old eyes and legs, never mind the coordination required between them. No wonder I am scared.

The moment arrives suddenly, when a space opens up on my side of the road, and by waiting until the last second before I dart across, the other side of the road might just open itself for me without my having to stop in the middle. I dart out onto the road, and thankfully the truck driver sees me and recognizes my intention and slows down. I underestimate one thing, however, and that is the weight of a backpack which makes sprinting a joke. As my pack bounces on my back I feel as if I am running through wet cement, and have to stop in the middle of the road after all, because the opposing vehicles are all rushing downhill, and are packed too close together to offer me a space to lumber the rest of the way.

Thankfully, no vehicles passing me on my backside sideswipe me as I now stand there waiting. Eventually my hoped for space appears, and I dart across the rest of the way, my pack bouncing crazily along. I reach the other side, bathed in sweat and exhausted by the mental ordeal of it. I know what I have done is utterly foolish, but my feelings turn quickly into anger that no provisions have been made by authorities for just such occurrences. How are pilgrims to manage in situations such as this when there is no alternative? I conclude there is a serious planning problem in Spain, or perhaps dying pilgrims are part of pilgrim lore, and we should just get used to it.

In my mind I have been idealizing medieval pilgrims in their perseverance through all of their likely hardships. They certainly had none of the options for comfort that we do today, and faced many dangers ranging from disease, robbers, and wild dogs. But none of them had to contend with dodging cars and trucks at high speeds, never mind "pilgrim" bicyclists who come barreling down these narrow trails and are on top of you before you any hope of reacting in time. Their shouts of "Buen Camino" as they race on by, are, at best, a warning to get the hell out of the way, and certainly have nothing to do with peace or tranquility.

If there is a danger to the Camino's future as a spiritual event other than the obvious danger of commercialization and sheer overuse, it is the collision between speed and serenity. This is not just about using speedy tourist options such as taxis, buses or trains, travel, but is also visible in the need one sees in many pilgrims to stay constantly connected electronically to their regular lives, even as they "pilgrim-on." I have walked behind some pilgrims for extended periods as they talked on their cell phones the entire time. Perhaps something of the Camino's quiet power is rubbing off anyway, but I seriously doubt it.

After 5 mi/8 km, with over two hours of walking along this congested, honking mess of traffic, I am exhausted need a break. A roadside rest area appears and although it is primarily intended for cars and trucks, it is the only place to rest that I can see. Close to the edge of this parking lot is some shade, in the middle of which is an abandoned water well, with a metal grate on it. It looks inviting and cool in the shade, so I plop down on the round well, pull off my backpack, and lay down on my back with a sigh of relief.

At this instant I hear a clanging sound coming from the well and see that my little Sony digital recorder has slipped out of my pocket and onto the grate with its open slits. My heart jumps into my throat as I see my recorder lying there about to fall into the chasm below. All of my verbal reflections and commentary from the Camino are on that recorder, since I often dictate as I walk. I am so frightened, I dare not move for fear of jarring it loose into the abyss. I slowly reach my arm toward it, keeping my body perfectly still, and then snatch the top of it and squeeze it firmly into my palm.

Once I have it in my hand, I jump up and am literally shaking from the tension of this moment. For me a miracle has occurred, since by any known laws of physics or probability, that tape recorder should have fallen through into the unreachable darkness below. Given the width of the spaces it would have been the easiest thing in the world for it to have fallen through, but it did not. I feel such a flood of relief and gratitude that I completely forget all of my fatigue and need for rest. I slap on my pack in record time, and no longer care about trucks or traffic and have a surge of incredible energy as I jump onto the trail. My pace is brisk and even though I am running the risk of more blisters, I don't care. As far as I am concerned, I have dodged death twice today, and I have the energy of a man just resurrected.

CHAPTER 12

No Room at the Inn

"I lift my eyes to the hills from where comes my help.
My help comes from the Lord." Psalm 121: 1-2.

"Hope is a commitment to the Horizon of
Transcendence"

William S. Schmidt

*G*iven my near disaster with the tape recorder at the well, it takes time for my heart to settle down, but within ten minutes. the trail has veered away from the road, and the rushing stream is again beside me. A minute or two later a point of easy access to the stream appears. This spot is bathed in wonderful sunlight and I rush down toward the water, throw off my pack, tear off my shoes and socks, and step into the icy flow.

Streams of Living Water

It is refreshing beyond belief and is a moment of incredible grace. As I find a place to sit the verse "I will give you streams of living water" rolls over and over in my mind. What a gift to sit in the warm sun with my legs in the icy stream after hours of walking next to caravans of trucks, along with two scrapes with near disaster. I am renewed so dramatically and quickly by this stream that I cannot fathom where all this extra energy I feel has come from. I am not going to argue with this unexpected blessing and deep renewal, so I put my socks and shoes back on, and keep walking for two more hours until I arrive at the village of Herrerias, at the foot of the final steep climb into Galicia.

Herrarias is an ancient hamlet which stretches along one street beside a lovely river. It is so incredibly quiet as I enter the village I wonder if the place is abandoned. According to my guidebook there is no Albergue here, so I take aim for the only hotel I can see, a modest place attached to a bar/restaurant. It is late afternoon but for some reason no one seems to be around. I wait and then wait some more in the reception area, move on to wait in the bar, and even the restaurant, all in futility, since no one appears.

Eventually my impatience gets the better of me and I decide I will search this building from top to bottom. Surely someone must be looking after this place. I start by heading for the kitchen, where an old woman is preparing vegetables for the evening meal. She speaks not one word of English, and with my few Spanish phrases, she figures out that I want a room and a beer, not necessarily in that order. We start with the room, and I take the first one she shows me. At this point, anything other than a dorm room with dozens of bunk beds feels like a five-star hotel to me. I head back downstairs for my beer, and take it down to the river to dangle my feet in the water as I indulge my thirst. There is something about total physical and emotional exhaustion that makes a glass of beer next to a stream seem like a gift from heaven. I take my sweet time in this lovely oasis, but eventually rouse myself to head back upstairs for my shower and clothes washing ritual.

In many rural Spanish hotels the bathroom is outside one's room, and is shared by two or more rooms. This hotel is no exception, so I grab my towel and slip down the hall to shower. The place seems completely deserted. Upon returning to my room I am finishing drying off when all of a sudden my door opens and two startled women are standing in my doorway. I am momentarily too stunned to know what to do, but cover up as best I can. As they pour out their profuse apologies, I discover that they are in one of the other rooms but became confused as to which was their door. All of us share some embarrassed laughter and as they leave I can only keep laughing at the absurdities of the Camino.

Later that evening, as I walk down the street looking for a place to eat, they spot me and exclaim: "Oh, there is the naked pilgrim." I can only smile back at them, and am pleased that my embarrassment stays under control. Further exploration of the hamlet reveals that there is a private hostel in operation, run by an attractive, esoteric young woman. Hanging around her is a young man who at one point has lived in Chicago where I reside. He "was" a pilgrim he tells me, but has temporarily settled here in Herrerias to work as a handyman for his exotic host. This is not the first time I have come across this arrangement, of an attractive female hospitaliero being "helped" by a male pilgrim, who has given up his trek to be of service. It is not a bad option, and I indulge a brief fantasy of such a role for myself given how handy a guy I am.

The quiet of my hotel allows me to sleep until after 7 AM, again a late wake up for Camino time. By 8 AM I am out the door, and am immediately climbing, first on a smooth paved road, which soon veers off onto a trail going steeply down over a creek bed, and then directly back up and up over very difficult and challenging terrain. Only a half hour later I am fully bathed in sweat even though it is cool and shady. This strenuous climbing goes on for another two hours when I finally reach O'Cebreiro, the peak of this mountain range.

O'Cebriero greets me with sun peeking through clouds with expansive views in all directions. The path takes me past the church of Santa Maria Real dating from the ninth century, one of the oldest structures on the Camino. The historic aura of this place is palpable but for some reason the place is overrun with pilgrims, especially bikers, who seem to be coming from the main road that runs past the village. The café next to the church is extremely crowded which is somewhat strange at this time of the day. I order my late breakfast/early lunch as more and more pilgrims arrive. There is no place left to sit. I become restless with all this commotion, and decide to put my remaining food away and hit the trail.

My haste no doubt contributes to my missing the marker directing me back to the actual Camino path, and before I know it I am on the asphalt road leading out of town. The guidebook confuses me at this point, because it looks as if I should be walking on a wooded trail alongside the road, not on the paved highway as I am. I am not exactly lost, since I see from the map that this road leads straight into the village of Linares, only 2 mi/3 km away. Nonetheless, I begin to berate myself again for my carelessness when leaving O'Cebreiro. This is accentuated by the fact that my feet are really hurting, surely compounded by the reality that they are pounding away on hard pavement, not on a nice, soft wooded trail, as was my expectation.

As I walk along there are numerous cyclists buzzing past me on the highway, so I have confirmation that I am not lost, but my emotional bombardment will not let up. Eventually the town of Linares appears, and, as expected, the actual pilgrim path reappears. My reaction to my "mistake" puzzles me, because I am unable to let myself off the hook for the extra hardship I created for myself. I am again staring my perfection demand full in the face, and I do not like the look and feel of it. I should be getting better at this by now. I began to smirk as the irony of my inner attitude dawns on me. I am not perfect at avoiding perfection demands. I take this moment of self-recognition as a graced moment, however, and clutch my wholeness stone as a reminder to take this moment more fully into my awareness on the journey toward fuller self-acceptance in the midst of my ever present imperfections.

I rest for a bit in Linares in order to get my physical and emotional equilibrium back, but also to gear up for the push to the Alto de Poio, the highest point in Galicia. I reach the peak with great effort, only to be met by a stiff wind as it rushes over these heights. I have been switching back and forth between hiking shoes and sandals and am simply unable to find comfort for my feet. Thankfully, this last stretch from Alto do Polo into Fonfria, my destination for the day, is flat, and so I should be able to stumble my way along for this last hour. I have already put 14 mi/22 km on these feet of mine today, half of which has been continuous, steep climbing.

Imagine my shock upon arriving in Fonfria to find the seventy bed Albergue full, along with both two small hotels in the village. There is a long queue of desperate pilgrims ahead of me at the hostel trying to find other arrangements. The poor overwhelmed person at the desk speaks only Spanish, but in time I make out that the next destination with available beds is Triacastela, a full 6 mi/10 km away. My heart sinks. Now what? A bilingual pilgrim talks to our host on my behalf, and he suggests I order a taxi to take me to Triacastella. In an instant, I gladly throw all pilgrim perfection aside, and have him order one for me.

I wait in the courtyard for my taxi and watch the horde of pilgrims trying to negotiate these tough circumstances. It is only 2:30 in the afternoon and the place is packed, with dozens of people already camping out across the street where they will spend the night in an open field. In the meantime, half an hour passes, then an hour, and I wake up to the fact that no taxi is coming. What to do? I look across the field, and see the cloudy sky above it, and immediately rule out joining the open sky campers. One night outdoors in a cold rain with no protection, and I will be heading for a bout with pneumonia.

At this moment an amazing thing happens. My spirit awakens inside me and says: "Get up, you can do this, you can walk 6 mi/10 km more. You are stronger than you think!!" It is as if a jolt of electricity has passed through me. I obey this voice, get up immediately, and strap on my pack with determination. I grab my hiking poles and without looking back, stride purposefully onto the trail. I realize I have in my possession an orange, one piece of bread, plenty of water, two tough feet, and an indomitable spirit. What else could I possibly need? I decide on a strategy of slow, meditative walking, and will set aside any goals for speed or destination. If it gets dark, no matter, I have a headlamp, and I will simply walk until I find a bed.

This moment of taking matters into my own hands feels liberating and freeing. My life reveals such moments of courageous choice making, and in some ways even the decision to walk the Camino in five weeks is such a choice. Most of the time these choices are arrived at over time, and have many layers of decision making in them. Today, in this small, but intense choice to launch out into the unknown, I experience in a microcosm the tension between the active and passive sides of my spirit. I notice that beyond any rational "cost-benefit analysis" approach to any decision, there is often a moment of distinct choice that then presents itself. To choose consciously, deliberately, and boldly in such moments is hard to do. But in that moment lies our freedom. Kierkegaard, of course, long ago demonstrated this point in his existentialist philosophy, but right now I experience in my freedom of choice a new clarity, and in that freedom I stride boldly, if slowly, on.

To lessen the risk of injury I decide to take a five minute break every thirty minutes or so, and soon take my first one. Even though I am in pain from my calves down, it is bearable, with slow walking. I am becoming aware of the interweaving of mind, spirit, and body in my pain management. If I have tended to live from a "mind over matter" approach to life thus far in my existence, I am becoming converted into a "mind with matter" approach. I am rather old to be just figuring this out now, but when my mind has done all this heavy lifting for me, it is hard to just give it up. Perhaps I have used my body primarily as a transportation vehicle for my mind, and so far it has cooperated fairly well. But on the Camino the body pushes back very quickly and old patterns crumble. In that disintegration good things can happen if at least one is awake. Thankfully, I have awakened.

Soon after my break my walking comes to a completely unexpected and dramatic end when suddenly a small, attractive hotel appears right next to the path. The hotel stands alone, although a farmhouse and barn are behind it. I think I am hallucinating, but the mirage seems real enough, so I tentatively approach, and surprisingly the woman behind the bar actually speaks flawless English. My sense that I am hallucinating is confirmed when she says yes, they have rooms. "Would I like to see one," she asks? I dare not interrupt the dream, so I go along with the trick being played on me. The room turns out to be the most attractive I have seen so far in my Spanish journey. It is made entirely out of stone, with a modern, lavish bathroom attached. The price? Thirty euro!! I do not recall how long it takes me to close my gaping mouth. Why she gives a room to such an idiotically grinning, hairy, dirty pilgrim, I do not know, but she does.

If it were not for the pain in my feet, I might have believed I was losing touch with reality, but my pain is real enough. A long, hot shower revives me enough stumble to the bar for my usual ritual of survival: a cold beer. I overhear a young couple at the table next to me speaking German. It is the first German I have heard in almost a week, so I do not hesitate to go over and introduce myself. Their names are Natalie and Philipp from Ludwigshafen, Germany, although she was born in Poland, she came to Germany as a child. We hit it off immediately, and decide to stay and have dinner together since we are all hungry, and it is already early evening.

By now I have lost all surprise at the Camino's ability to sweep away age barriers, and this encounter is no exception. Natalie and Philipp are both students in their mid-twenties, and therefore younger than two of my sons. Perhaps age becomes so irrelevant on the Camino because we are all sharing the same experiences and the same vulnerabilities. But my new friends are not quite as willing to lower the barriers around ethnicity, since they seem really down on the Spanish. Their negative reaction may have roots in some typical German perfectionism related largely to cleanliness and order, those nonadjustable standards by which the rest of humanity must be judged.

But the real source of their cynicism may have a point in its favor, having to do with the meaning of the Camino itself. I have learned from my Spanish pilgrim friends, with whom I have had dialogue about life in Spain, that many Spaniards walk the bare minimum of the Camino for largely cultural and "self-promotional" reasons. Walking the minimum kilometers gets one the precious "Compostella," the certificate of completion, which can become a form of resume' padding, and supposedly can even help someone with promotions and salary raises. This factor irks my new German friends.

I, on the other hand, disagree with my companions, and see it as rather culturally enlightened. Imagine the helpful cultural benefits which would accrue if our respective home cultures would give us raises or promotions if we hiked to monasteries or other spiritually or culturally sacred sites, and underwent personal, cultural, and spiritual growth as a result? It might do many of us more good than some of the useless seminars, workshops, and courses that we take, which we also use for our own hollow resume padding and self-promotion. So, I am not as quick to write it off as my young friends are. After all, since I am much older and wiser, I am allowed to judge their judgment.

After several hours of lively banter, we head off to our respective rooms and I write in my journal before exhaustion overtakes me, and I attempt to sleep. As exhausted as I am, I cannot find sleep because of intense throbbing in my feet. My nerve endings are jumping down there and seem to be discharging all kinds of tension. This is a new phenomenon for me, and I do not know what to make of it, other than the obvious reason that I overdid it today, but mostly I am annoyed that I cannot sleep. I eventually get up and give them a cold foot bath, which seems to help, and eventually blessed sleep comes.

Morning always seems to arrive quickly on the Camino, which may be in direct proportion to the degree of fatigue from the day before. In that case, I must have been very tired yesterday. I roll out of bed very slowly, and need extra time to time to come to full wakefulness, which really only occurs after I receive my eternally blessed Café con Leche. The entire Camino would come to a grinding halt if it were not for this holy drink. At 8 AM I finally step out into the early morning sun to be startled by shouts of "William, William!" coming from across the patio below the hotel. There is Gregor, my Polish professor buddy, running to give me a big hug. This is now our fourth unexpected encounter. He seems to be my only "starting point" fellow pilgrim left on the trail, and we revel in this serendipitous encounter.

He is having breakfast with Manuel, a German from Stuttgart, a city near my birthplace, and we all decide to walk together today. It turns out the two of them spent the night in the overcrowded Albergue in Fonfria which had turned me away yesterday. They report it was quite the zoo, with the overflow campers also needing to use the showers and toilets in addition to the many pilgrims jammed into every nook and cranny. I did not have the heart to tell them of my lovely 30€ room.

We depart my blessed palace in the wilderness in bright sunlight that shines onto brilliant white clouds filling every valley below us as far as the eye can see. We are literally walking above the clouds on the high mountain ridge that forms this portion of the trail. The view is so majestic and sublime it forces us to stop every few minutes to take pictures. It is absolutely heavenly, and in the cool, fresh mountain air, is the most transcendent nature focused moment I can recall from the entire journey.

Walking Above Clouds

We cover hardly any ground during the first hour due to our picture taking, being so in awe of the view. Eventually the trail begins to descend as we head toward Triacastella, a 2000 foot/750 meter drop in the Valley below. We now need to navigate carefully downward what we so agonizingly had to climb for the last two days.

Our conversation slows and soon ceases altogether as we focus on the steep rocky trail under our feet. I am following Gregor on the narrow trail, with Manuel some distance behind me. After some distance of careful downhill treading, I notice that Gregor has a single woman's sandal dangling from the back of his pack. When we finally stop for a break I ask if there is a story behind this single sandal. He answers with only one word: "Cinderella!"

I offer a raised eyebrow as my response. He hesitates briefly, but concludes it is safe to continue to tell me the sad tale. His romantic life is pathetic, and he is seeking the woman of his dreams. He was confident that the Camino would deliver, but so far, nothing. There is only a week left, and he is getting desperate. He found this shoe on the trail a few days ago, and has been carrying it on his pack ever since, looking for its owner. The shape of the shoe and the size of the foot convince him that it fits a beautiful woman. When she sees him carrying her shoe, and discovers the trouble he has taken to find her, she will swoon with delight and fall into his arms. I burst out laughing, not because the plan is so completely absurd, but because the Camino is unpredictable enough that such a plan could actually happen.

I do point out some flaws in his thinking, however. Since he is moving with the flow of pilgrim traffic, and pilgrims do not just stare at each other's backpacks, he may already have overtaken this Cinderella, who at that moment may not have been looking in his direction. Furthermore, being the heroic specimen of maleness he is, he has probably out-walked his Cinderella and is moving further and further ahead of her. He is stunned by my insight, and quickly realizes I may well be onto something. I suggest finding a popular pilgrim stopping point up ahead, where he could pin the sandal with a note in various languages attached, including his contact information. He is overjoyed at my helpfulness, and slaps me on the back in gratitude.

A hard two hours later we arrive at Triacastella, and adjacent to the Albergue in the town center, we find a suitable message board next to a popular restaurant. I write a note in English with all the necessary information, and he provides a German and Polish version. We are very happy with our work, convinced that such a degree of devotion to a cause is sure to delight the gods of love. At this point we part ways, with Gregor and Manuel deciding to take a 4 mi/7 km longer route to visit the oldest monastery in Spain, the Benedictine monastery of Samos. I decline to accompany them, since I have already stayed in two monasteries, and have thereby more than fulfilled my monastic quota for this pilgrimage. Two such stays is enough for me. Besides, I intend to make it all the way to Sarria today, a further 12 mi/20 km away, and I have no time left for detours. If I make it, it will become one of my longest distances, a full 19 mi/30 km on one day. After the rousing voice I received yesterday mobilizing me into action, I intend to keep moving. I am trusting that my more integrated body/mind/spirit will find the rhythm, balance, and stamina that will be required of me.

Leaving Triacastella at noon means I will need to commit to five more hours of steady walking, but with enough breaks thrown in to give my feet some "fresh air" time, I should be okay. Walking in my sandals is one way to accomplish this, but, at my first attempt to switch into my sandals, I am shocked to discover that one of them is missing. I always carry my sandals on the outside of the pack, since there is no room on the inside, but now one has gone missing, and could be anywhere along the path I walked today. That sandal is gone, and the irony of my situation hits me right between the eyes. All morning long Gregor and I have amused ourselves with his Cinderella fantasy and the missing sandal. Now I am the one walking with only one sandal all day, and didn't even know it.

As troubling as this loss of sandal is, with likely dire consequences for my feet, I burst out laughing. The gods are easily amused on the Camino and show their trickster nature by turning the tables on their little earthlings. This trick is a real back slapper for them. For a while I laugh along with them. Here is this pilgrim making jokes at his silly companion with only one sandal, when all the while he himself has only one sandal on his pack also. But then I get angry, although not with the gods. I am angry at myself. How could I not secure that shoe better this morning? Sandals have saved my feet from obliteration. Besides, they are all I have to wear in the evenings when my heavy, wet walking shoes must come off.

I begin to repeat the self-flagellation that happens all too regularly for me on the Camino. Mistake—self-blame! Bigger mistake—bigger self-blame! I decide on the spot to not take this emotional path this time. I have other options available to me, the first of which is to purchase a new set of sandals. How impossible can that really be? There is a small supermarket store across the street from where I am standing so I take my advice and go to check it out. They only have simple shower sandals, nothing that could remotely handle a rough trail. I leave the store discouraged, but not disheartened. I realize the struggle here is every bit as much about the state of my "soul" as it is about my "sole." I am experiencing the challenge of accepting myself gracefully, right where it is most difficult: in failure and shortcoming, in disappointment and vulnerability. I am determined to find a different way home to myself today, and my missing sandal has led the way.

One street beyond the store the pilgrim path begins by heading off into the woods. At this moment, Israel, the lame Spaniard who had to abandon his pilgrimage in Rabanal a full four days ago, comes striding toward me. I am shocked to see him since he was completely flattened when I last saw him. The lame do walk again on the Camino. He is full of excitement as he tells me of his modest recovery after an additional day of complete rest, which then allowed him to continue. He has now made up in three days, the distance I covered in four. But that is not the real source of his excitement. He is effusive in his description of the effects the entire Camino experience has had on him, in particular a sense of joy, energy, and a freedom he has never known before.

He elaborates by describing how deeply he has been impacted by his early encounter with two Hungarians and their spiritual practices, such as prayer and meditation. He was intrigued and began such practices himself, and feels himself coming home to his spiritual center. He has continued to send his daily e-mail updates with pictures back to his office which his coworkers eagerly devour. They are continuing to text him back, and report how moved they are. His story gives me a partial answer to my lingering question of how the Spanish might renew their spiritual life, which, at least at a formal, religious level seems rather comatose. I see in Israel a microcosm of the spiritual hunger that his generation is experiencing, which can only be satisfied by the direct experience of the sacred. I see more clearly than ever how the Camino is a vehicle for this renewal.

I also quietly mull over the fact that my lost sandal is the catalyst for this unexpected re-encounter. By lingering those extra fifteen minutes in town, fussing over my shoe situation, this encounter happened. Since the trail divides into two directions at that point, it is surreal that we met at that division of the path. I claim no divine string pulling in such moments, but see our freedom to choose as leading to a variety of possibilities of which this was one. These serendipitous moments can become particularly loaded with meaning if we are willing to search for that meaning. The psychologist Carl Jung calls this synchronicity. This is what happened for us.

We walk together for over two hours at a brisk pace, but given that Israel is at least twenty years younger than I, and an athlete, I know I cannot sustain our pace any longer. We say goodbye hoping we may see each other at the Albergue in Calvor another 4 mi/6 km ahead. I take a long break before resuming my walking because those fast-paced hours with Israel have over-extended me. The distance I have covered is nice to have behind me, but I cannot repeat the hard lessons of my first days on the Camino.

Arrival in Calvor an hour and a half later reveals that the twenty-two bed Albergue is full. It is already 4 PM after all, and given my experience of being locked out yesterday, along with the crowds on the trail, I should not be surprised. I am shocked, however, when the host tells me

William S. Schmidt

that every one of the five Albergue's in Sarria, the next major town, is
full. Now panic sets in, until I hear the rest of the sentence, informing
me that the three-star Alfonso Hotel in Sarria has one room left which
they will hold if I can get there in one hour.

It is amazing how motivating it can be when one is told you can
have the last apple on the tree, but you need to climb it in record time
to claim it. That is the situation in which I now find myself. I actually
have serious doubts I can walk 4 mi/6 km to Sarria in one hour, but
what choice do I really have? I immediately say yes to the hospialiero,
who passes on my bold claim to Hotel registration. There is no time
to waste so I do not even bother to ask if Israel has already registered
here. I desperately need to find a bed for the night, and everything else
is secondary for me now as I pull on my pack, grab my poles, and head
out the door as quickly as possible.

I am momentarily confused where the trail is, and absolutely
cannot afford to waste time going in circles looking for it. Two local
Spaniards are fortunately not frightened off by my desperate hand
gestures, and with some additional rounds of pointing, headshaking,
and head nodding, I am finally heading in the right direction. In spite
of having walked over 15 mi/25 km already today, I am striding with
determination. The thought of a guaranteed bed spurs me on, with
increasingly protesting feet. I am also experiencing some knee and hip
pain which should be cause for worry, which I immediately force out
of my mind. All my promises to myself for integrated mind/body/
spirit walking as recently as yesterday are thrown to the wind. Today, I
am going to pound these feet into the ground if I have to.

As I draw near to Sarria, I know I can make it, but by now I am
walking with an unsteady gait, literally stumbling over a curb or two as
I enter the outskirts. I curse the fact that the hotel is close to the center
of town and not here at the perimeter. I curse the fact that I did not
demand to be given an hour and half to walk instead of this damn
single hour. I curse the Camino for becoming a race! All my cursing
aside, virtually on the minute of my hour, I plop my sweaty elbows on
the hotel reservation desk. The relief is enormous as I am given my
room key in what are sumptuous surroundings. My anger and intensity
gives way to tremendous exhaustion given all the energy that I have
expended today. I just sit on the bed unable to wash, unpack, or go for
my reward beverage. I am even too tired to lie down.

I eventually accomplish my tasks of cleaning, and while I am not exactly refreshed, I am able to put one foot in front of the other again. Since the Spanish siesta is now over, and I am in one of the few remaining larger towns before Santiago, I decide to try my luck at finding a shoe store. I cross the lovely foot bridge over the river in front of my hotel, and to my amazement a shoe store is just around the corner. Not only is it a shoe store, it actually specializes in athletic footwear. I am already completely willing to call this a miracle, even before I see staring me in the face on the rack in front of me, my missing sandal. Of course, it is not "the" sandal, but one of the exact same make, color, and size as the one I lost. These grey Teva's on sale in front of me are an exact duplicate of those I purchased in Chicago. I just cannot stop shaking my head all the way to the cashier.

I now have a grand total of three sandals in my possession, all of the same size, make, and color, although there are two left foot shoes, and one right. I resolve to keep all three because there is a reasonable chance I will lose one of them at some point. This does not worry me in the least because then I will still have two sandals left. Even if this literally means two "left" sandals, I am completely at peace about it. My feet have taken such a pounding, they will never notice such a minor inconvenience as two left shoes. From now on three sandals will be dangling from the back of my pack.

I take my unexpected treasure out of the store and look to find a restaurant in the lovely pedestrian zone along the river. There are plenty of pilgrims mixed in with the locals, but I recognize no one and so dine alone. I am learning to keep my own company on the Camino, but it is not always easy. The experience of solitude takes me into zones of pain more quickly than zones of joy or delight. I am not sure if this is because I have a natural tendency to focus more on pain than pleasure, or if I am simply responding to current moments of distress of which there is plenty. Either way, I am aware of my pain, emotional and physical. The key, it seems to me, is to remain in a place of observation about it, not immersion in it. If I begin to wallow in my pain, I can stay there forever and become lost in it. Rather, if I can keep a dialogue going with it, by understanding its source and it's context, but also respecting it as a reflection of my aliveness, then it tends to find a safer place inside me and I can move on again.

With these musings I finish my meal and take my weary bones back across the river and off to bed. I again find that excessive fatigue is not the best inducement to sleep. My body is aching so much it keeps me awake for the second night in a row. Even as I lie there I am first and foremost in awe of what my body is able to endure. I think of all the countless pilgrims through the ages who have endured deprivation and hardship far beyond my own. I now also better understand why there were so many hospitals along the Camino route, including pilgrim cemeteries. There are limits to what our bodies can endure, and I seem to be flirting with those limits on a daily basis.

It is part of human nature to want to impose our will onto reality, yet we can do so only to a point. Finding that point is one of the key ingredients of maturity and wisdom. Reality always pushes back against our will, and I want to be in harmony with this push back. My personal intentions and desires need to be more clearly informed by both inner and outer reality. The Camino, I am discovering, is God's special laboratory for bringing about an awareness in all of us unconscious pilgrims of what is most real and true for us.

Sleep finally comes, although more restless than usual. When I awake I discover why. I have red welts on my arms and legs and realize that my three-star hotel has a bed bug problem. The problem seems modest enough, but I still a jump out of bed in record time. Thankfully all my clothes are packed away in my backpack, so I hope to avoid becoming a carrier of the problem. I certainly am developing a new appreciation for Michelle, the bed-bug vigilante. My itching arms and legs do not stop me having a full breakfast in the hotel restaurant, but I find the morning news on the large TV screens annoying. I realize with some surprise that I have been weaned of my normally enjoyable "news addiction," an unexpected change the Camino has induced in me. If I am losing my rabid interest in current events, what other unexpected transformations might this pilgrimage be forging?

CHAPTER 13

Camino Variations

Pilgrims Prayer

Codex Calixtinus—12th Century

God, You called your servant Abraham from Ur In Chaldea watching over him in all his wanderings, even as you have guided countless peoples as they too crossed their barren lands. Guard these your children who travel desolate paths seeking your fuller intentions for their lives. Be their companion on the way, their guide at the many crossroads they encounter; be their strength in weariness, their defense in dangers, their shelter on the path, their shade in the heat, their light in darkness, their comfort in discouragement, and the firmness of their intentions; that through your guidance, they may arrive safely at the end of the journey and, enriched with your grace and filled with your virtue, may return to their homes in joy.

> Paraphrase of my Pilgrim Passport,
> Credencial del Pelegrino

*B*efore leaving Sarria, I ask the woman at the hotel registration desk to make a reservation for me tonight by calling ahead for a hotel in Portomarin, my destination for the day. Among my realizations over dinner last night is that the Camino has essentially become a race for beds. For three days now I have been driven to exhaustion, far exceeding my mileage for the day, just to have a chance at a bed. I cannot continue in this mode. I notice that many people, especially the newly arrived Spanish pilgrims, all seem to carry cell phones and merrily call ahead to reserve their spots. They are almost all much younger than I, and have no compunction whatsoever at securing a bed for themselves. Whatever "romance" I enjoyed in the early weeks of the Camino, trusting that a bed would be found somewhere for me, has now flown out the window.

I am becoming more and more willing to set aside my Camino "purity" for the practicality of getting there in one piece. Besides, I think to myself, if a medieval pilgrim had been given the option to make a reservation and sleep in a tent on a given night, vs. sleeping under the open sky, he would have gladly chosen the tent. For me it is high time that I give up my pilgrim perfectionism. Portomarin is still 15 mi/25 km from Sarria, and I should not extend my mileage past that distance. So, it is reservations for me from this point on if at all possible.

My fatigue of the last days has left me grumbly this morning. After crossing the river next to my hotel I begin climbing seemingly endless stairs into the old town, only to have to climb back down the other side of the hill that marks the other end of the city. Normally this scenic route would find me interested, if not fascinated, but today, even though it is still early, I am tired and am fighting against gravity all the way. This is not a good sign.

My sense of strain today becomes very noticeable midmorning as the biker traffic increases. The terrain is very hilly, and in spots the trail is very narrow, barely enough for one person to pass. I have found when climbing I do much better leaning into the hillside and really pumping hard. Momentum is the key. Of course, bikers also like momentum, and on this occasion no less than ten bikers in a row pass me, most grunting a garbled "Buen Camino" as they announce their desire to pass. Since they take virtually the entire path, I am the one who must stop and step aside to let them keep their precious momentum going. I, on the other hand, am pushed into often prickly bushes to make way for these speed merchants with their fancy rainbow outfits.

Besides the obvious safety issues, and my own need for room on the trail, the deeper question for me is the nature of the Camino itself.

Is it a spiritual event or a sporting event? Perhaps it is both, and if so, can these dimensions truly coexist, or better said, how can they coexist in one person, never mind on the entirety of the Camino? I try to operate in life from the principle that before one judges others one should always undergo some rigorous self-examination first.

When I apply this test to myself, I recognize that I am not only on the Camino for "purely" spiritual reasons, whatever they might be. I too test my physical limits, my athleticism if you will, every day. I am certainly doing it more slowly than a biker, but even for me the physical is a doorway through which the spiritual and the emotional appears. So the question is not really physical vs. non-physical, or spiritual vs. sporty, but openness to the fullness of the experience. So, I grudgingly grant my biker trail mates the status of pilgrims, but I still don't like being pushed into the bushes.

The trail out of Sarria becomes increasingly more hilly and this challenge is intensified by light drizzle. As I climb the wind picks up and soon begins driving the drizzle into my face. It is time to put on my poncho and before long the drizzle has become a steady rain. I find it so much harder to walk in the rain, and I am so thankful that I am "only" going to have to ask for 15 mi/25 km today from these legs and lungs.

I come up behind an older Pilgrim walking very gingerly, painfully even, and notice he has a Québec flag sewn onto his pack. I cannot pass up an opportunity to meet a fellow Canadian, and strike up a conversation. It turns out my slow moving trail mate is Guy from Laval, Québec, Canada. He is 63 years old, and began walking from Le Puy in France two months ago. He is clearly in distress and describes his aches and pains in full detail. His body is breaking down, so much so, that he has had to take two full five day breaks, the first still in France well over six weeks ago, and the second most recently in Leon.

I am fascinated to learn how he and three others have formed a spontaneous "walking community" of pilgrims who have met each other on the pilgrimage. Of the four, two men and two women, two have since stopped walking because of their physical problems, and only Guy and one woman are still trekking, although he does not know where on the trail she might be at this moment. The two non-walkers have rented a car and driven on ahead to secure beds for all of them at a prearranged destination, as is their daily pattern. I admit this is an ingenious solution to their circumstances, which also reveals how naturally solitariness morphs into community and back again on the Camino.

As Guy I walk slowly on in the now steady rain, he affirms the pilgrimage for its capacity to bring reflection into our lives, but also laments its increasing commercialization, especially now as we are nearing Santiago. I find myself agreeing with Guy on his Camino diagnosis, but above all am struck by his determination. He would have every reason to quit, since he is probably damaging his body at this point. He has an easy way to get to Santiago by simply joining his two other friends who are already driving. But here is, stubbornly walking these final few days into Santiago. I admire his fortitude and see a lot of myself in his determination.

We walk together for a full two hours or so even though his pace is much slower than mine, as we finally join a crowd of muddy, cold pilgrims in a small café for lunch primarily just to get out of the rain for a while. I bid my goodbye when we leave the Café, since I will need to pick up the pace in order to secure my room in Portomarin by my 5 PM deadline. Perhaps the focus on the community Guy and his companions created for themselves have stirred up my feelings, but as the afternoon of solitary walking wears on, I find myself fighting with familiar feelings of loneliness and isolation. Besides, I am walking in a sea of Spanish speakers regularly now, and seem to find fewer and fewer potential conversation partners. The morning with Guy is becoming an exception it seems.

Arrival in Portomarin by late afternoon under leaden skies secures me a simple, but adequate room in one star Hotel Villajardin. It's real drawing card, however, is a small balcony which offers a view of the large reservoir Lake which surrounds Portomarin. I feel much less tired today than in previous days when I overdid my mileage count. I may even have enough energy left to look for a barber to help clean me up.

A Hairy Beast

The Spanish must have an aversion to barbershops or hairdresser salons because I have been looking for one for over a week now, to no avail. I completely shaved my head and face prior to departure as a ritual of preparation, but that is now well over a month ago, and I have not shaved since. At this point I am certainly unkempt and wild looking, perhaps seeming even dangerous, which may help explain my isolation. My persistence finally pays off when I see a small poster in a window that looks hair related, and sure enough, it is a small one-person shop run by a middle-aged Spanish woman.

Since I have absolutely no idea how to ask for what I want, I am reduced to gestures and simulations. Thankfully there is no one else in the shop because they would have found my theatrics amusing, if not weird. The proprietor does not understand I want to have my entire head shaved, and she repeats my gestures several times looking more uncertain all the time. When I insist, she reluctantly begins, and either because of fear or total lack of experience, she works excruciatingly slowly. The slower she is, the more anxious I become, because I have no direct view of what she is doing. As far as I can tell, I have no blood trickling down my neck, although I am starting to sweat which makes me less certain. By the time she finishes, we are both exhausted. I thank her profusely, and leave her a huge tip, more out of relief than gratitude, and escape into the cool early evening air.

Virtually a few steps from my hair-raising adventure is a restaurant with an outdoor patio. I spot sitting there ready to dig into their Pilgrim meal, but Natalie and Philipp, my young German friends. They beckon me over, and are delighted when I ask if I can join them for dinner. They seem lonely for a familiar face and common language, just as I am. I have barely sat down when I spot an older "Camino couple," Ulli and Marc whom I befriended a few days ago, who are walking by right here in front of us, and once I get their attention, wave them over. They too are delighted to see me and are happy to join us. So now we are a group of five. Within minutes wild-haired Christopher with the two young women from Chile in tow, spot me, and rush over to say hello. They also eager to share a meal with us, and are happy to be drawn into the circle.

By now we are a group of eight and have pulled over a second table to make room for the newcomers. We come from Poland, Luxembourg, Germany, Belgium, Chile, and U.S.A./Canada, and only have the German language and the Camino in common. I smile on the inside as I realize I seem to be the common denominator for all these connections, and the instigator for this serendipitous encounter. I may have to change my self-perception of being this solitary wanderer. People seem to know me and like hanging around me. Perhaps my loneliness is distorting what is actually happening in my life. I get lots of kidding about my now clean-shaven look: how much better I now look, too bad for the scratch marks on my head, and so on.

I dish out the kidding every bit as much as I receive, since everyone's quirks are rather obvious to me as mine seem to be to them. This relational ease with less pretense is one of the Camino's treasures, and we all seem to be blessed with more freedom and spontaneity than we are normally accustomed to, for which the warmth and laughter is ample evidence. I lose track of time in the midst of our comradery, but within a few hours or so the party seems to be winding down, and the group begins to disperse. I am the only one not walking with someone on the Camino, and since we are all staying in different places, I take my leave to walk around the old town for a bit, before heading off to bed.

On the other side of the market square from our restaurant is the large and very ancient 12th century Romanesque Church of San Nicolas. I have been observing people entering the church from my perch on the patio, and decide to head over for a look. As I push open the ancient doors an amazing sight awaits me.

The church is packed with well over 150 young people. They are clearly all on pilgrimage, and are in the middle of celebrating Mass. Two young priests are presiding and there is a palpable vitality and energy in the congregation. The officiating priest invokes laughter and verbal shouts of affirmation from his audience. The singing is vibrant with guitars and percussion and rhythm instruments joining in. I am swept up in the joy of the celebration, and my own heart sings along. As Mass ends my surprise and delight only doubles. As the two priests disrobe each other and hand their vestments off, the young congregants rush to the altar and begin dancing around it as they sing.

I can only stare in wonder at the latent spiritual power and energy that has burst forth so unexpectedly here on the Camino. They are living the joy of their faith, and have broken free of the morbidity and spiritual deadness I have so often observed here in Spain. I cannot bring myself to leave until the event has completely ended. By this point I have concluded that I need to trust the power of the Spirit to break into and through our human deadness much more than I have. Maybe this can be true in my personal journey also. With these spiritual thoughts swirling in my mind, I step into the darkness and coolness of the evening and wind my way back to my hotel lodging.

My sleep is interrupted in the middle of the night by loud snoring which I truly did not expect to hear since I am sleeping alone. The sound is loud and penetrating and for the life of me I cannot figure out where it is coming from. It is literally penetrating walls which do not seem all that thin. This person's particular snoring resonance must hit some unique wave length which sets all the atoms in this building into vibration. Fitful sleep eventually returns only to be stopped for good by the sound of furniture being moved in the rooms above me. It is 5 AM, and I cannot believe my bad luck tonight. This hotel room is louder than any Albergue accommodation I have had even in rooms holding dozens of people. Adequate sleep is so restorative and necessary, I am not sure how this lack of sleep will affect me, given the hard day that awaits me tomorrow.

I do not wait for the sun to rise on this morning, but am out the door by 6 AM. This will be the last hard climbing day before Santiago with only three more easier stages to go after that. My destination today is Palas de Rei, a full 27 km (16.5 miles) to go. Because I had someone call ahead for me last night to reserve a room for tonight, I am not worried about having a roof over my head, but do need energy for the climbing I will do today. The day dawns gray and heavily overcast as I leave Portomarin and its lovely lake. One long bridge crossing later, I am in dense woodlands, and in the faint early morning light I must pick my way carefully.

Perhaps between the gray sky and little sleep, along with the recognition that I am in my final Camino phase, all conspire to generate waves of sadness and aloneness that wash over me this morning. Mixed in with this and this are strong and unexpected feelings of rejection and unloveability. This becomes intensified by my fears about aging. Old rejection fears have quite a durability I am noticing, and they have new fuel beyond the rejection that comes with divorce. My aging is truly accelerating these feelings, and even though I have outpaced many a younger person on the Camino, my age has become so visible to me these last weeks. This fear I realize is not simply about physical capabilities, but about one's place in the kingdom of love. Does getting old still grant one access to this kingdom? My faith offers assurances about the infinite reach of God's love, but it is the absence of human love that I lament this morning.

I am interrupted in my preoccupation with the love-vacuum in my life by a field of beautiful yellow and purple flowers next to the trail. They seem to shout out joy, and are radiant in their wholeness, just as they are. I recall Jesus' message about the lilies of the field reveling in the joy of their maker, without worrying about their future status, even as fading flowers. I take their message to heart and release my morning morbidity. Oddly, my thoughts turn to my backpack, where I still have three sandals flopping along behind me; the two new ones, and the third odd one I am keeping in reserve. I decide on the spot that this extra shoe must go. All the footwear I now use is new, all of it having been purchased in Spain. This third sandal is my one holdover from Chicago. The symbol of what I must do becomes immediately clear to me. I need to release old ways of walking in order to walk in newness of life. The changes this requires in attitudes, habits, and choices is becoming much clearer to me. Above all, these changes require the vulnerability which the Camino has so powerfully broken open for me.

I take the opportunity to prayerfully remove my third sandal from my pack, even as my attempt to have a serious ritual is interrupted by my laughter at the ridiculous picture I have been portraying for a week now. For some reason, the image three sandals flopping around on my pack all these days strikes me as incredibly funny, and all my "holy" thoughts flee my mind. But perhaps that is the best spiritual food I could use right now, to not take myself too seriously. I don't have the heart to just throw my sandal into the garbage can at the side trail, which I might add, are few and far between throughout the Camino. So, I lean the sandal on the outside of the can as a kind of Pilgrim trophy, a witness to our trials and tribulations, and the goofiness which often accompanies our attempt to make sense of our lives.

The climb out of Portomarin is truly steep, and by 11 AM I have run out of gas, and need to rest. A café at the side of the road works just fine as a place to stop, and with limited tables and seats, I plop down on the last chair next to a weary looking Pilgrim, perhaps a mirror of myself. His name is Sebastian, a Frenchman from Paris, who has walked from home and is on his second Camino. He has been walking for well over two months now, and is desperate to finish. He is forcing himself to walk 26 mi/40 km a day so no wonder he looks so worn out.

I find him to be a very astute commentator on the power and pitfalls of the Camino, and he describes for me the depression he believes often follows the completion of the Camino. I can't help but wonder if he is also describing his own experience, and given the intensity with which he is walking, I can imagine he might be heading for just such a repeat depression. I have the inclination to walk with him for a while to explore his experience a bit further, but realize very quickly that his pace will be too fast for me, so I bid him adieu as he steps back onto the trail.

As I sit there finishing my coffee I realize that before I can resume walking I need to do a bit of shopping related to foot care. My challenge today is to buy a new package of feminine napkins as I was directed to do by Madame Rancal. This is my third effort to secure this vital product, and you would think I would have figured out an easy way to do this by now. The first problem is to find the item, since there is no rhyme or reason to product placement in many Spanish stores. You would think it would be next to the tissue section, or perhaps next to the lotion or feminine products section, but no, today it is next to shampoo and soft drinks.

Once I have found the product, the next challenge is to get past the checkout attendant with minimal awkwardness. Today, I use the camouflage of buying fruit, toothpaste, and a small drink. My attempt at subterfuge is a complete failure, as her raised eyebrow gives me away. Fumbling with my change only makes me feel more conspicuous. So what, I conclude, she must find her amusement somehow, and walk out the door as slowly as I dare. As I leave the hamlet, it dawns on me that my mornings exertion has brought me to the high point of the days climb. Not only that, but it seems that I have done my last serious, extended climbing of the entire Camino. It is not exactly all downhill from here, but all the heavy climbing is over.

Going downhill sounds easy, but it is certainly more treacherous than going uphill. One takes more risks going downhill, and often at greater speed. But if walking pilgrims pick up a bit more speed when going downhill, the biking pilgrims become true speed demons. Their desire for speed is not directed toward the paved roadways that are often adjacent to the trail. No, they want maximum speed on the rough and narrow walking path they demand to share with walking pilgrims.

After weeks of observation, I have concluded that Camino cyclists have invented a new game I am calling: "**Pilgrim Bowling**." The sport is quite simple really, and proceeds in the following way. The first requirement is to find the down slope of a hill with a narrow trail, and a few scattered walking pilgrims strung out along the path. The cyclist must pick up as much speed as possible roaring down the hill, to see how close they can get to the walking pilgrim before they shout "Buen Camino" in the pilgrim's ear as they race on by. The alert and nimble pilgrims tend to jump quickly enough and in the right direction, opening up the path, allowing for even more speed. The slow and dumb pilgrims tend to jump in the wrong direction, but are useful in their own way because they become an instant obstacle the cyclist can try and avoid. Besides, those moments become a great way to test their brakes.

The most hilarious situations, however, are the ones where the pilgrims just jump straight up and down because they don't know what to do. They are like grasshoppers and can jump amazingly high sometimes. It gets most interesting toward the end of the day, when everyone is more tired, and pilgrims are staggering along. At this point, they tend to jump both right and left simultaneously, with arms and legs flopping everywhere. The game is best observed from the top of a hill, and with all the jumping, scattering, and shouting, there is always something interesting happening. A good time seems to be had by all, and since no one is wearing helmets or any other protective gear, it must be an eminently safe sport.

Virtually my entire afternoon is spent on gently rolling terrain, with soft wooded paths. I pass occasional small groups of pilgrims, but even here, nearing Santiago, the trail is surprisingly uncrowded. I do have an unexpected moment of surprise, however, when I come across two women relieving themselves in a field right next to the trail. The sheer fact of their need is of course not surprising, but their choice of location is, since there are stone fences and trees in the near vicinity where privacy could have been found.

We even make brief eye contact, and there is seemingly no shame or embarrassment experienced by any of us. What is noteworthy for me is how the raw demands of our bodies, male and female, so override all other norms on the Camino. Our definitions of privacy, modesty, dignity, and personal space, all get challenged and adjusted. This shifting of our norms is of course one of the Camino's great challenges, and if we are fortunate, it's great gifts.

The evening in Palas de Rei is quiet and solitary in contrast to the camaraderie of friends in Portomarin just one night ago. It remains an eternal mystery of the Camino how people can simply appear and disappear in a flash. Friendships that form quickly and deeply can only be held in their immediate moment, likely not to reappear again. And, when one least expects it, there they come again. Or not. So it is in Palas de Rei. I am alone in a sea of humanity I have simply not yet befriended.

As I wander around the village, I realize I am only three or four days from Santiago, and somehow the recognition of the near-ending of this major life event plunges me into my most intense dismemberment yet. Of course, the Camino has worked on me all these past weeks, dismantling and reassembling my sense of myself. But tonight I am overwhelmed by a sense of the absurdity of everything, and by all that I call "my life." What is the point of anything and everything? My lost marriage of 35 years is the most obvious candidate for this question, but tonight everything is up for grabs. Many things in my life do not make much sense to me right now.

It is not that I have lost touch with all the goodness and blessings I have known, but at this moment all of my reasons and rationales for purpose and meaning seem hollow and meaningless. I sense the inadequacy of my mind to hold the so-called good and bad simultaneously. It flips from attaching itself to either one or the other state constantly, and is forever judging and weighing all that comes its way. Religious traditions, both East and West, both have their useful "answers" to this problem of making life meaningful, but tonight I am not interested in any such answers. Right now they all seem to be convenient rationalizations, a kind of spiritual seduction needed by my mind for temporary comfort.

Strangely, I am not in a state of despair about this, but more what I will call a necessary purging. Perhaps I use my mind too heavily for providing justification for my actions, in other words I may use it primarily for motivation and rationalization purposes. With my life circuits overwhelmed my familiar working "reasons" for my choices seem inadequate. The odd thing is, I don't seem to "mind" this paralysis at this point because it seems necessary somehow to cleanse me of an over reliance on constructed meaning. Do I really need "meaning" all the time to attend to the conditions of my life? Perhaps I am being asked to simply give myself over to whatever is at hand, regardless if it makes particular sense or not, and to trust from a much deeper level.

What seems more fundamental to me than the reasons I bring to any action, or even the reasons I derive from it, are the **intentions** that guide me in the first place. If I carry intentions toward "goodness" in other words, toward compassion and kindness, then I can let the outcome be what it may. To live without such constructed "reasons" is actually a call to a greater freedom, an invitation to fuller living and loving in the presence of what simply is.

You would think that falling asleep by questioning the validity of my mind would result in restless, if not impossible sleep, but to the contrary, it is my best sleep in days. It surely did not hurt that there were no bedbugs. I also heard no snoring; and the mattress was first rate for a change. Even so my good night's sleep does not change my mental state of last evening, that life is not necessarily supposed to make sense, and I am at peace with that conclusion at least for now.

It again dawns heavily overcast and I can find no place for breakfast, but I don't seem bothered by this since I now often begin walking without eating. At the same time I have no food with me, so I may become very hungry today. The path is heavily wooded this morning, and given the overcast sky, quite dark. I pass two groups of pilgrims of over twenty persons each, with one group younger, perhaps a church youth group singing and laughing, and the other an intergenerational group including numerous children. Both groups seem to be on a devotional pilgrimage, and I am struck by how different our respective experiences on the Camino are.

For pilgrims who walk in groups, the group itself becomes the container of their experience and offers much of the focus. It provides support and belonging, and takes care of many of one's needs. The group helps with motivation, and determines the pace, perhaps not always welcome, but there is a consistent looking out for its weakest members.

The individual Pilgrim on the other hand, has to contend with the existential challenge of aloneness and the risks that entails. When alone, we are the container for our experience, and the challenges, the isolation, the constant vigilance regarding the trail are on our shoulders alone. This is also compounded for those who do not speak the local language which greatly intensifies the experience of personal challenge. In many ways these contrasting ways of walking are reflections of the two ways of walking the path of life, the solitary and the communal. None of us walks exclusively on one or the other, but the Camino offers the opportunity to practice both ways of being on the human journey.

By late morning I am desperately hungry and am grateful to have passed the pilgrim hordes along the way, because the first café that is open already has quite a pilgrim crowd inside it when I arrive. It is my good fortune to have been served my baguette by the overworked solitary employee, when the first of the groups straggles in. At this point the place becomes packed so tight it takes forever just to work my way out the door to find some open space, just in time to see the second group heading straight for us. Had I been behind either group, I would have been walking to the next town on an empty stomach.

Perhaps because the trails have felt so crowded this morning, I do something unusual and stop at a church in the village of Furelos. A completely unexpected and compelling sight awaits me inside, namely a Jesus figure hanging on a cross. There must be thousands of depictions of Jesus hanging from crosses across Spain, but this depiction reaches deep into my soul. In this instance the artist has Jesus hanging on the cross with only one hand nailed to it, while with the other he is reaching down to us standing his feet. One is not sure, is he reaching out for help, looking to us for assistance to be taken down, or is he reaching out to help us up to join him on the cross? Both are legitimate interpretations and both are potentially true for me.

Am I perhaps hanging on some crosses beyond any redemptive task that once led me there? For how long should any of us hang on the crosses of our failures and shortcomings, and for how long should we hang on a cross for those we love, whom we hope to save? Does working out our salvation require a lifetime of cross-hanging?

Conversely, what crosses am I avoiding through self-assuredness and self-sufficiency? Am I so whole, so redeemed, so pure, so happy to be comfortable, that all cross hanging is banished from possibility? I think not. I do not believe I am called to follow a path of spiritual morbidity, but I am called to embrace reality, and that means getting up on some crosses. The crucifixions of our lives do not necessarily announce their final redemptive purpose in order to make it easier for us to climb up. Rather, they call out to us in the midst of our total unknowing. They are invitation to trust the process of dying so that the new life in us can be born.

Perhaps this is one answer to my growing crisis which came to a head yesterday around my struggle with collapse of meaning. I am not supposed to know the meaning of all that comes my way, because that would turn my mind and it's "reasons" into an Idol with an explanation for everything, a false god if there ever was one. I need to live through and beyond what I believe are "reasons" or the "why" of anything, into the reality of just being.

With my brief "lunch break" all too suddenly behind me, I am nevertheless grateful to be out ahead of all the groups that crowd the trail on this final stretch before Santiago. As if my recent days have not had enough odd sights, with everything from groups of singing pilgrims, guitar-plucking pilgrims, to bathroom-going pilgrims, I now come across two women leading the smallest dog I have ever seen. This miniature dog's legs are at most two inches long, and are moving so fast they are a blur, with the two women simply walking their normal pace in front of me. As I reach them I notice the dog is also decked out in pilgrim paraphernalia, such as a tiny gourd around its neck, and a scallop shell stitched into a tiny scarf around the dog's neck. I have observed increasing pilgrim kitsch the closer I get to Santiago, but we have now entered the ridiculous range I think to myself.

When I engage the women in conversation I am stunned to learn that this little dog has walked over 60 mi/100 km so far with these two. I have no reason to doubt them, but now I am dumbfounded. This dog with his tiny legs must surely take forty steps for every one of mine. Of course, he has four legs, while I only have two, which has to count for something, but nevertheless this dog's accomplishment is extraordinary. Perhaps this dog is the truest pilgrim of all, who faithfully obeys the call of his master. And yet the whole thing seems terribly neurotic to me. As I say my goodbye to them I find myself thinking that I hope they have enough money saved for the veterinary bills which are sure to follow.

By midafternoon I have slowed down from walking to plodding as so often happens at this point of the day. I have decided to stretch my mileage today by aiming for Arzua, rather than the tiny Rabadiso, a small but pretty village which has only one very popular Albergue, which is sure to fill up early. Arzua is the last major town before Santiago, with multiple accommodation possibilities, and I will much rather take my chances there.

As I turn a corner on the trail I am brought to a sudden standstill by a sight just as strange as the one I encountered barely an hour ago. Here is another woman walking a dog, only this dog is even smaller than the first. Fortunately, this dog is spared the embarrassment of wearing Pilgrim garb, but I can't help but stare at the flurry of little feet scampering to keep up with its owner and her nice, easy strides. What are these people thinking to bring toy house dogs onto a rough trail with their little legs a sheer blur? I come to the only conclusion available to me, namely, that the Camino is no cure for craziness.

My day of oddities serves up one final encounter, perhaps lower down on the strangeness meter, but fascinating in its own way. Shortly after my second toy dog encounter, I find myself following two young women walking side-by-side, both talking on cell phones. I presume they are not talking to each other, but for the thirty minutes or so in which I walk behind them, the cell phones do not leave their ears. In and of itself this is not odd, but on the Camino it feels out of place. On the other hand, technology is so present in our lives why should it not show up on pilgrimage? After all, my friend Israel's use of daily blogging captivates his co-workers, and became his way of recording his transformational journey. This recollection allows me to quickly set aside my judgment of the cell phone talking women, and affirm that they too are on their own path, and are seeing fit to communicate their experiences in real time, while I do it in delayed time via a diary and tape recorder. Who is to say that one has greater merit than the other?

My last hour of the day brings me to a steeper climb out of Rabadiso into Arzua than I have bargained for. I am more tired than usual today, probably because early in the day I was walking at a faster pace than normal, which has everything to do with trying to get ahead of the many groups I keep encountering. These groups of pilgrims tend to be chattering, laughing, singing, shouting, a kind of pilgrim mayhem. I can enjoy all the commotion at a distance, but when one is on an introspective or reflective pilgrimage as I am, it can be jarring to be surrounded by a group with a different energy, therefore I try and out-walk them. Today I may have pushed it too hard.

Entering Arzua brings me into a town stretching out along a long and narrow main road. Most of the roadways and sidewalks in the town are dug up for major construction which makes for an unexpected obstacle course. The benefit of my fast pace today pays off in that I find a modest hotel which still has one private room available. Once the groups I have passed today begin arriving, it will be game over as far as accommodations in this town are concerned.

I walk from one end of town to the other checking out possible places to eat, but am saddened by not seeing one familiar face in my entire exploration. There are lots of places to eat, but no one to eat with. In disappointment I plop down at a table in front of my hotel for my beer refreshment, and unexpectedly rolling up next to me on her bike is Joan. True to its nature, the Camino has offered up another of its endless surprises, this time in the form of a completely unexpected friend. I last saw Joan on a remote stretch of path way back on the Meseta, well over ten days ago. We laugh about how an old walking pilgrim like me is out-pacing a young biking one, but then again, I have cheated a bit since we last met, by taking a bus for a stretch, while Joan probably walks as much as she bikes, not including her detours.

She notes that all the hostels in town are full, and she cannot find accommodation, but there is talk the town may open a gymnasium for the overflow crowd of pilgrims. I have a fleeting thought to invite her to share my room if she wishes. Yes, there is a double bed, but sharing is not what I have in mind. I contemplate taking the floor and offering her the bed when I realize I carry no extra mattress, nor is there room on the floor, so I dismiss the thought. She seems happy enough to check out the overflow option, so we say goodbye and agree to a dinner rendezvous in an hour or so.

An hour later Joan petals up with the good news that a sports hall has been made available, and while she will be sleeping on the floor, they do provide mattresses, so her accommodation is secured at least for this night. There are plenty of places to eat, and with her fluency in Spanish, I know I can avoid an ordering disaster as I am prone to experience from time to time. We again find our way into significant and rich conversation. I continue to be surprised at my degree of transparency and even more so how easy it is. A lifetime of work as a therapist makes it very natural to receive the stories of others, but more difficult to share one's own. Between that and a sense of privacy, reticence has been the norm.

Now, in contrast, I am reveling in this new freedom and that it is not just a byproduct of Camino anonymity, but also suggests I have less need to protect myself. At least this is my hope. What also makes our sharing easier on this night is that we are both experiencing a sense of deconstruction of our familiar sense of self. It is happening for us at very different developmental stations: for Joan at an earlier stage of the identity and intimacy quest; for me at a later stage of life review and coming to terms with my story. Yet our process is similar, and we recognize it in one another. Our evening ends relatively early as is typical for tired pilgrims, yet I have been given another gift in this unexpected exchange.

My satisfaction at getting the last private room in my hotel has turned into teeth-grinding frustration by 2 AM as I toss and turn at the noise emanating from below. It turns out my room is directly above the hotel restaurant. They sure know how to party in Spain, and closing time is a foreign concept. There must be a fiesta going on, because the noise is not just coming from below, but also from down the street where a music stage has been set up. I am surrounded by noise and my ear plugs cannot stop the vibrations. Perhaps I dozed off from time to time, but it sure seems as if I had a sleepless night when I get up at the crack of dawn with a heavy head, and no energy.

A very similar all-night party happened three weeks ago in Azofra when Horst and I were kept up all night on the feast day of Mary Magdalene. On that day I was ill and feverish, and still made it through the day, so I take comfort in the hope that I probably do have reserves I can draw upon today. There is no one around as a step out onto the street at 7 AM, except a few teenage boys kicking beer cans down the road. They seem a bit aggressive to me and are quite drunk. They call out to me and I respond in English by letting them know I am from Chicago. They make the usual association to gangsters, and all of a sudden I am their best buddy. That is not a connection I intend to foster with them, so I toss out words like "Michael Jordan" and "Chicago Bulls," but they are not interested in basketball. So I let the gangster label settle on my broad shoulders. I had no idea I look so tough.

The big beer can they are sharing is running out, and now they are getting aggressive with each other, so I pick up the pace and they quickly lose interest in me. A female pilgrim close to my age comes around the next street corner and falls into step next to me. She is Italian, but even with her broken English I learn that she has not slept a wink either. Her room was across the street from the stage where the music was blaring all night and she looks completely worn out. This is likely the second last day for us and the physical and emotional toll the pilgrimage has taken is visible in our faces.

Walking at our own pace is a truth any pilgrim who has walked this far has long ago realized, so we part ways quickly since I walk faster than she. I find myself alone in an old oak forest, when the realization dawns on me that I will arrive in Santiago tomorrow. Of course I "knew" this day was coming. But at this moment I feel it at another level altogether. I stop in my tracks for a few moments as a bundle of tangled feelings erupt. I feel this intense mixture joy, anticipation, deep sadness, and gratitude.

In many ways I am in stunned disbelief that I am almost there, that this profound event of my life is almost complete. It has asked so much of me, and given me so much in return. I know I am not "healed" of the loss of my marriage, but I sense that I have been made ready to receive the healing yet to come. I have been prepared for the transitions which are on their way, if not already here. The first of these is the transition away from the Camino itself. I find myself glad to be walking this final stretch into Santiago, rather than taking the bus as I had contemplated some weeks ago. I am also grateful that I will have two days in Finesterre following my arrival in Santiago in order to have that final and much needed closure.

I am pulled out my thoughts by the sight of a pilgrim just ahead of me walking with his right arm in a sling. There is a small bag slung over his left shoulder, and as I pull up next to him I find out his name is Sebastian from Italy. He fell several days ago and has separated his right shoulder. Since he can no longer carry his backpack he gave it away with most of his belongings, keeping only the most basic essentials in the small bag he drapes over his good shoulder. Quitting is simply not an option for him.

Meeting Sebastian while in the middle of facing the ending of the Camino has a strong effect on me. He mirrors for me the wounds we all carry. Some wounds are more visible than others, of course, but the journey toward wholeness requires meeting pain directly and walking with it for a time. While this may seem masochistic or morbidly neurotic, it reflects deep wisdom. When we hold pain in a certain way our spirit incubates it, and thereby lets it be transformed into something we can relate to, can take back into ourselves, whereupon it becomes a gift. It may bring new direction, a new vision, new hope, a new purpose, whatever it may be that we may need. It is a product of the alchemy of the soul.

My early morning start and the extra mileage I added on yesterday, has me arriving in Arca by 1 PM, although I am feeling very exhausted given my sleeplessness. I seem to be ahead of the pilgrim horde today, and arrive in town early enough to find a lovely (quiet) room in a small new hotel. I have a view overlooking a lush valley and the hills beyond, but I cannot take it in right now because I only have energy for a quick shower, and gratefully drop into bed for a two hour nap.

By 4 PM I awake refreshed and begin exploring the main Street to find Ulli and Marc the "Camino couple" working on two huge beers at a street side table. We are surprised and delighted to find one another again. Pilgrims always have much to catch up on given our many adventures and we plunge into our debriefing. This town of Arca is a true pilgrim magnet and funnels everyone on toward Santiago. We must be sitting in a prime spot because soon the two Chilean women walk on by, although by now they have lost Christopher.

Two Canadian women join us whom I have just passed at midmorning. They are a mother-daughter duo from Ontario. What makes them noteworthy is that the mother has two very swollen black eyes and looks as if she has been on the losing end of a tough fight. When I saw her on the trail early this morning I fantasized that here is an abused woman who is on the Camino for healing and recovery from trauma. Now my fantasy can be replaced by the real story.

The mother tells me of her sudden fall two days ago. She fell directly on her face. Thankfully, nothing was broken, although her face was terribly bruised. As she lay on the ground moaning and crying for help, a pilgrim just walks on by, ignoring her cries for help. Later that same day, she meets the stranger and confronts him: "Did you not see me laying there right next to you where you were walking?" While he was very apologetic, he admits, that no, he did not see her, he was so engrossed in his own thoughts and inner process, he was oblivious to what was happening around him.

This woman's story is an enactment of the Good Samaritan story, right here on the Camino, only in this version there is no Good Samaritan. Her narrative reveals two sides of the spiritual quest. On one hand, we are compelled to travel deep into ourselves, so deeply as a matter of fact, that other aspects of life can fade, if not disappear altogether. Awareness of one's neighbor can become a casualty of such extended introspection. My observations and experiences on the Camino tell me that this danger is an exception, yet the possibility is real enough. One's own introspective process does take intense focus, commitment, and a necessary solitude from time to time, but the cry of the neighbor must also be heeded, and, unfortunately, can sometimes be too easily dismissed.

We are joined next by Marianne, a Swiss woman close to my age, who is one of the long walkers I am so in awe of. She has walked almost double my mileage, and has the aches and pains to show for it, but then again, so do I. She comments that her main life theme is her tendency to over extend herself, and the Camino has been her vehicle for trying to address this difficulty. One could wonder why someone needs to over extend themselves in order to face a pattern of over extending themselves, but perhaps that is the only true way we ever face something. Maybe one has to stare one's problem in the face, and consciously address it on a daily basis, not unlike the alcoholic who needs daily AA meetings to find the necessary awareness and support to overcome a chronic entrapment.

While most of my tablemates this evening are new to me, it feels like a family dinner. We are family now, a family of seekers, deeply impacted by what we have undergone, and have all had a good number of our pretenses stripped from us. On this final night before reaching Santiago we share freely, poignantly, and truthfully. There is a lingering sadness in the air as we realize that a profound, unrepeatable experience is about to end. This feeling is matched by excitement over what tomorrow will bring. We break for the night earlier than usual, since most of us are aiming to arrive in time for Pilgrim Mass which begins at noon every day in the great Cathedral of Santiago.

There are about 13 mi/20 km to go from Arca to Santiago, which can be walked in four to five hours, so a 7 AM start is a must for those wishing to arrive in time for pilgrim Mass. I am uncertain about my plans for tomorrow. If I have learned one thing on the Camino it is not to be rushed nor driven by deadlines, not even pilgrim Masses. I know I will need contemplation tomorrow, whatever else the day might bring, and that will remain my priority.

CHAPTER 14

A Visit With St. James

"Let us go singing as far as we go: the road will be less tedious."

Virgil, Ecologues

I awake by 7 AM which is late by pilgrims standards, but I have already decided during the night to skip the pilgrim Mass in Santiago so there is no need to jump out of bed and join a race to the finish line on my last official walking day. I have much to reflect on and want to gather myself in contemplation today and not be driven by deadlines. Besides, there are Masses scheduled later in the day which I can attend if I wish.

With this resolved, I settle in for a leisurely breakfast in the hotel restaurant and meander out the door by 8:30 AM. Within a few steps I am in a dense eucalyptus forest with massive trees and a canopy so thick the sun does not reach the ground. It is calm and the rich scent of eucalyptus fills the air. The trail is carpet soft from years of layers of leaf and bark. Most surprisingly, the forest is empty of people. No pilgrims are visible in Arca as I leave town, and none are encountered anywhere in the forest. I have an entire forest to myself on the doorstep of Santiago.

The incredible silence and beauty surrounding me simultaneously drives me deeply into myself with remarkable sharpness and clarity. The Camino has done its work of dismembering me, and I see the themes of my life in all their fullness and pathos. Loss, hurt, the need to forgive and be forgiven, my values, the shape of my priorities, the now family-emptied unknowns of my future, are all seen and felt in their full power.

All of this comes with pain which is the path by which all this awareness and ownership has come. I do not feel overwhelmed, however, but fully held in my experience. I feel secure in a way I cannot explain but only sense. The hymn "It Is Well With My Soul" again comes to mind and I begin to sing, softly at first, and with each repetition I sing louder until I sing with full volume from deep in my gut:

> When peace like a River attends my way
> When sorrows like sea billows roll
> Whatever my lot, You have taught me to sing
> It is well, it is well, with my soul.

Now the trees begin to sing back, and the forest comes alive with sound. I am one voice in a great choir of affirmation of the goodness of creation, and of the grace that lives at the heart of our pain.

One's sense of time shifts at such times, and I can only determine how long I was in that forest by calculating backwards from my map, and it was likely one hour. I am only sprung from my soul celebration as the forest opens briefly in what can at best be called a small cluster of buildings with an open café and some pilgrims milling about. Suddenly, I hear shouts of "William, William," with Gregor, my Polish friend from the very first night on the Camino in Orisson, France, running toward me. He has a new set of friends, which include the ever present young women from Chile. We embrace as the brothers we are, and decide on the spot to walk to Santiago together. We have now run into each other for at least the fifth time in the vastness of a 500 mile/800 kilometer journey.

Here, most unexpectedly, on the very last stretch into Santiago, we cross paths again, as the last remaining members of our original Pilgrim troupe of twenty or so of us who began five weeks ago. We take the time to extend our coffee break, and then step onto the trail for the final few hours into Santiago. There is much to share between us, and we quickly proceed to talk about recent meaningful moments we have each experienced. This theme takes us somewhat unexpectedly into a conversation about images of Christ which deeply impacted us along the way. We become so engrossed in this conversation, that at a fork in the path, we suddenly realize that no Camino arrows are to be seen anywhere. We are lost, and have been led astray by Jesus Christ.

A young pilgrim blazes past us, and he certainly looks like he knows where he is going, and so we follow him, happily continuing our conversation. About a mile/two kilometers later, we realize there are still no Camino markers visible anywhere, and this fellow we are following likely has no clue where he is either. I race after the young man to find out if he knows where he is going, while Gregor heads up a hill where cars are parked to see if he can get directions.

I finally reach the young fellow and am out of breath by the time I get there. I ask him in English and German if he knows where the path to Santiago is, and strangely, he does not answer me in any human language, including sign language. He actually keeps eating an apple the entire time and says not a word. I am not sure if he is deaf or mute or both, or in an altered state of consciousness, but I can get nothing out of him.

In frustration I find my way back to Gregor, and he has had no luck either. We can't believe we are lost with Santiago virtually in sight. We are not truly "lost" since we know where Santiago is, but we have certainly taken a huge detour and a still need to figure out how to get there. We have different ideas about how to proceed, with Gregor convinced the path is further up the hill next to a TV tower, while I am certain the road next to us leads into Santiago, and I do not want to take any further chances. We cannot agree on the right solution and so we choose to each try our own route and hopefully will meet up again on the path, or if not, on the Plaza in front of the Cathedral.

The irony of our situation is not lost on me as I trudge along the highway into Santiago. Not only the presence of friends, but even high powered spiritual discourse, can lead one astray right at the threshold of one's goal. I find myself chuckling at the absurdity of walking hundreds of miles without getting lost (with one minor exception), only to now, with at most 4mi/6 km to go, be wandering confused along a busy highway.

All of a sudden on my left there is an opening between buildings in the village of San Marcos, where I spot the familiar scallop shell and know I have found the path. I quickly run across the highway and I am back on track. In barely five minutes I arrive at the crest of the hill called Monto Gozo, where stands a massive sculpture, and the panorama of Santiago spreads out before me. This is a good spot for lunch, and a vendor selling American style hot dogs is selling his wares. I decide to lower my sausage standards on this occasion and have one. Gregor is nowhere in sight and if he has not already passed by, is sure to come this way. About twenty minutes later Gregor appears, looking a bit sheepish, but as relieved as I am that our unexpected detour has ended.

We take a few moments to examine the sculpture erected in honor of Pope John Paul II's pilgrimage to Santiago, and both agree it is ugly and out of place. We proceed down the hill and soon find ourselves on the outskirts of Santiago. With each step we have become more quiet and focused on our own thoughts and feelings. I find myself in disbelief that a journey so long in the planning, so intentional in the preparation, so intense and challenging in its execution, is coming to an end. I am filled with excitement, relief, and anticipation, but also a not unexpected sadness. A great spirit adventure is coming to an end.

Gregor wishes to check into an Albergue on the way into the city, and so we take temporary leave of one another since I intend to find a hotel room somewhere near the center. His legs are twenty five years younger than mine and walking back and forth to the suburbs from the center of Santiago is not something I intend to do. I am going to stay put for a while. My legs have paid their dues.

I walk on, with scallop shells in the pavement and walls guiding me, but I do not really need them since the spires of the Cathedral are impossible to miss. I am about to reach the Cathedral when three street musicians playing guitars and flutes grab my attention. I linger for a bit to take in the atmosphere in the city. It is festive, alive, and a buzz of excitement fills the air. This Camino route, arriving as it does from the East, takes one to the back side of the Cathedral. Its gray stone walls show their 900 year age. Even from the tight confines of alleys and passages the Cathedral's vastness seems overwhelming for a pilgrim who has been slogging it out for weeks over field and mountain, with only hamlet and village the bulk of human habitation one encounters. As the final corner is turned a breathtaking sight stops me in my tracks. A vast open plaza is spread before me as the western entrance of the Cathedral with its double stairway gleams in the sun.

Pilgrims and tourists mingle in the hundreds, yet seem spread out in the great expanse of the square. I move to the center of the square and sit on the flat paving stones as seems to be pilgrim custom. I peel the backpack off my sweaty back and use it as a pillow as I lie down on the cool stones and gaze slowly around me. Many others are doing the same thing which is the only ritual I need right now. More pilgrims drift in, some alone, some in groups, often accompanied by shouts of joy, hugging, and great rejoicing. A group of six or eight cyclists arrives. They drop their bikes and begin an orgy of backslapping and dancing with others joining in. I feel everyone's joy mingling with my own even as I sense an intense loneliness at this moment.

I have scarcely begun to take in my surroundings when Gregor appears. We embrace on the plaza as two life wanderers who have found home, if only for a moment. The rejoicing runs deep because much has been endured and much life material has been faced on this journey. We take many pictures of the Cathedral, ourselves with fellow pilgrims, virtually all of whom are unknown to us, all in an atmosphere of exuberant celebration. There are some rituals left to take care of such as embracing the life size statue of St. James which adorns the main altar of the Cathedral; going down into the crypt to view the silver reliquary which supposedly holds the Saints bones; but perhaps most importantly, obtaining the "Compostella," the certificate of completion that all pilgrims walking the last 60 mi/100 km are eligible to receive.

Gregor and I decide to delay all these rituals and find a restaurant to have a feast of celebration. Besides, we are famished all of a sudden, as if we haven't eaten in a month. A lovely tapas restaurant just off the Cathedral Square looks inviting, and in spite of the crowds, a great table on the patio is available. We order one of their most expensive bottles of champagne which starts our celebration off rather nicely. After five weeks of pilgrim meals the tapas choice is perfect. It is as if a diet of bread and water has been replaced by an endless flow of delicacies, and we savor them all one after the other. There is a feeling of unreality in the air, of disbelief, that such a journey has been accomplished and even more so, that it is over. Joy is mixed with subtle sadness, all of it welcomed, all of it honored.

We agree to accomplish one final ritual together, namely, to get our Compostella certificate. The office creating the documents is just up the street. We notice that the line waiting to get in is much shorter than the usual hours long queue, so we join the throng and spend only an hour or so lining up with hundreds of other pilgrims patiently waiting their turn. I receive my Compostella gratefully, and hold it very gently, noticing how my name is written in Latin in full calligraphy. I purchase an appropriate tube and insert my precious document for safekeeping for the journey home.

Descending down the street with my proof of success clutched in my fist, two of the famed "long-walkers," Wolfgang and Heinz from Salzburg and Swabia respectively are standing there. They look no less haggard than they did on the trail, but happiness and relief is written on their faces. A round of hugs and back-slapping follows, and of course, pictures must be taken! I have no place to put my Compostella, so I place it on a window sill while I work my camera. We briefly share our stories of arrival, but we all have separate needs and so soon say our goodbyes. I have a desire to visit the Cathedral, do some modest shopping for souvenirs and perhaps a gift or two. Gregor and I agree to meet the following morning to take a bus to Finesterre, the "end of the earth" destination on the Atlantic coast, which for many pilgrims is the true end station of the Camino. According to legend it is there where St. James' casket floated onto shore and where pilgrims have congregated even in pre-Christian times.

Two long-walkers flanked by Bill and Gregor

But first I must complete my ritual journey here in Santiago by visiting the saint in all his bejeweled glory. A Mass is underway as I enter the vast chamber that has received the spiritual hopes and pains of so many millions of worshipers over the centuries. I sit and absorb the cool, soft atmosphere around me. The Mass is in Spanish and I find I cannot emotionally enter into it, but nevertheless, to my delight and surprise in the middle of the high altar stands the life-sized figure of St. James, with a steady stream of pilgrims hugging him, kissing him, putting their heads on his shoulders, all while Mass is proceeding around them.

I get up to join them since the Mass is not drawing me in today. I may join a later service, but first I must complete my ritual journey. Standing in line has never felt more peaceful as I await my turn. Everyone seems to respect the time each person needs with the saint, and I am glad to be standing in line with them and slowly ascending the stairs to meet our pilgrim patron.

My turn arrives and it feels utterly natural to hug the human sized figure of St. James. I feel an unexpected sense of continuity with the gospel story, all the details of which don't seem to matter very much right at this moment. I feel myself to be one with all these countless followers of this Jesus, of whom James was one of the first. Like James, I too went to foreign lands out of a sense of calling in response to the Jesus story although I did not get my head chopped off for my troubles. If anything, I have been handsomely rewarded for my efforts, although not without pain in life. So I hold the saint with gratitude and deep joy.

Descending from the altar deposits me literally at the doorway that leads to the crypt where the saints' bones are said to rest. Down steep steps I go to find myself standing in front of a silver reliquary behind an ornate gate. It is quiet and serene in the vault in contrast to the intensity of hundreds of people milling about in the Cathedral directly above me. As a serious skeptic in matters of relics, I absolutely do not believe this reliquary contains the bones of St. James. At this moment, however, I find this does not bother me in the least. I am not here for the bones in any case, but I am deeply moved by the devotion of the millions of pilgrims that have preceded me to this place, regardless of the content of their beliefs.

Bones of St. James

All of us carry our longings and spiritual yearnings deep within us, and whether the lure is devotional, sublime, infantile, archaic, or mythic, it hardly matters to me. I am here to honor that force deep inside me that says "yes" to my existence, and "yes" to the Creator-Spirit that fashioned me. Everything else is superfluous for me and at this moment I can only honor in myself that universal impulse to say "yes" to something sacred, however vague or clear the object of our devotion might be.

The pilgrims queuing behind me give me time and space to linger with my thoughts for a few moments, but in time I must move on to make space for those who follow me. This too is its own spiritual lesson and I smile quietly to myself as I contemplate this insight. Ascending the stairs takes me back to the main sanctuary where Mass has ended and the queue to visit the statue and bones of the saint has become much longer. I wonder how patient this pilgrim group will be, but they seem no less peaceful or serene than I. Perhaps we have all been transformed by the commitment that brought us to this place.

I take my time to walk around the Cathedral, taking in the art, numerous chapels, and of course the huge swinging incense dispenser, the **Botafumereiro**. This device is so large that it takes a group of up to eight men to set it swinging over the heads worshipers and smelly pilgrims on feast days. By now it is early evening and I exit the Cathedral by the west doorway into the setting sun. The square is emptying and I look in vain for a familiar face to greet. Several pilgrim acquaintances have mentioned coming to the square as a rendezvous point to meet for dinner, but in over a half hour of milling about, I recognize no one. My feelings of loneliness have been building for several hours now, but have become especially intense in the vastness of the square with no one around with whom to share my joy.

It is almost 8 PM and I realize it is time to find my hotel and get ready for the night and the excursion tomorrow. I step into a few restaurants along the way in the off chance that I might find some pilgrim friends, but no such luck. I stay in the last restaurant I enter since I should eat something, even though I am not particularly hungry. As I sip my solitary glass of wine, I discover again how closely our joy and sorrow reside beside one another. In a few short hours ago I was celebrating with Gregor, rejoicing with Heinz and Wolfgang, and now I am feeling the pain of loneliness. All our feelings are intensified at noteworthy moments such as this, but what I am discovering right now is that aloneness and togetherness are always present to one another as the two sides of the one coin of human experience. We can of course seek to avoid our awareness of either one or the other depending on personality, but neither one can be escaped for long.

Returning to my room finds me really struggling, not just with aloneness, but with loss. My room is small and spartan, and while its austerity may be fitting for a monk's cell or a pilgrim's penance, tonight it feels like an isolation chamber where I have been given a life sentence. I miss my life partner so badly. She would understand what this means to me; she knows the context of my life, and gets what moves me. But not only is she not here, she has moved beyond our shared story. The full force of this awareness allows my tears flow as freely as at any other time on my journey. I am greatly surprised at the depth of my grief at this very moment, and can't stop crying. Somehow the end of the pilgrimage opened up the full force of the ending of a lifelong relationship and it seems more than I can bear. Sleep eludes me this night and I toss and turn. I am in a battle within my soul, and I do not want to let go of my soul friend. But she is gone and I spend my night staring into this reality. Only the first glimmers of dawn grant me two short hours sleep before my alarm clock rouses me into the day. Today I go to "the end of the earth." Perhaps there my spirit can be revived.

CHAPTER 15

The End of the Earth

My lord God

I have no idea where I am going. I do not see the road ahead of me. I cannot know for certain where it will end. Nor do I really know myself, and the fact that I think I am following your will does not mean that I am actually doing so. But I believe that my desire to please you, does in fact please you.

And I hope that I have that desire in all that I am doing. I hope that I will never do anything apart from that desire. And I know that if I do this you will lead me by the right road though I may know nothing about it. Therefore will I trust you always though I may seem to be lost and in the shadow of death.

I will not fear, for you are ever with me, and you will never leave me to face my perils alone.

Thomas Merton, Thoughts in Solitude, 1956, p.81.

*M*y night of tears has one further jolt in it when in a flash I remember leaving my Camino credential, my certificate of completion, on a window ledge as I was taking pictures with my pilgrim buddies yesterday afternoon. I jump out of bed looking for the certificate, and in my spartan, empty room it does not take long to realize it is not here. How could I be so foolish as to leave it sitting on that window ledge, when so much toil and pain went into getting it? I find some equilibrium about it fairly quickly, however, as I rationalize that perhaps it is still there and I can find it on the way to the bus depot in the morning, or if not, I can get back into line when I return from Finesterre and get another. With this small bit of comfort I settle again into my few hours of fitful sleep.

Morning finds me eager to get underway. I pack in a flash since by now I can do so blindfolded. While my room was far too austere for my mood last night, the hotel has a lovely breakfast that seems indulgent by pilgrim standards, but now it lifts my spirits, never mind my energy level. There is a time and place for ascetic renunciation, but perhaps that time has ended. Why not mark its ending with a good breakfast?

I adjust my route to the bus station so I can swing by the Cathedral Square and the spot where I left my credential. It is gone as I feared. Somehow I am not unduly upset. I can get another credential upon my return from Finesterre since I will have a final day in Santiago before I fly home. Arrival at the bus station finds me again in the company of pilgrims who are also on their way to Finesterre. Gregor is among them as we arranged to rendezvous here. Many pilgrims walk the 40 mi/60 km of rugged terrain to Finesterre in three days, but those of us taking the bus today look like we have already paid a high price for our spiritual enlightenment, and have nothing left to prove. I for one absolutely do not have three hard days of walking left in me.

Unfortunately, the bus breaks down before it even leaves the station and so we all pile out waiting for a replacement. Over an hour later we are finally underway. Another hour or two later comes my sudden first glimpse of deep blue water, spotted at the end of a narrow, steep valley framed by towering trees. My spirit leaps for joy at the beauty that opens up before me. The bus hugs the jagged coast from this point on, and the collision of green hills, blue sky, and azure water, draws me into its majesty. I can't take my eyes off the shoreline as it seems to mimic my own heightened boundary sense. I feel deep in my bones how vital it is for me to complete my journey in this way. Numerous coastal villages are traversed and in another hour or so I see an enormous bay opening up, with a long finger of land protruding out into the ocean. A tiny town is nestled into the curve of the bay which must be Finesterre. Sure enough, we pull into a bus stop at a slight widening of the road. The hills surround us as they spill into the ocean. Right next to the bus stop is the Albergue where Gregor plans to stay, while I spot a hotel across the street with balconies overlooking the harbor. It looks perfect!

The hotel has cheaper rooms facing the hills behind the hotel, but I am only going to settle for ocean view with balcony. I have seen enough hills for a while. My room is all that I hoped for and more. Stepping out onto the balcony opens up a panorama of deep blue water matched by an equally blue sky, a large stone mountain across the bay, seagulls swooping above me on their circuits, and a soft warm breeze wrapping itself around me. I can't stop grinning and am becoming a quick believer that there may be such a thing as heaven on earth. Of course it helps to have suffered a while first, and perhaps that is a preliminary criterion for any heavenly quest, not that I am necessarily seeking heaven for its rewards. I intend to let God take care of the outcome of my life, and for today I am being blessed by this divine embrace.

I sit and take in the peace that surrounds me and find a deep gratitude welling up inside me. I am in gratitude for both pain and renewal, and have experienced so much of both on this journey. The challenge has been to trust this rhythm, not just on the pilgrimage, but in all the particulars of my life. The magnitude of the challenge I have undertaken grabs me so fully, yet it is really only a small microcosm of my life. But given its concentrated form on the Camino, it has uncovered in sharp detail the pathos which shapes my and all our lives, and from which we discover deep truths about our existence. For me a core truth is that I am finite and frail, yet somehow imbued with a strength and a dignity and a grandeur that is not my own, but a freely and wonderfully given gift.

Sitting here at the "edge of the earth," I feel as if I have crossed a threshold and am looking back through a veil into the nature of my existence. My life is so small and not even really "mine." Yet, paradoxically, it is unique and particular as the grain of sand that is me. It wants to shine brightly and thereby reflect its author.

I am roused from my musings by a knock on the door. It is Gregor, who has been denied entry to the Albergue because he has traveled to Finesterre by bus, and only foot travelers are eligible to stay there overnight. It seems there are criteria after all to enter the kingdom of heaven, but the universe seems willing to offer alternatives, which for Gregor turns out to be the room across the hall which I had shunned in order to take the one with the better view. We are happy to be neighbors once again. As I discovered very early in my relationship with Gregor, he has hordes of pilgrim friends and even in his first few minutes in Finesterre, he has already found some of them who are staying at the Albergue. We agree to go meet them for beers just down the street and head off to join them.

By now it is late afternoon and a decision must be made as how we will ritualize the ending of our journey here in Finesterre. There is a lighthouse at the outermost point of land jutting into the sea. Most pilgrims find their way to that spot and utilize various rituals of completion. These include a burning of one's pilgrim clothes as a kind of purification ritual; others find scallop shells on the beach as a take home icon of their experience; while others jump into the waters of the Atlantic as a death/rebirth ritual.

I for one am not about to burn my clothes on any beach, since I have only one pair of pants left. Three of us, myself, Gregor, and Christian, a high school teacher from New York and a friend of Gregor's, decide that our ritual will be a feast at the lighthouse where we will watch the sun go down into the Atlantic. Our first task is to buy the necessary food items we need, so we embark on a trek to find a grocery store. We are in luck, and find one just up the street. Because we are poorly equipped pilgrims, with no utensils other than knives, we adjust our menu accordingly. We decide on exotic cheeses and sausages with ample wine, with various breads and pastries to round out the menu. As we discuss our cheese preferences amongst ourselves, and old man approaches me and addresses me in German. He has a gnarly, weathered face with rather tattered clothing.

I am first of all struck that he addresses me in German since I am only speaking English with my friends. He excitedly tells me I should not view the sunset at the lighthouse, but rather proceed up a hill behind the lighthouse to a bluff where I will find large "Celtic boulders" from which I must view the sunset. These stones, he says, are on the east-west vortex, and are on an energy line with the bald stony mountain across the bay, the mountain he calls the "Celtic Olympus." He adds that as the sun sets into the Atlantic it simultaneously "rises" on the mountain as the shadows of the setting sun rise up this Celtic mountain.

My first reaction is that he is a crackpot and I gently but firmly brush him off to return to my cheese selection. He seems to get my point and moves away. My friends and I realize this store has no bread as is true in many Spanish grocery stores, and so I volunteer to find a bakery and am told by the cashier that it is only three stores down the street.

As I step into the street the old German is waiting for me, and is insisting I follow him. I decide to humor him since I am walking that way anyway. He takes me up the street to an opening between buildings to show me where I must go. Turning across the bay he points to the Celtic mountain which is impossible to miss since it is the largest landmark on the horizon. He then draws an imaginary line from this mountain across the bay to the vicinity of the sacred "Celtic" stones. That line is the energy center, he declares, the implication being I would be a fool to ignore his recommendation. Well, why not, I think, that bluff looks very dramatic even at this distance, and I decide to try and persuade my friends to take this final trek. I complete my bakery responsibilities and head back to our rendezvous point. My friends are amused at my story and have no particular objection to this alternative destination, although we all wonder why my unsolicited guide made such a fuss about it.

By now we are extremely hungry and begin our hike up the coastal road to the promontory point. The lighthouse itself is over 2mi/3 km away and we must pass by it to get to our "Celtic stones" and with the entire stretch uphill, I am soon straining. We are loaded down with more food and wine than I can imagine even three hungry men finishing, but who knows? Since I supposedly know where I am going, I lead the way, but with many paths and trails crisscrossing, the exact route is not easy to find. A few wrong turns and a full hour later, we reach the lighthouse and aim for the boulders high up on the hill behind it. A final brief but steep climb later brings us to our destination.

The view we have claimed for our troubles is spectacular. The entire ocean spreads as a vast panorama before us. The lighthouse is far below, and to our left across the bay is the sacred mountain, the "Celtic Olympus" shining in the evening sun. The blues and greens are soft and layered but brilliant in their depth. As one's eye moves away from land toward the horizon, blue upon blue reveals the deepening depth of the ocean. Adding drama is the howling wind at this elevation. We find shelter in the huge boulders which are over waist high. Were it not for the shelter of these massive stones our food would fly away. We see a large group of people gathering at the lighthouse for their sunset ritual. We, on the other hand, are alone, savoring the power of wind, water, and light. Maybe there is an extra measure of spirit energy in this place.

There is a drama to this place, with each of us bringing his own meanings and intensifications. I, for one, am drawn into what I can only describe as a visionary state, an awareness that is mediated by my very surroundings. As the sun sinks lower into the sky it creates a wide "river of light" dancing on the ocean below, a highway of light aimed directly at me. My eyes follow that road of light from the shore to the setting sun and I know that I am on that road spiritually and with my entire being. It is as if the eternal has broken into my awareness and I know myself to be on the path toward this light. We are all walking in our lives toward this light, with joy and sorrow, on this vast highway of life. Each of us walks independently yet we are all on the same road.

River of Light

Our destiny is a shared one, even in our unique journeys. To have been given such a vision of the eternal is profoundly joyful for me and I am giddy with delight. I experience an incredible sense of continuity with all the countless pilgrims that have gone before me, as well as with the endless number who will follow me. I know deep in my soul that this is not simply a moment of Camino closure, but is a revelation of our human journey to our wholeness and sacred home. Even ancient pilgrim sojourners intuited this, which is why this location of Finesterre marked the transition point from this world to the next for people in many eras.

My companions have had their own sacred realizations and we share with one another as much as the howling winds will allow. We have also discovered that, while we may have experienced moments of heightened awareness, sand can still get into one's cheese. Enlightenment always runs into our earthly reality, and reminders of our dust nature are never far away. Luckily we have plenty of wine with which to wash down our sandy cheese, and it is quite possible that because of our ample wine supply, we became even more enlightened as the evening wore on.

By now the sun has set and dusk is fully upon us. We gather our few remaining morsels quickly, in part because navigating down this rock strewn hill is treacherous in the dark, but even more so because Christian will be locked out of the Albergue if he arrives after curfew. We walk the entire way back in the dark, but the lights of Finesterre guide us from the shoreline below. We contemplate helping our friend climb the fence if he is in fact locked out, and although we do arrive after curfew, a kind soul has mercy on him and lets him in. Gregor and I take our leave and by now are eager to return to our rooms. An incredibly rich day has unfolded and we each seek our privacy and our rest.

The sun rises over the tip of the Celtic Olympus mountain in reverse of the shadow that enveloped it last evening. My waking rhythm is still on Camino time and so I am up early and fully awake and ready to savor the sunrise. I don't want to miss a thing and so go downstairs to the hotel kitchen and bring my breakfast back upstairs to enjoy on my balcony. The sky is again cloudless as a few fishing boats slowly work their way out of the harbor to their destinations. The gulls are busy as usual and I entertain myself for a while by tossing left over bread from my perch and take my delight at their mid-air calisthenics. They miss not one morsel, but our game must end, and I am to meet Gregor for a beach excursion, before he departs for Santiago this afternoon, and then goes back home to Poland tomorrow.

The beach in Finesterre is wide and sandy, and even in the morning sun the temperature is hot, with the sand unbearably so. The water, however, is another matter. Even now in late summer it is extremely cold. Gregor enters up to his knees and has had enough. But I will not let the temperature deter me from a final ritual. I need to enact a baptism of sorts, and as an ex-Baptist I need to undergo complete immersion in order for it to count. Of course I have no swimming gear with me, but I am wearing hiking shorts and they could use a ritual washing as much as I do.

I enter the icy waters gingerly at first but this is just slow torture. Only a full plunge will do, and one deep breath later, in I plunge. I scream with shock and delight but also become instantly energized. I can't believe it, but I am completely loving this moment. I swim with full vigor and head into deeper waters which become even colder. No matter. I dive deep and feel the strength of my stroke and the renewal of healing waters. I feel myself to be undergoing a true baptism, with an old life being washed away. I have no illusions that pain is permanently washed away, but I also know that the new is coming. As I swim I sense with clarity why I had to come to Finesterre. I am not magically 'healed' in the sense that my physical or emotional pain is gone. The painful scenarios of my life are as real as they were before I began the Camino, but I have been birthed into new life by God's grace. These waters enveloping me at this moment represent that new birth. The cold slowly begins to penetrate my bones and I must return to shore, but I sense my ritual journey is complete.

Gregor and I have one last event together, an "end of the earth" fish lunch. We savor the local cuisine and offer each other final reminiscences. After all, we were companions on day one, and now on day thirty four, we must take our leave. A spiritual brotherhood has grown between us that is intergenerational, multi-ethnic, multicultural, and ecumenical. This is the mystery of Spirit, and in that mode we say our goodbye.

I spend my remaining afternoon outdoors walking the beach and climbing the bluff above the town. The dinner hour finds me back in Finesterre, and I see a whole new crop of pilgrims arriving, checking in to the Albergue across from my hotel. I have the fantasy that a familiar face may appear, but I recognize no one. The river of humanity flows on, and I must soon take my leave. I am alone, but I am peaceful and content. I experience no further need to return to either the lighthouse or the Celtic mound that was our shrine last night. My balcony becomes my final perch as darkness appears and harbor lights flicker on as the final boats slip back into their moorings. Tomorrow I return to Santiago and my final full day in Spain.

I awake early as is now my habit and have two hours to get ready for my 9 AM bus trip to Santiago. The hotel restaurant is closed this morning so I walk down to the beach cafeteria for breakfast. I chat briefly with a German pilgrim at a table across from me, when the door opens and Philip and Natalie, the young couple from Germany walk in. Our paths have not crossed for over two weeks or 150 mi/250 km ago, yet here we are meeting in a little café at the end of the earth. They join me and we quickly launch into mutual updates. They have walked to Finesterre from Santiago for three grueling days in bad weather, and are heading back to Santiago today on the same bus as I. They are not as chipper as before, and seem worn out by this last stretch. It confirms the wisdom of closing my Camino experience in a gentler way by taking the bus. Our updating takes longer than I realize and once I notice what time it is, I bolt out of the café to rush back to my hotel to gather my things and catch our bus.

A "short" 45 mi/60 km bus ride back to Santiago takes almost four hours of excruciatingly slow travel. I must already be transitioning back to city rhythms because I am surprisingly impatient with our slow pace. Admittedly, I also have some final agendas to take care of in Santiago, such as getting a replacement "Compostella," and don't want to cut my last hours short, but I still hope I am not losing my hard-won patience this quickly.

Arrival at the bus depot in Santiago gives me the opportunity for a last trek into town and on the way I make my final hotel selection, only this time I go for quality. I am tired of austerity and am going to end the Camino in style. Walking back into the inner heart of Santiago takes me into the pilgrim crowds once again, with thousands of new faces all around me. I don't feel lonely anymore it seems, and I feel a sense of peace at the completion of my journey. It was and is full, and I need nothing more from it.

In my contemplative, wandering mode I decide to take some time to visit the pilgrim museum in Santiago, and out the corner of my eye I spot a familiar face in the crowds. It is Joan, the Irish "biking" pilgrim, who surely has the record for the slowest bike-traveled Camino ever. We are completely surprised to see each other again, especially in the midst of so many people at this very moment. A shift of only one minute either way, and I would have been inside the museum or she would have been already on her way and lost in the crowds.

We quickly grab a table at a nearby bar and can't talk fast enough in our eagerness to catch up. She is on her way to the ocean today to find her closure near the water much as I have done. The arrival in Santiago for us as pilgrims is almost too much to integrate after all the weeks of struggle to get here. We seem to need the boundary experience of a shoreline to bring the full awareness of ending and of closure to bear on our personal sojourn. Because the Camino drives us so deeply into ourselves, we seem to need a physical reminder of boundary which a shoreline represents, to more fully enter into the final task of closure and ownership. This is certainly the sentiment I sense in so many of us pilgrims as our journey ends.

Joan has a bit of time before her bus leaves, and decides to join me at the museum, which provides us with an excellent historical overview of this pilgrimage, and a genuine appreciation of the continuity we share with millions of other pilgrims through the ages. An hour or so later we part ways, feeling even stronger solidarity with that vast community of seekers and wanderers who have followed the call of the pilgrim spirit inside them. I move on deeper into the alleys of Santiago to buy a few gifts and souvenirs, and slowly work my way back to the office where the Camino credentials are issued and I take my spot in line.

This time the line is twice as long as before and I am told I have a two hour minimum wait ahead of me. As I stand there, a tap on my shoulder interrupts my daydreaming. It is John, from Belgium, who has recently arrived and is thrilled to find another familiar face. His Camino girlfriend is now history, which suggests that Camino romances can have a short, if intense, life. He looks tired, but happy nevertheless. When I first met him in our early Camino days way back in Larrasoana, it looked like he wouldn't make it, yet out of his original group of six, here he is, the only one who finished. I sense a quiet confidence in him that I did not see before.

Thirty more minutes pass as I stand in line and I begin to feel increasingly restless and ridiculous even. Why am I standing here wasting my final hours in Santiago, waiting for a stupid piece of paper to tell me I have finished the Camino? I already have a credential: it is written in my heart, and the Camino is forever sealed there. I know I have finished my pilgrimage and have been challenged, blessed, and strengthened beyond imagining, so why do I need a silly credential to tell me so? The answer is clearly that I do not need such confirmation, and since no piece of paper can tell me what I have gained, I boldly step out of the line and feel amazingly liberated as I step away. My credential seeking days are over perhaps.

Barely five minutes later as I am meandering down the street, another familiar face appears. It is Heinz from Vienna, one of the long walkers who has trekked for over ninety days from his front door, and has even been to Finisterre and back on foot. He embraces me as an old friend and seems almost desperate to talk to me. Heinz is leaving for home tomorrow as am I, and asks if I can spare the time to have a cup coffee with him.

We have barely sat down and he pours out a story of marital pain. His wife has been having an affair with his friend for several years, and furthermore, that he and his wife were close friends with the other couple. Heinz offers me a detailed marital history, and tells me of the love between he and his wife, but also of the pain between them, including a history of conflict-avoidance, and now the rupture of betrayal. His desire to go on pilgrimage was immediate upon the disclosure of the wound, and within days he was literally walking out his front door. Heinz is very clear with me that he did not walk thousands of kilometers for healing, but to get perspective. I am intrigued by this and ask him to elaborate. He tells me that his deeper need, beyond obtaining simple pain relief, is to find a way forward, to gain a vantage point from which to discover what to do. This he has seemingly found in the form of an inner desire to forgive. He wants badly to reconcile, and has been receiving subtle signals of hope in that direction in his recent calls home.

I cannot help but think of myself as he talks. Yet his situation is very different from mine, not the least of which is the fact that I have received no such signals of hope in my communications. Nevertheless, our feelings and our inner process is similar, and Heinz is moved and yet not surprised by my own sharing with him. Even as I sit with him, I cannot help but wonder what it means that the last Camino story I am taking with me is one of marital pain and distress.

Just as is true for Heinz, marital pain is the predominant story I brought with me as I entered my Camino. Yet in many ways my outcome is different. While I have certainly had intense pain along the way about my broken marriage, I have also come to realize that my Camino was not simply about my marriage. The Camino was ultimately about me, and my relationship to myself as embodied finite self, as a person with feelings, as a mind-and-spirit self, all in the context of my relationships. My life is more unsettled about where it is headed than at any time in the last twenty years. Yet I am at peace about that unsettledness in ways I could not imagine before the Camino.

I know I am re-entering the same life I left, but I am entering it as a more thoughtful and trusting person. I know more fully that God is present to me in all that comes my way. What is asked of me is to be open to every hill and valley. Heinz and I must eventually say goodbye to one another, and while I am saying goodbye to a friend in pain, he is even more so a friend in hope for a renewed future for each of us.

Leaving Heinz behind I step slowly away, deep in thought. I decide to take a final walk past the Cathedral, but have no further need to enter. As I walk through the square I end up walking right past a table where John is seated with two of his French friends. I sense both of us know we have already said our final goodbye, because he does not invite me to sit with them for a last glass of wine, nor do I ask to join the circle. I know it is time to leave the world of the Camino behind.

It is almost 8 PM in the evening and I want to ritualize my last moments in Santiago with a final glass of wine, with a toast to myself and the sacred presence that guided me here. I climb the high stairs behind the great Cathedral and see a comparatively small church up ahead and decide to enter so I can offer a final prayer of thanksgiving before my wine ritual. Upon entering I am shocked to discover a full church, where a concert of sixteenth to twentieth century Spanish classical and sacred music is about to begin. An open seat is there waiting for me, and I settle in for two hours of heavenly musical bliss washing over me.

I am first offered an appetizer of classical guitar, with a salad of string quartet music, followed by main courses of organ and choral works, with dessert including an encore of various additional selections. The composers featured this evening include Joaquin Turinam(1763-1832), Pablo Bruna (1611-1679), and Oscar Espla (1886-1976), among others. To be transported into a heavenly state while fully on earth is nothing one can necessarily plan for, which is why it comes to us as gift, as grace. Such transcendence that enters our lives is so real, so direct, yet it is nothing we ourselves manufacture by ourselves. But it does require an openness to be transported into that awareness, and so it is for me this night. I find myself lifted out of all the so-called "good" or "bad" details of my life, into a unity that holds them all. There is a wholeness in the Universe that I intuit, and have come to know more fully, yet which can so easily elude me, but now it comes to me again, unsummoned and unexpected. The unity stone which I now feel in my pocket came to me as a first prompting for this awareness, and so many more such moments have been given to me, with this concert just one more in a long line of such gifts.

I know I was guided to enter this space as a final gift, a gift of blessing and closure for my journey. I am overwhelmed by the realization that this sacred journey, so intense and so challenging, is closing in such a sublime way. I am in awe as I leave the church and although it is late, I still find an outdoor bar to offer my final toast to the sacred Spirit with my long delayed last glass of Rioja wine. By 11 PM I find my way back to my room for a final short night.

I sleep peacefully and calmly even as my early morning flight time forces me out of bed at 5 AM for a thirty minute walk to the bus station and the shuttle service to the airport. It seems surreal that only two weeks ago, I had a similar pre-dawn walk to the bus depot in Leon, where I skipped the next two walking stages to give me the extra days in Finisterre. How differently I felt on that day. I was in such turmoil about the Camino, about my life, and my seemingly unresolvable pain issues. Today I feel so different. I walk in peace today and am ready to leave. My Camino is finally over. Or is it?

I arrive at the bus depot and while looking for a coffee shop, Christopher, the Belgian music teacher appears, this time without a crowd of women around him. We hug and laugh. I tell him, "This damn Camino never ends!" "How do I get out of it?" He replies: "The Camino never ends. It just moves to the next chapter." I nod my assent and chuckle at the wiles of the Camino. I have gone through about five Camino "endings" in the last twelve hours, only to be tapped on the shoulder and be told one more time: "Not so fast, your Camino is just moving locations, so don't get so cute with yourself that you think you get to decide when or where it ends." It only ends when I stop walking, and I am not going to be allowed to stop walking just yet.

We become quiet as we sit next to each other with the bus winding its way to the airport in darkness. Our final goodbye is at our respective gates, as Christopher is on a flight home via Munich, while I am flying to Madrid to make my further connections. It is 9 AM, Friday, August 14, as I board the plane. My next Camino is about to begin.

A MEDITATION ON STONES

*W*hile our Earth is predominantly made up of water, its watery vastness is bounded by stone. The first acts of creation involved the containment of formlessness and void through stone. Stone gives form and substance to our Earth, and ultimately to our very own being. Much of the time we give no thought to stones. They are ubiquitous and we generally have no occasion to even give them a second thought. The exceptions to our unconsciousness regarding stones are of course, geologists, the scientists of stone, who understand the history and nature of stones in their raw objectivity. But there is another community of people who relate to stones in a more subjective and intimate way, namely those among us who are serious walkers, whose feet pound away on the trails we frequent, and who of necessity must pay attention to the paths of stone which we trod.

One such path which has known millions upon millions of feet, is the pilgrimage to Santiago, Spain, a stony trail if there ever was one. As a matter of fact, the entire reality of "the Camino" is framed by stone. Spain is a country of stone. Stone houses, stone barns, stone churches. Stone streets, stone paths, stone everything. When you walk hundreds of miles on stones of every size and description, all day and every day, you get a particular sense of stones and your relationship to them. There are sharp stones, smooth stones, loose stones, flat stones, stones of many colors, slippery stones, cracked stones, and on and on, but what they all have in common is that they penetrate into you from the ground on up, way into your soul, when you walk the Camino.

At the beginning of most every day of my thirty three days of walking those 500 miles/800 kilometers, I generally felt oblivious to the effect of stones. But after only an hour or two of walking, I could tell through the feelings of pressure or pain in my feet, the shape of the stone. The power of stones is that they directly impact our walking, whether secure or shaky, firm or slippery, easy or hard, all of which forces us to look at them. I probably spent 80% of my walking time on the Camino looking down at the path, a practice which I surely share with all other pilgrims. Looking at what? Stones, and how to render my walking safer, easier, firmer, softer, etc. Many stones became steppingstones, securing my climbing or descending; others, like pebbles, were welcomed because they are "softer" and more helpful to the foot because they mold to it.

There is a reason why we call someone who is inebriated "stoned." He has been hammered into submission into a lower form of himself. The Camino does this through the feet. It takes you down into the earth of your being and knocks on the door of your soul. If you don't open in good time, it will smash the door open and get your attention the hard way. Stones are Earth's first true form, and consciousness was eventually born out of softened stones. We ultimately return to the stones out of which we were made, as the Earth's plates suck into the deep, the bones of our being. Perhaps this is why we so value certain kinds of stone in the form of diamonds and all manner of precious stones, in that they have been birthed under great pressure into the radiant forms of their colored beauty.

Stones as Pathway to Consciousness

We often desire the smooth paths of our lives. Certainly car driving is enhanced by a smooth road, and as any driver in northern climates knows, a road made uneven by freeze and thaw cycles soon becomes so rough as to be able to rattle one's teeth. When walking, however, I found the opposite to be true. The smoother the path, the more my feet protested. Walking for long stretches on pavement or concrete often became excruciating, especially when walking through towns or cities. When one added the factor of the heat of the sun-baked stones into one's pavement pounding, each step felt worse than the last. My feet never became as tired on uneven paths as they did on smooth ones, perhaps because the unevenness allowed for the foot and the path to mold into one another, to "roll together" in a way which a flat, hard surface never allowed.

I draw from this a life analogy, that "smoothness" in life, i.e., a firmness won through becoming hard and tough, is a poor environment for the suppleness our soul requires. To live from our soul requires a certain unevenness, an uncertainty and unpredictability even, because in that uncertainty lies our freedom. To have it all nailed down and locked up may feel secure, but it is in fact too hard an environment for our souls to flourish.

At first glance this seems counterintuitive. How could all the unevenness of our lives, the vulnerability, be "better" for us than smooth predictability? The answer has to do with the necessity of challenge to forge our selfhood. By challenge I am highlighting our unfinished-ness, in that we are forever "on the way" to authentic selfhood. We are creatures both contained and shaped by time and space, yet we transcend them through our spirit of freedom. We live in both dimensions, the bound and the unbound, and must harmonize them for better or for worse. Walking and navigating a stony trail, either long or short, is a great way of simulating this life task. This is one of the secret benefits of walking, and is the true essence of walking meditations.

When I was walking the Camino, there emerged a quality of consciousness that is akin to what I will call the "observer" self. In normal consciousness we operate on the one hand with an intense focus on something outside of ourselves, our tasks, our agendas, or the necessary life concerns that need our attention. Or, we may focus on our inner reality, what we think, feel, believe, or conclude about ourselves and what we are currently living. But then there is a deeper consciousness that is able to observe us both in our inner and outer preoccupations.

In this third form of consciousness I hover over both my body and my inner life, as well as my surroundings. This state is not dissociative, but detached and engaged. When walking, I felt the pain of every footprint, but I also became an observer of what was happening to myself. This is a very distinct position or vantage point to arrive at, and meditative practices in general are a seasoned way to get there. The power, or I might call it "the gift," that comes from being in this space of mind-body duality and the heightened awareness which flows from it, is insight.

Insight is the capacity to see more deeply, and in this seeing lives our truth. I affirm that this is truth with a small "t" because it claims no universality or absoluteness. It is contextual and grounded in our ever-changing reality, but it is "true" because it sees more, and sees it non-manipulatively. It sees, and says yes to what it sees. It let's be what it sees. This is the power of insight, and walking on stones became a way for me to get there.

Stones as Protection for our Souls

Analogies are tricky things in that they can be taken too far, yet they reveal truth within the limits of the meaning they intend to convey. One such meaning is visible in the protective function of stones. Wherever stones are available, people have tended to build their houses with stone, and even in areas where wood is the preferred material, stone is valued as a decorative and "symbolic" enhancement of a home, by revealing and affirming the home's protective and enduring features.

An ancient and abiding narrative surrounding the protective function of stone is found in the encounter of Moses with God on Mount Sinai. Not only are the Ten Commandments written on stone, but the very encounter of Moses with God is potentially dangerous and annihilating for Moses, so much so that God secures Moses, and protects and shields him in the cleft of the rock, these eternal stones of God's holy mountain.

> Then the Lord said, "Here is a place beside me. You must stand on the rock and when my glory passes by, I will put you in a cleft of the rock and shield you with my hand while I pass by. Then I will take my hand away and you shall see the back of me; but my face is not to be seen." Exodus 33:22

Stones are a supreme symbol of permanence and durability, yet their creation reveals the enormous forces of nature that have been unleashed upon them to make them what they are. This Mount Sinai stone has been split asunder, enough to protect Moses, and as such is a stone that has undergone much in its evolution into the shape it now manifests. This ravaged stone has endured the forces that shaped it, and is now conscripted by God to protect Moses from that which would overwhelm him.

I take from this that protection for our souls, even when encountering God, is taken from the raw materials that surround us, which are themselves God's creation. Stones are symbolic of the deep and abiding structures of mind and spirit, those elements forged in the fires of suffering and endurance. These features of our humanness have been purified in the furnace of the birth and development of consciousness, and are present in the deep structures of our psyches. There, in the mythic underworld of our being, live the impulses of truth-seeking, freedom-awareness, hope-orientation, and transcendence-yearning. We are sheltered in our souls by God's hand, even as the dangers are profoundly real. Stones, for me, are symbols of hope, that the shelter needed for our souls is every bit as real and robust as the dangers which also lurk there. This is not a Pollyannaish or magic-based protection, but a protection that appears most fully when the struggle is fully entered. This is my experience of encountering the principalities and powers that threaten to overwhelm my little life. In the midst of that struggle, God provides the protective stones in the form of the spirit-gifts that buffer, shelter, and guide the little ship that is our soul.

Marker Stones

Christian Scripture abounds with references to stones as foundational markers for life. Perhaps the most noteworthy of these analogies is the use of "cornerstone" imagery to suggest the necessity of building a house with a proper cornerstone, so that the entire structure remains aligned, secure, and thereby stable. Paradoxically, this vital cornerstone is actually a stone which has first been rejected by the house builders.

> The stone which the builders rejected has proved to be the keystone. Psalm 118:22

> He is the living stone, rejected by men but chosen by God and precious to him; set yourselves close to him so that you too,

> the holy priesthood that offers the spiritual sacrifices which
> Jesus Christ has made acceptable to God, maybe living stones
> making a spiritual house. I Peter 2: 4-5.

The motif of the rejected stone within the Christian tradition refers to Jesus as a living stone, the full embodiment of the Sacred. Jesus, whose journey of faithfulness toward God's claim upon him took him into the domains of darkness and alienation, fully manifests the inverted path which God seems to utilize to bring about wholeness and salvation. Out of brokenness, God forges healing and wholeness. Out of powerlessness and radical vulnerability, God generates strength. What the world labels foolish, God reveals as wise. What dies is born into new life. God's power of reversal is fully manifested in the life pattern of Jesus. This pathway of his faithful living and dying in response to God reveals a cornerstone for our own being, a cornerstone which becomes the basis for our spiritual habitation, but which also points the way in our daily choice-making.

To have the way revealed brings both light and illumination, but also direction. To have a sense of direction does not necessarily reveal much about the final destination. But having an effective compass orients one enough to allow the daily steps to be reasonably strong and sure. Too much of contemporary life is driven by calculation, by goals and outcomes that are perhaps at odds with deeper values and yearnings. Orienting oneself to sacred guideposts keeps our daily walking more grounded in that which is most deeply held and true.

This is the symbolic power of the countless "cairns" of stone one finds on the Camino. We leave our stones on growing piles which are often begun by another. When walking the unknown path which is our one and only life, there are cairns left by others, namely, the love, wisdom, guidance and modeling, that others have been for us. They too have felt the quandaries of their choice-making, and are implicitly supporting us in our here and now dilemmas.

Cairns are primarily meant for forks in the road where we have options and choices we need to make. Do we choose path A or do we choose path B? Do we walk this way or another way? Which path is more authentic for us, and it is often unclear which is the better way. Our commitment to the truth quest is our compass, and when on the Camino we pilgrims not only left stones behind, but we also left deep conversations behind. Deep conversations are the "Cairns of the spirit," and they are beautifully illustrated by the narrative of the two grieving disciples on the road to Emmaus (Luke 24:31). They shared their verbal "cairns" with one another as they walked, through the shared story of lament and wonderment which was nevertheless experienced uniquely by each of them. In this sharing a slowly dawning recognition emerged. Only at the end of their encounter did they come to recognize that Jesus was in their midst as he broke bread with them. Virtually simultaneous with their recognition of him he departs from them, suggesting that the gift is in the recognition, in the "aha," and not in the holding on or clinging, even to a figure as sublime as Jesus.

Deep spiritual discourse, as modeled by these wandering disciples, deposits living stones in our hearts, which serve as guideposts for ourselves and others in all the vicissitudes of life. Perhaps that is the truest expression of any pilgrimage, whenever and wherever it is undertaken, namely, to be in deep discourse with one another on whatever road we happen to find ourselves. Out of that sharing living stones are exchanged, and our way is made more sure, if only for the challenges of the day. In this confidence we walk boldly and in truth.

ABOUT THE AUTHOR

William (Bill) Schmidt is a German born Canadian who serves as Associate Professor in the Institute of Pastoral Studies of Loyola University Chicago. He has worked as a Chaplain, Counselor, and Psychotherapist for thirty five years, and has had an avid interest in Pilgrimage as a resource for spiritual growth and renewal. He is the author of two books and numerous articles in the fields of Counseling and Spirituality. He is currently the Editor of the <u>Journal of Spirituality in Mental Health</u>. He is the father of three sons, and lives in the Chicago suburb of Bridgeview, Il.